TARTANS

TARTANS

Brian Wilton

Aurum

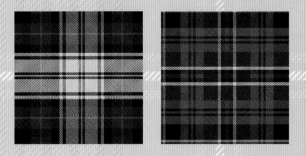

First published 2007 by
Aurum Press Limited
7 Greenland Street
London NW1 0ND

www.aurumpress.co.uk

A catalogue record for this book is available
from the British Library.

ISBN-10: 1 84513 098 7
ISBN-13: 978 1 84513 098 5

10 9 8 7 6 5 4 3 2 1
2011 2010 2009 2008 2007

Designed by Rich Carr

Maps by ML Design, London, www.ml-design.co.uk

Printed and bound in China

CONTENTS

Acknowledgements

In a work of this breadth that draws information from so many sources – rare and contemporary books, archival materials, museum records, clan histories, the ubiquitous Internet and the rapidly diminishing number of tartan experts – paying homage and giving credit can be rather fraught. References are frequently vague, shrouded in mist or totally absent. So, for any failure to acknowledge a source, or inadvertent plagiarism, I – in the words of a Victorian historian – 'crave the victims' indulgence'.

Thanks must first go to the National Trust for Scotland for having the wisdom to appreciate the important role that tartan has played in the last 300 years of Scotland's history *and* that of her kinsmen dispersed around the globe. Thanks also to Colin Hutcheson of Edinburgh for introducing me to this project.

Special thanks must go to author, weaver and tartan specialist Lt Col Peter Eslea MacDonald of Crieff for drawing on his encyclopaedic knowledge to cut through the obfuscation and inaccuracies surrounding some clan tartans. I thank him also for checking that tartan names and images match each other! The risk involved in raising my head above the parapet has been greatly reduced.

Thank you, too, to Alistair Campbell of Airds, and Crescent Publishing of New York and Shepheard-Walwyn of London for permission to use material from their books.

Across the Atlantic there are many worthy recipients of appreciation: the late Bill Johnston for the hugely valuable bequest to the Scottish Tartans Authority of his library and woven samples, very many of which have been scoured for information; his colleague and friend Dr Philip D Smith Jr of Tennessee for his perennial support and his scholarly reference works; our great friend the late 'Chuck' Bearman for his unstinting support of the 'tartan world'; Matthew A.C. Newsome and James 'Al' Bullman of the Tartans Museum in Franklin, North Carolina; Todd Wilkinson of Springfield, Missouri;

and the many unsung correspondents too numerous to mention who have replied to emailed queries.

The biggest debt of gratitude, however, is to Jamie Scarlett MBE. Now in his mid-eighties and living in an isolated Highland croft, Jamie is a self-effacing but scholarly oasis in a rapidly encroaching desert of academic paucity regarding Scotland's unique tartan identity. Still fluently writing articles and booklets on his favourite subject and freely dispensing sound advice and encouragement, he has provided friendship and support of inestimable value.

The Scottish Tartans Authority (STA), or rather those who conceived and supported the concept from its inception in 1995, must also take a string of curtain calls. Without their resolve to preserve the past and promote the future of Scotland's national fabric, the country's history *and* economy would be very much the poorer. Blair Macnaughton Snr of Pitlochry, a towering figure in industry, was the progenitor of the STA, and he was quickly joined by academics, weavers and major retailers who have enthusiastically supported it over the past decade. Without that faith and considerable financial input, much of Scotland's heritage would have been lost and this book would not have been written.

The copyright holders of the diverse range of excellent photographs are too numerous to mention individually but I must pay homage to two of them. Ken and Maureen Lussey of *Undiscovered Scotland* have created a superlative website for potential visitors to Scotland and have let me rifle their photographic treasure chest. Michael Macgregor of Michael Macgregor Photography of Ardnamurchan has supplied some of his stunning landscapes which have given real substance to many of the tartans discussed.

Finally, I must thank my wife Isobel and children Lyle and Tilly for their forbearance at my being a stranger for so long. The very many months of lost weekends and early morning starts are over!

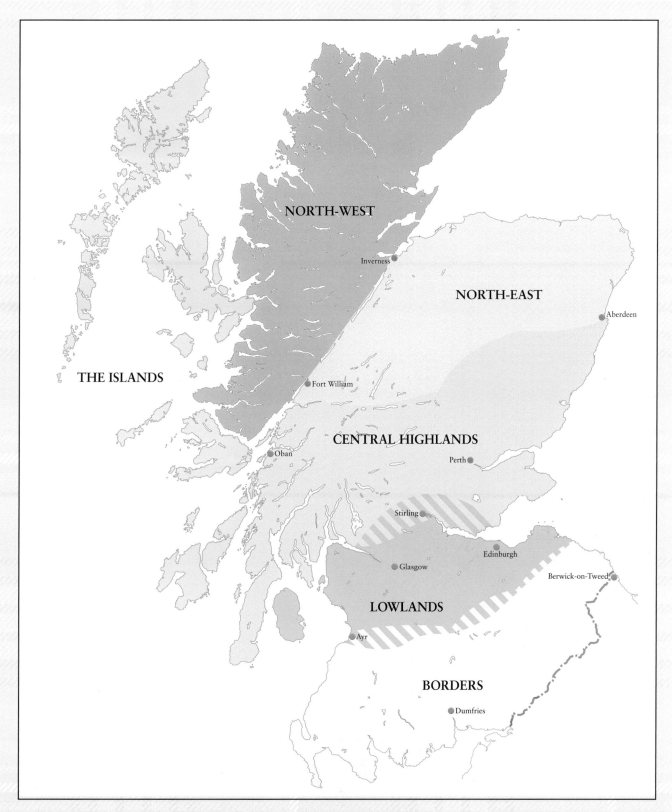

NORTH-WEST

Inverness

NORTH-EAST

Aberdeen

THE ISLANDS

Fort William

CENTRAL HIGHLANDS

Oban

Perth

Stirling

Edinburgh

Glasgow

Berwick-on-Tweed

LOWLANDS

Ayr

BORDERS

Dumfries

Map Key

Allocating clans to specific areas is a very inexact science. The maps provided are designed to give an approximate indication of landholdings and/or areas of influence and should not be regarded as either accurate or comprehensive.

INTRODUCTION

In modern times, tartan's unique place in the world is best typified by
its unique place *out* of the world – on the moon! If the next manned visit
to that celestial body lands in the Ocean of Storms, one of the many unusual
sights the crew will see should be a small tartan flag – deposited there in
1969 by Apollo 12's lunar module pilot, Commander Alan Bean.

No other textile design in or out the world acts as such a powerful symbol,
an ever-burning beacon to celebrate that dour, indefatigable island race
that has sent its sons and daughters around the globe to explore, to fight,
to teach, to invent, to colonize, to convert and to multiply. Today it's
estimated that the far-flung Scottish Diaspora numbers some 60 million –
twelve times the population of the 'old country'.

The world-famous Edinburgh Military Tattoo set against the backdrop of Edinburgh Castle
offers an annual feast of music, spectacle . . . and tartan.

Their disproportionate achievements have gifted a great legacy to very many nations and it should be very humbling to native Scots that so many 'foreigners' move heaven and earth to prove that they have some Scots blood in them! If and when they find it, their first thought is invariably 'What's my tartan?'

From tartan's ancient Celtic roots – the oldest sample ever found is around 3,000 years old – to its current international status is a long and fascinating journey. How it came about that rough wool plucked from native sheep, dyed with seaweed and lichens and woven on simple handlooms in isolated Scottish glens has achieved such prominence has as much to do with the art form itself as with the culture that embraced it.

The very nature of tartan offers seemingly infinite design possibilities that can permutate up to six or more colours plucked from the spectrum and then lay them out in an equally infinite number of ways. Swathes of colour are interspersed with contrasting and complementary lines and bands that produce subtle new shades at their crossings. All these variables allow each and every tartan to take on its own distinctive identity, transferable to the individuals or communities that wore it.

In the 18th and 19th centuries, events in Scotland serendipitously combined to establish tartan as an identifier for many of those communities, Highland and Lowland. A trickle of around 30 clan tartans quickly grew to a stream of over 100 and then in the 20th century spread out around the globe to a flood of thousands.

Up until the second half of the last century, the tartans that predominated represented clans, families and districts but as the choice of printed and broadcast media expanded, tartan's flexibility as a

A New York cab celebrates Tartan Day, America's joyful homage to its Scottish roots.

The '45 and the Tartan Ban

The 1745 rising of the clans which culminated in the Battle of Culloden – the last major battle to be fought on British soil – was probably the most disastrous event ever to overtake Scotland.

THE rebellion began when Bonnie Prince Charlie landed in Scotland in August 1745 in an attempt to claim the throne for his father James, son of the dethroned James II of England (and VII of Scotland). Many of the Highland clans hastened to join him, and after a failed attempt to invade England the 5,000-strong Jacobite force was brutally defeated at Culloden Moor, near Inverness, by a mixed English and Scottish army led by the Duke of Cumberland, second son of King George II.

After the dust of battle had settled, it's reported that 1,200 of the Prince's army were dead – including many slaughtered as they lay on the battlefield. Over 100 combatants and Jacobite supporters were later executed, and over 1,100 transported to the West Indies to end their days in slavery. Nor was that all. As historian David Nash Fords records,

> Cumberland gave orders for the systematic extirpation of all 'rebels' who were found concealed in the Highlands. All houses where they could find shelter were to be burnt and all cattle driven off. This was interpreted to mean the killing or burning of all Highlanders found wounded or with arms in their hands.

Many of Cumberland's Scottish troops took advantage of their orders to settle old scores with their fellow Scots and indulge in widespread murder and pillage.

The aftermath was long and bitter. Existing schisms were widened even more, with clan set against clan and community against community. The carrying of weapons, and the wearing of tartan and Highland dress were banned, and whole communities pillaged and sent into the hills for no crime other than an inability to speak English. This was 18th-century ethnic cleansing with a vengeance.

A medal struck to celebrate the Duke of Cumberland's victory over Bonnie Prince Charlie in the 1745 Jacobite Rebellion. Cumberland's brutality saw thousands of Highlanders lose their homes, if not their lives.

The tartan ban, enforced by means of the 1746 Dress Act, was a determined effort on the part of the British government to stifle rebellion, humiliate the Highlanders and crush the power of the Chiefs and put an end to Gaelic culture. Ironically, however, it also elevated tartan to almost cult status. As so often is the case, the act of banning something made it seem more rather than less important, and the Highlander devised many ingenious ways of evading it.

By 1782 it was judged by the Government that meaningful Jacobite resistance was at an end – Bonnie Prince Charlie was by then 60 and still in exile in Florence – and an era of reconciliation had dawned. George III gave assent to the repeal on 1 July 1782, and a much promulgated announcement in Gaelic and English read:

> Listen Men. This is bringing before all the Sons of the Gael, the King and Parliament of Britain have forever abolished the act against the Highland Dress; which came down to the Clans from the beginning of the world to the year 1746. This must bring great joy to every Highland Heart. You are no longer bound down to the unmanly dress of the Lowlander. This is declaring to every Man, young and old, simple and gentle, that they may after this put on and wear the Truis, the Little Kilt, the Coat, and the Striped Hose, as also the Belted Plaid, without fear of the Law of the Realm or the spite of the enemies.

George IV's Visit to Edinburgh

THE BBC website's history section sums up George IV thus:

> Although one of the most gifted of royal princes, his obsessive self-interest and vast expenditure on palaces and pictures, militaria and mistresses, parties and pageants meant that, by the time of his accession to the throne in 1820, he had become a byword for senseless extravagance and a national joke.

Included in these excesses were 'the colourful, pseudo-historic pageants he devised for his coronation of 1821 and his visit to Edinburgh of 1822'.

It was the first time a reigning monarch had travelled to Scotland since 1641, and no expense was spared. Sir Walter Scott choreographed the visit, presenting a glittering nationalist pageant that built on the popularity of his novels and poems, which had already made the Highlands a focus for European romantic sentiments. A bewildering kaleidoscope of traditional and newly acquired tartans was on display, providing a huge boost to the weaving industry and a superlative marketing tool for Scottish tourism, both of which have lasted to the present day.

Another medal, this time to commemorate George IV's 1822 visit to Edinburgh – a much happier occasion and the beginning of tartan's heyday

textile design and as a marketing tool became very apparent, as did its inherent ability to proclaim to the world at large: 'I come from this country … this is my family … my clan … my city, state, province … my district, company, regiment, college, primary school, football team …' The list is endless!

Similarly, there is no other textile that allows its designers to incorporate elements of personal or corporate significance — the colours from a sports team or company logo; a grandfather's medal ribbon; a national flag; a wedding date; a line for each of the children; a red for blood spilled; a black for mourning … the possibilities are limited only by the designer's imagination.

As perhaps befits such a complex and evocative fabric, tartan's history is littered with 'grey areas', with unknowns and guesses and carefully crafted caveats. So many historical references are riddled with omissions or highly debatable statements that some of what now passes for history may prove in time to be, at best, honest conclusions based on past errors (in computer parlance, 'rubbish in – rubbish out') and at worst, ill-informed opinion. As Jamie Scarlett, prolific author and the doyen of tartan studies, said recently: 'I never believe anything I see in print, even if I've written it myself.'

Many favourite clan tartans are known forgeries from the minds and pens of the brilliant Sobieski Stuart brothers of the 19th century with their *Vestiarium Scoticum* (see page 6). Many others were the closest fashion tartans to hand on the shelves of Lowland weavers William Wilson & Sons when panicky clan chiefs couldn't identify their tartans. But, just as in the political world where the terrorists of today are the statesmen of tomorrow, so too does time lend credibility to upstart tartans.

This book covers over 400 tartans in a wide range of categories and frequently flies off on overseas tangents just to show how international tartan has become. With over 4,500 tartans to choose from and a finite space available, deciding what to include hasn't been easy. What can be guaranteed will be the posse of aggrieved parties demanding to know how it was possible that their tartan was omitted!

In a work of this breadth that draws information from so many sources – rare and contemporary books, archival materials, museum records, clan histories, the ubiquitous Internet and the rapidly diminishing number of tartan experts – putting pen to paper or fingers to keyboard can be likened to tattooing cross hairs on one's forehead and then gazing over the parapet at an approaching Redcoat charge. There will be errors and there will be arguments but that is the nature of tartan.

Those readers looking for conventional clan histories will be disappointed. Although there are snippets here and there, the subject has largely been avoided. Whilst individual clans are immensely proud – and rightly so – of their history, they will tacitly admit that there is an inevitable sameness to each and every one of them: vying for position, marrying for power, stealing cattle, fighting with the neighbours, severing heads, supporting or opposing Charlie, losing lands, being hung, drawn and quartered and fleeing the country! The formula therefore merely dips in to clan histories to look for individuals and places that give some substance and soul to the tartans.

In any case, tartan has quite enough history of its own. Over the past centuries it has been silent witness to Scotland's long and turbulent struggle to achieve harmony and prosperity. In 1946 Dr George Fraser Black, bibliographer and historical scholar at the New York Public Library, wrote of his forebears:

It is surely a paradox that a nation which, in the making, had the hardest kind of work to extract a scanty living from a stubborn soil, and still harder work to defend their independence, their liberties, their faith from foes of their own kindred, should be best known to the world for the romantic ideals they have cherished and the chivalrous follies for which their blood has been shed.

Tartan has survived a Royal ban, travelled to the moon and been emblazoned on passenger jets and Formula One racing cars. It has seen some of the greatest acts of bravery and sacrifice in modern warfare and yet is equally at home in children's nurseries and on fashion catwalks. Chivalrous folly or romantic ideal, tartan is truly the 'Fabric of a Nation', and it is here to stay.

From King of England to Queen of Pop – Madonna struts her stuff in a becoming tartan miniskirt

Tartan numbering

THOSE tartans that have numbers up to around 2,700 use the original numbers allocated by the now-defunct Scottish Tartans Society. Subsequent numbers are those of the Scottish Tartans Authority. The master database holds over 6,000 entries, many of which are just slightly different versions of the same tartan recorded by researchers over the last century and a half. Of interest only to academics, those are excluded from the conventionally accessible database to avoid confusion.

The Sobieskis and *Vestiarium Scoticum*

In about 1820, two stylish and charming young brothers came to settle in Scotland. Their names were John Hay Allen and Charles Stuart Hay Allen, and before long rumours began to circulate that they were the legitimate grandsons of Bonnie Prince Charlie, who had died in Rome in 1788. It was alleged that in 1773 a son had been born to the so-called King Charles III and his much-younger wife Princess Louisa of Stolberg Guedern. For fear that the baby might suffer harm at the hands of the Hanoverian government in Britain, still apprehensive about another possible Jacobite uprising, the baby was immediately spirited out of Italy and brought up in England by a naval officer identified as John Carter Allen, later to become an Admiral. The child, known as Thomas Allen, grew up to be a naval lieutenant and the father of John and Charles.

WHILST the brothers never openly made claims to their royal lineage, neither did they deny the excited rumours in Scottish society. They changed the spelling of their surnames to 'Allan,' the accepted Scottish version of the name, and poetry by the elder brother John tended to give even greater credibility to the whispers. The thought that the Scots might again have a Jacobite 'king' amongst them opened many influential hearts, doors and no doubt purses. In the 1830s the Earl of Lovat granted them a hunting lodge in Inverness-shire, where they surrounded themselves with royal paraphernalia and took on the names of John Sobieski Stuart and Charles Edward Stuart, the Sobieski deriving from the name of Bonnie Prince Charlie's Polish mother, Maria Clementine Sobieska.

In 1822 the brothers had let it be known that in their possession they had some ancient manuscripts giving details of many old clan tartans, not just for the Highlanders but also for those in the Lowlands and Scottish Borders, hitherto regarded as tartan deserts. After the enthusiasm for tartan kindled by George IV's 1822 visit to Edinburgh, the brothers' claims fell on even more receptive ears and in 1842 they published a compilation of the relevant tartans, edited by John and illustrated by Charles,

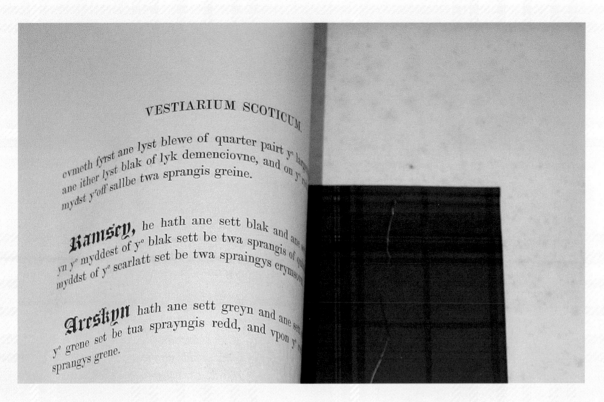

VESTIARIUM SCOTICUM.

cvmeth fyrst ane lyst blewe of quarter pairt y^e lar...
ane ither lyst blak of lyk demenciovne, and on y^e r...
mydst y'off sallbe twa sprangis greine.

Ramsey, he hath ane sett blak and ane w...
yn ye myddest of y^o blak sett be twa sprangis of ...
myddst of ye scarlatt set be twa spraingys crymso...

Areskyn hath ane sett greyn and ane set...
ye grene set be tua sprayngis redd, and vpon y^e ...
sprangys grene.

The 1842 Vestiarium Scoticum showing the 'Clan Stuart' tartan which is cracking with age

Opposite: A pencil sketch of the Sobieski brothers, John and Charles. This appeared in a slim 1848 privately printed publication that featured a scholarly debunking of the Vestiarium Scoticum and a vigorous defence, presumably from John Sobieski Stuart.

by the name of *Vestiarium Scoticum*, a magnificent leather-bound tome measuring 15 inches by 11 and made available at 10 guineas. It was the first book to effectively illustrate tartans by using an ingenious pantograph system developed by the Smith brothers of Mauchline, using ranks of pens to scribe coloured parallel lines onto black paper; the Smiths went on in later years to use their invention to illustrate their own much-valued book *The Authenticated Tartans of the Clans and Families of Scotland*.

The *Vestiarium* was seized upon by clan chiefs and the weaving industry with equal fervour. Very few thought seriously to question its contents (Sir Walter Scott, who was told of the Sobieskis' 'archive' before his death in 1832, was a rare sceptical exception) and it wasn't until almost 140 years later that an analytical study of the book was undertaken by D.C. Stewart and J.C. Thompson, and published as *Scotland's Forged Tartans*. Its conclusion was that the talented and ingenious Sobieskis had perpetrated a monumental hoax upon a gullible society and the vast majority of 'old' clan tartans came only from the fertile imagination of Charles the illustrator. The only one of his 'sources' ever seen by outsiders

was the so-called Cromarty MS, of which photographs were taken in around 1894. Modern inspection of them throws up countless clumsy alterations and inconsistencies that tend to confirm its highly dubious provenance.

It's possible that some of the 75 tartans may have been based on historical samples that the Sobieskis came across. Modern historians tend not to judge the brothers too harshly; they didn't seem to embark on the project for financial gain; perhaps it was to further their social position but was there any need? The rumours of their birthright had already attracted notice in abundance. Another theory suggests that they themselves were the unwitting dupes of a shadowy puppet master ... but who?

Calculating impostors, social poseurs, gullible innocents, well-meaning dupes ... whatever the Sobieski brothers were, the impetus they imparted to the clan tartan culture came just as the new Queen and her Consort paid their first visit to Scotland. The enthusiasm of Victoria and Albert set the royal seal of approval on everything to do with the Highlands — including all of Scotland's 'forged tartans', many of which are still in use today.

Cape Wrath

KEITH Thurso

SINCLAIR

MACKAY Loch Naver GUNN

MACLEOD

SUTHERLAND

Loch Shin

Coigach Lairg

Ullapool

ROSS

MACLEOD

MUNRO Cromarty

DAVIDSON URQUHART Morzy Firth

MACKENZIE Inverness

MACDONELL
MATHESON

CHISHOLM

MACRAE
MACLEOD

MACDONALD
OF GLENGARRY

Mallaig

MACDONALD
OF CLANRANALD CAMERON
Loch Moidart
Loch Shiel Fort William

MACINNES

0 10 20 30 40 50 kilometres
0 10 20 30 miles

THE NORTH-WEST

In 1848, just 16 miles south of Scotland's north-west tip of Cape Wrath, the 380-ton barque *Ellen* dropped anchor in Loch Laxford. Chartered by the Duke of Sutherland of Highland Clearance infamy and captained by Dugald McLachlan, the *Ellen* took on 155 passengers bound for the 'New Scotland' – Nova Scotia. It's not surprising to learn that of those passengers – all of them reportedly tenants of the Duke's – almost three-quarters were from clans traditionally indigenous to that area.

These MacKays, MacKenzies, MacLeods, Gunns and Keiths were following in the wake of their forebears who had made their way into the history books in 1773 as the very first Scottish settlers of Nova Scotia. 227 years later a replica of their sailing ship *Hector* was launched at Pictou on the coast of Nova Scotia and amongst the subscribers were those very Highland clans who first travelled in her. Appropriately, the very first Canadian Provincial tartan was that of Nova Scotia – designed exactly 180 years after the first Scots' landing there.

Wick harbour and town. The name comes from the Norse for 'bay', indicating the town's Viking roots.

| Sinclair | 1436 | Sinclair of Ulbster | 339 |

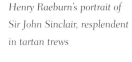

Henry Raeburn's portrait of Sir John Sinclair, resplendent in tartan trews

SINCLAIR 1436

In the far north-west of Scotland, around Wick and Thurso and north to the Orkneys and Shetland, the Sinclairs held sway. Their progenitor was William, son of the Comte de Saint Clair; he came to England in 1066 with William the Conqueror and first settled at Roslin, south of Edinburgh. William Sinclair founded Rosslyn Chapel, the subject of renewed attention as a result of the novel and film *The Da Vinci Code*.

A famous descendant was Prince Henry Sinclair who inherited the Jarldom (Norwegian earldom) of the Orkneys and Shetland. His discovery of America 94 years before Columbus landed at San Salvador is said to be one of the best documented of all claims. Henry is reported to have landed in what is now called Guysborough Harbour on the eastern end of Nova Scotia on 2 June 1398. He explored Nova Scotia whilst living amongst the local MicMac Indian tribes, visited parts of New England and left a memorial to one of his knights etched into a rock at Westford, Massachusetts.

With the death of the last Sinclair of Roslin in 1778, the Earls of Caithness became representatives of the family. The clan tartan first appeared in a portrait of Alexander, 13th Earl of Caithness, *circa* 1850 and it agrees with the Smiths' illustration of the tartan in their *Authenticated Tartans of the Clans and Families of Scotland* of the same year.

SINCLAIR OF ULBSTER 339

Taken from the trews in Sir Henry Raeburn's 1796 portrait of Sir John Sinclair of Ulbster, who is portrayed as a colonel in the Rothesay and Caithness Fencibles (1794–1802). Sinclair is best known for his monumental *Statistical Account of Scotland*, published in 21 volumes between 1791 and 1799, the forerunner of the modern census and the first systematic attempt to compile social and economic statistics for every parish in the country. Today, the account provides a unique record of life at the end of the 18th century. From 1815, Sinclair lived on George Street in Edinburgh, where he died. He is buried in the ruins of Holyrood Abbey and his statue is prominently displayed in Thurso in appreciation of the work he undertook to improve the town.

Where Did Tartan Come From?

One of the problems with charting the birth and progress of tartan is that the word itself is relatively modern and restricted to the English language. Many other countries had – and still have – no such word, so we have to be content with 'painted . . . variously coloured . . . several colours . . . divers colours . . . sundry waies devided and mottled garments'.

EVEN where the description 'tartane' is used, it needn't necessarily mean tartan as we know it today – it was, for quite a few generations, used to describe a type of cloth and not necessarily the design in which it was woven.

The elements are also against the tartan historian in that cloth is a very transient artefact – a mere speck of dust on the archaeological timeline – except when it happens to end up in a medium that preserves it such as a peat bog, a salt mine or an arid desert. It is the last of these that we have to thank for our earliest tartan remnant, which was woven between 1200 and 700 BC – about the same time as the Fall of Troy and the end of the Bronze Age.

So where did tartan disappear to between then and the sixteenth century, when it was next mentioned? The eminent tartan historian James Scarlett MBE thinks that it was always there but no one thought it unusual enough to mention, and it wasn't until visitors began to venture into 'North Britain' and saw the 'Scotch savages' in their quaint dress, that it became noteworthy. In their European travels, Scottish mercenaries also excited great comment about their outlandish dress and even back then, what they wore under it was a matter of great conjecture amongst the ladies of the day.

Why did it only survive in Scotland? Once again we turn to Jamie Scarlett for the possible answer: 'I believe that tartan is essentially an ancient art form of the Celts that thrived in isolated communities such as can be found in mountainous areas where travel from one valley or glen to another was extremely difficult.'

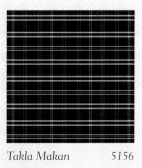

Takla Makan   5156

History suggests that the Celts originally came from the south-east of Russia around the Caspian Sea and gradually expanded westwards – once they arrived in mainland Britain they couldn't progress any further west than Scotland, Ireland, Wales, Cornwall and Brittany (France), and so there they remained.

The location and topography of western Scotland and the Highlands meant that Highlanders were more isolated than their southern kin and so the old skills survived for much longer – long enough for the rest of Britain to notice the quaint costumes and for happenstance to enter the arena in the form of George IV, Sir Walter Scott, the Sobieski brothers and Queen Victoria, all of whose enthusiasm for Scotland, the Scots and the tartan-clad Scottish regiments ensured worldwide immortality for tartan.

TAKLA MAKAN   5156

On the ancient caravan route through the heart of Asia – the Silk Road – illness or natural disaster overtook a group of travellers and they were swallowed up by the shifting sands of the Taklamakan Desert in Xinjiang, western China. 2,500 to 3,000 years later a Swedish explorer, Sven Heden, discovered the burial place of what were, by then, exceptionally well-preserved mummies. Despite being in western China, their faces were Caucasoid with long slender noses, reddish brown or brown hair and fair skin. The textiles found in their burials were exquisitely woven of wool yarn and amongst them were perfectly preserved, complex tartans!

| Sinclair Hunting | 889 | Gunn | 708 |

SINCLAIR HUNTING   889

The American website for the Sinclairs claims that the Sinclairs wore a green tartan at the Battle of Flodden (1513), where, apart from the drummer, the entire contingent was killed. Be that as it may, the first outing of the Sinclair Hunting was in the *Vestiarium Scoticum* in 1842.

GUNN   708

The Gunn tartan was first documented in 1810, so between them the 16 Gunns on board the 1848 exodus were bound to have some of their own rough-spun shawls and plaids ready for the cold 39-day crossing of the North Atlantic. It was said in the 19th century that the story of Clan Gunn was as gory as the red stripe that ran through their tartan. Known as the *MacGregors of the North* and the *Desperate Gunns*, the clan claimed descent from the Norsemen and was renowned for its bravery and the beauty of its womenfolk.

In the 15th century the seventh chief was the prosaically named George Gunn, *Am Bàrisdeach Mór* – the Great Brooch-wearer, from a large silver brooch which fastened his plaid. He held a prominent position as Crowner or coroner of Caithness and was said to have lived with barbaric pomp in his castle at Halberry, south of Wick.

Of George's seven sons the eldest, James, was the progenitor of the MacHamish Gunns; the second son Robert was the ancestor of the Robson Gunns; John

From R.R. McIan's The Clans of the Scottish Highlands (1845). McIan's fellow author James Logan commented – with delightful Victorian verbosity – that 'a fine dark pattern . . . served so well to conceal an ambuscade among the sombre-coloured and luxuriant heath and mountain herbage'.

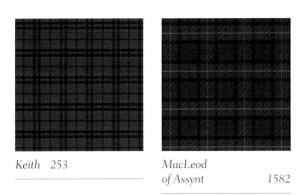

Keith   253

MacLeod
of Assynt   1582

the third son fathered the Gunns of Strathmore, Henry fathered the Caithness Hendersons and William the Williamsons and Wilsons. This shows well how early clans got their names: MacSheumais (pronounced *MacHamish*) – son of James; Robson – son of Robert; Henderson – son of Henry; and Wilson or Williamson – son of Will or son of William. One can also see from this how other quite unrelated clans of the same name could be formed in other parts of Scotland named after sons taking themselves off to form their own dynasties.

The Gunns' history in the 16th and 17th centuries is peppered with ambushes, guerrilla raids and cattle-lifting – all seemingly attended by brutal killings. Here and there in the midst of the bloodshed are contrasting moments of quiet humour which indicate the divisions in Highland culture. One Alexander Gunn, on being asked to attack a neighbour and set fire to the harvest, declared that he was prepared to kill the factor (the estate manager) but burning corn was no job for a gentleman.

At another time the Gunns surprised a group of Keiths eating around a fire. Their leader was picking his teeth and Henry Gunn 'sped an arrow on its way with a cry "Try this for size, Keith!"' In a further chapter of their feud with the Keiths, the Gunns ambushed a Keith party and shot their arrows at close range with a polite 'The Compliments of the Gunns to the Keiths.'

Perhaps the ancient feuds between the Gunns and the Keiths were forgotten on the barque *Ellen* since aboard, also travelling to Nova Scotia, was a large family of Falconers – a sept or dependent family of the Keiths. One of the children was called Henrina – possibly bestowed upon the poor girl by disappointed parents hoping for a boy!

KEITH   253

Strangely the structure (the sett or pattern) of the Keith tartan is not too dissimilar from that of their arch-enemies the Gunns, with a black band traversing the green rather than the gory red one. It's sometimes called the Keith and Austin tartan, which hints at the fact that it's shared between no fewer than four clans – Keith, Austin, Falconer and Marshall. The likely explanation for this is that they were all from the looms of Wilsons of Bannockburn!

The name Marshall brings alive the ancient hereditary title of Great Marischal of Scotland which was held by the Keith family from the 12th to the 18th century. *Marischal* (from the French *maréchal*) is the Scots spelling of marshal and the Great Marischal was the King's Marshal – Scotland's premier general with a wide portfolio of duties, the main one being to display military genius when required.

One Keith who was notably true to that tradition was Francis Edward James (1696–1758), who rose to the rank of general in the Russian army, field marshal in the Prussian army and then Governor of Berlin.

MACLEOD OF ASSYNT   1582

Although essentially Islanders, the MacLeods didn't confine themselves to Skye and this branch settled on the mainland in Assynt – that great coastal land mass between Ullapool in the south and Kylesku in the north. In Highland memories – which are famously long – the MacLeods of Assynt are considered the black sheep of the family for betraying James Graham, Marquis of Montrose, who was fighting for the would-be Charles II against the Covenanting army in the later stages of the Civil War. Montrose had fled to Assynt in 1650 after the Battle of Carbisdale and trustingly placed himself in the hands of MacLeod of Assynt, whose betrayal of him resulted in his trial and execution in Edinburgh.

Tartan Terms

Most skills have their own technical language and tartan weaving is no exception.

These basic terms are useful in describing the process and the tartan itself

THE **warp** comprises the longitudinal threads of any woven material, whereas the **weft** is the horizontal threads interwoven with the warp by a **shuttle** moving back and forth across the loom.

Tramlines are two parallel lines close together like tram or train lines. **Guards** or guard lines are two narrow lines of the same colour, one on each side of a stripe of another colour – 'guarding' it.

Comparing tartans can be quite confusing to the untrained eye and one excellent method used by tartan academics was the production of a colour strip – a visual slice through the warp that showed the arrangement and proportions of the colours.

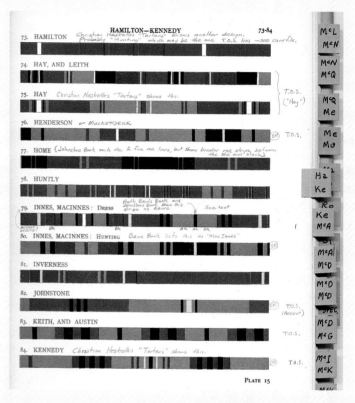

Above: Examples of colour strips, a technique invented by Donald Calder Stewart to define and record different tartans

These colour strips were the invention of Donald Calder Stewart (1893–1977), a towering historian in the field of tartan. They were the nucleus of a recording system for tartans called Sindex (Stewart-Index) which is used to this day by tartan academics. Nowadays computer programs can easily reproduce this tartan slice, but before the advent of such technology, each tartan was painstakingly recorded using coloured pencils or – when they were invented – felt pens.

Left: A length of black and white Menzies tartan on the loom.

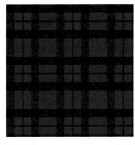

MacKay

The original clan territories of the MacKays were called Strathnaver – the valley of the River Naver which flows out of Loch Naver in Caithness in the far north of Scotland. The staunchly Protestant MacKays fought against the Stewarts in the Jacobite Uprisings of 1715 and 1745 and supported the Hanoverian forces against the Jacobites.

The MacKays of Strathnaver were especially remembered for the famous 'Mackay Regiment' raised for the service of the Dutch and Swedish Crowns during the 17th century, and many MacKays settled in Holland and Sweden, giving rise to a number of noble families there. In the 19th century the close links with the Continent and Holland resulted in the title of Lord Reay passing to Baron Eric Mackay van Ophemert in the Netherlands. His nephew Baron Aeneas Mackay, Prime Minister of the Netherlands, was the great-grandfather of the present chief.

MACKAY 703

This is the MacKay clan tartan, a sample of which was signed and sealed by the Chief for the Highland Society of London in 1816. It shows a marked similarity to the Gunn tartan in all but the colour of one line, suggesting a shared territorial origin – or, of course, demonstrating the marketing ingenuity of weavers Wilsons of Bannockburn who produced the earliest specimens of both.

This comes from a tartan coat in Inverness Museum described thus by the then curator, Miss M.O. MacDougall: 'period c. late 18th century, was in possession of a Strathnaver MacKay whose ancestors wore it as MacKay tartan. The design is that of the Campbell of Breadalbane with brown instead of black . . . it is possible the brown may be faded black.'

As Margaret MacDougall quite rightly said, this is Campbell of Breadalbane, which connects neatly to a note from an unknown source saying that this was later called the 'Duchess of Argyle' and used for dresses for boys and girls in charity schools. The relevant Duchess of Argyll, whose husband was hereditary Chief of Clan Campbell,

This McIan portrait demonstrates the wearing of the 'targe' – the Highland shield. The central spike, though only short here, was often up to 12 inches long and, coupled with a dirk held in the same left hand, proved a formidable weapon in battle.

Saving the Capercaillie

IN autumn 2006, the Scottish Tartans Authority joined forces with the Royal Society for the Protection of Birds in an effort to save one of the country's best-loved but most threatened birds from extinction. There are fewer than 2,000 capercaillies left in Scotland, down from 20,000 in the late 1970s, mostly living in the ancient pine forests in the north. The tartan was designed by Alistair Buchan, chairman of the Scottish Tartans Authority, who used the capercaillie's own striking colours as the basis for his design. The RSPB will receive a percentage fee from all products made using the capercaillie tartan, and hope that this revenue and the related publicity will help in their quest to save the beleaguered bird from extinction.

Capercaillie   6857

A capercaillie, one of Scotland's most beautiful birds, in its natural habitat

could well have been Princess Louise, fourth daughter of Queen Victoria, who married the Marquis of Lorne, heir to the Dukedom of Argyll. The Duchess – as she became – was much involved with charitable work both in Britain and Canada and the adoption of a tartan connected with her husband would have been very appropriate.

However, this can't explain how that selfsame tartan migrated from the southern Highlands up to the northern extremities of Scotland to be claimed as a MacKay. There were, of course, MacKays of Argyll, but history insists that they were not related to the MacKays of the north.

MACKAY OF STRATHNAVER   2037

This was designed about 1952 by Wm. Andersons of Edinburgh and Lord Reay – Chief of Clan MacKay. (The Lordship of Reay was created in 1628 and Donald MacKay was the first holder of the title.)

This very unusual tartan features the seasons of the year and uses nine or ten different colours – depending upon the reference source used. Although a modern tartan, this commemorates the Aberach branch of the MacKays whose story here is gleaned from the Chebucto Community Net website from Nova Scotia:

The Aberach Mackays who occupied Strathnaver were the oldest Mackay group, descended from Ian Aberach Mackay; they had the reputation of being the most fearless section of the clan and were known for their honesty and fair play to their allies. The expression *Ceartas nan Abrich*, 'The Justice of the Aberachs', was a well-known slogan in their rich history.

In 1433, when the Reay Country was invaded, Ian, half-brother of Neil, the Chief's imprisoned heir, took command and after the battle assumed the chieftainship but refused to claim the position permanently, maintaining that he was only holding it in trust for his half-brother. Neil escaped from prison four years later and Ian Aberach gave the chieftainship back to him. In appreciation Neil gave him all the heights of Strathnaver, from Mudale to Rossall, on both sides of the River Naver.

MacKay of
Strathnaver   2037

MacKay   264

Dutch   1134

MacKay 264

Often called the Blue MacKay or Morgan. The design comes from the *Vestiarium Scoticum* of 1842 but it didn't enjoy enough popularity to replace the conventional 'Green' MacKay.

This has now become better known as the Morgan, that name being an integral part of the clan from the 12th century. Indeed there has been argument as to which name came first, Morgan or MacKay.

The well-known expression 'the real McCoy' actually comes from the MacKays. According to www.wordorigins.org:

This term meaning the genuine article derives from a brand of whisky. The phrase *the real MacKay*, referring to a brand of whisky of that name, appears in 1856. It was officially adopted as an advertising slogan by G. Mackay and Co. of Edinburgh in 1870. In the US, it became *McCoy*.

The first general (non-whisky) use is by Robert Louis Stevenson in 1883. Stevenson uses the *MacKay* spelling.

Many claim that the term derives from Norman 'Kid McCoy' Selby (1873–1940), an American champion boxer who was convicted of murder in 1924. An 1899 issue of the *San Francisco Examiner* refers to Selby as *the Real McCoy*, but as the term was well-established by this time Selby is not the origin.

Alternatively, it is often suggested that the term derives from Elijah McCoy (1843–1929), an inventor of a type of hydrostatic lubricators [for use in steam trains] in 1872. Although he is earlier than Selby, he is not early enough to be the origin. But while clearly not the origin of the term, both Selby and Elijah McCoy may have influenced the change in spelling from *MacKay* to *McCoy*.

Dutch 1134

When it came to designing a 'Dutch' tartan in 1965, the Lord Lyon of the day, Sir Iain Moncrieffe of that Ilk, advised the designer, Dundee-based John Cargill (foreman in a carpet factory and weaver of many fine silk tartans), that a Dutch tartan should be based on the MacKay because of that family's long and illustrious connections with the Netherlands. Both the Dutch and Dutch Dress follow that advice and incorporate large areas of orange to reflect the colours of the Dutch royal household.

Sheep being shepherded south of Durness in Sutherland. It was sheep like these that replaced the Highlanders during the infamous clearances following the Battle of Culloden.

Sutherland

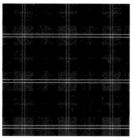

Sutherland   930

Sutherland of Duffus

3232

Sutherland Dress   1426

Sandwiched between the MacKays, Gunns and MacLeods was Sutherland country stretching from Helmsdale on the coast to the inland railhead of Lairg on Loch Shin. The history of Clan Sutherland and that of its illustrious regiments are inextricably intertwined: the First Sutherland Fencibles were followed by the Second and Third Fencibles; then came the 93rd Regiment of Foot later known as the Sutherland Highlanders who eventually became the Argyll and Sutherland Highlanders.

Seven Victoria Crosses were won by the 93rd at the siege of Lucknow in India; five by the Argyll and Sutherland Highlanders during the First World War and three more during the Second World War. At Balaclava in the Crimea in 1854 the Sutherland Highlanders formed the famous 'Thin Red Line' that faced and repulsed a charge by the Russian cavalry in a magnificent stand. A Russian cavalryman commented, 'We expected to have to fight soldiers, but not red devils.' Later in the century and in complete contrast must have been the simple task of quelling a rebellion by the boys of Winchester College: 'forty men of the 93rd advanced at the double against the boys, who thereupon fled in panic'.

Not so illustrious was the record of the Duke of Sutherland, whose clearances of the inland settlements to make way for sheep were the most notorious in the Highlands.

SUTHERLAND 930
The Sutherland clan tartan is from the 1842 book *Vestiarium Scoticum* and the basic pattern resembles the Black Watch tartan with red and white lines superimposed. It came into use soon after its publication, despite there being no evidence of its authenticity before the 1829 manuscript version of the *Vestiarium*.

SUTHERLAND OF DUFFUS 3232
The Clan Sutherland website describes this as the oldest of the Sutherland tartans, perhaps worn by the clan prior to 1746. It appears in a portrait of Kenneth, 3rd Lord Duffus, one of the Sutherland lairds, painted *c*.1715 by Richard Waitt. The problem with that assumption, of course, is that portrait painters frequently kept odd bits of tartan in their studio for just such occasions and it may have no connection whatsoever with the sitter!

SUTHERLAND DRESS 1426
This would appear to be a dress version introduced before 1980 by the Edinburgh kilt maker Hugh MacPherson, who specialized in providing kilts for the Highland dance world.

Sergeant James Sutherland, Adam Sutherland and Neil Mackay, in a MacLeay portrait. James Sutherland wears the uniform of the 3rd Sutherland Rifle Volunteers.

Caithness	2466	Munro	974	Red Munro	1204	Urquhart	1086	Urquhart	623

CAITHNESS 2466

Sutherland's partner, Caithness, had to wait about 200 years before it acquired a district tartan, designed in 1991 by Trudi Mann of Wick. It incorporates the colours of Caithness, including the unique blue-grey Caithness flagstone, used in cities around the world.

MUNRO 974

Southern neighbours to the Sutherlands were the Munros and just like the former, they appeared to gravitate to a military life. Their Chief and many of his men served as mercenaries in defence of Protestantism in MacKay's Regiment in the early-17th-century wars of Gustavus of Sweden ('the Lion of the North') and Christian IV of Denmark. It was recorded that amongst the Munros at that time were three generals, eight colonels, five lieutenant colonels, eleven majors and more than thirty captains of the name.

Confusion surrounds the Munro tartan and its very close cousins the Dalziel and the George IV. It was manufactured by Wilsons of Bannockburn as the 'Locheil Tartan' (i.e. Cameron of Locheil) and how it became a Munro tartan is a bit of a mystery. Despite that, this sett has long been regarded as the correct form of the Munro tartan. In early versions (as shown here) bright pink replaces the crimson between the three green lines.

RED MUNRO 1204

This is the name given to the Munro tartan conjured up by the imaginative Sobieskis. 'Monrois. Thre blak stryppys vpon ane redd feyld and throuchovt ye redd sett ain strypp of quhite.' Although an invention of brother Charles, it was a very attractive one and is still woven today as an alternative sett for the Munros. Like the Sutherlands, the clan also wears the Government or Black Watch tartan as an 'undress' or hunting tartan.

URQUHART 1086

Just to the south-east of Munro country lay Urquhart lands in a 20-mile-long and 9-mile-wide peninsula known as the Black Isle where the Urquharts were hereditary sheriffs of the town of Cromarty. Bounded on the north by the Cromarty Firth and on the south by the Moray Firth, it's neither an island nor black – the latter is said to have come from the area's past association with the black art of witchcraft.

'Schyr Richarde Urquharde Knychte' was alleged to be the author of the original manuscript from which the Sobieski brothers claimed they compiled the *Vestiarium Scoticum* but modern research suggests that he was yet another figment of the Sobieskis' imagination.

This is the Urquhart of Urquhart tartan as confirmed by the Chief in 1981 and filed by the Office of the Lord Lyon. It was first recorded in the Cockburn Collection of 1810 and is a variation of the Black Watch tartan with an additional broad red overstripe.

URQUHART 623

This is another of the Sobieski Stuarts' *Vestiarium* inventions and uses the same basic design as the Sutherland. This 'Urquhart white line' version was also recorded in the Lyon Court Book in 1981 and is now more widely worn than the older tartan from the Cockburn Collection.

Raphael Tuck's 1906 postcard of the Urquhart tartan with Urquhart Castle in the background

The Paintings of R.R. McIan

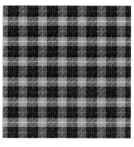

Davidson   1332   Davidson of Tulloch   1360

THE Victorian era was the great age of Romanticism, and nowhere was this more evident than at Queen Victoria's Scottish home of Balmoral Castle on Deeside. She and her consort Prince Albert were ardent fans of all things 'Highland' and enthusiastically embraced the world of tartan.

Born in 1803, Robert Ronald McIan became an actor and he too grew enthralled with tartans. McIan was also something of a painter and with the encouragement and collaboration of his great friend James Logan, utilized those skills to produce *The Clans of the Scottish Highlands* (1845).

McIan's stage background is evident in many of the book's illustrations, which are theatrical in the extreme. They're also lacking the great detail of the miniaturist McLeay but they do form the most complete record of Highland dress of the day and are perennial favourites wherever Scottish theming is called for. Painting tartans is notoriously difficult and like many of his artistic colleagues, McIan didn't always get them right!

McIan's depiction of the Munro tartan. His collaborator James Logan points out alongside that the clan's war cry is "'Caisteal Foulis na theine" – "Castle Foulis is in flames" – enough to rouse the ire of every clansman'.

DAVIDSON   1332

The chief of Clan Davidson was the hereditary keeper of the royal castle at Dingwall on the western edge of the Black Isle. Unlike many Highland clan names which begin 'Mac', Gaelic for 'son of', the son of David took the Anglicized form of 'David son'. The propensity of the Scots to squabble amongst themselves should never be underestimated. In 1370 when the Davidsons went into battle with their allies the MacPhersons against the Camerons they had a dispute with them as to who should lead the right wing into the battle. In umbrage, the MacPhersons withdrew and the Davidsons suffered heavy casualties. As a result of that and even more losses in the famous Battle of the Clans in Perth – where only one Davidson is said to have survived – the clan's power became greatly diminished and the remnants were scattered.

The tartans seem a little scattered as well since there were four contenders, the one shown here being the most recent (*Vestiarium Scoticum*, 1842) and registered as the official clan tartan in 1961 with the Office of the Lord Lyon. Other contenders were an 1822 version from Wilsons (now known as Davidson of Tulloch) certified by the chief of the day and then a couple of 1847 variations also from Wilsons of Bannockburn.

DAVIDSON OF TULLOCH   1360

The Davidsons of Tulloch in Ross-shire are one of the main branches of the Davidson family and the current clan chief is from that branch. This sett is an early-19th-century tartan held in the Highland Society of London records. The simplicity of the blue, green and black design has been the basis for numerous tartans over the decades and this particular one is likely to be considerably older than the 1816 Highland Society specimen.

HARLEY-DAVIDSON 5816

An iconic memorial to the Davidson name is of course the unmistakable Harley-Davidson motorcycle, the forerunner of which was built in a small shed in the Davidson family's Milwaukee backyard in 1903. It's thought that the family origins may have been in Dingwall in the far north of Scotland and whether or not it was in recognition of that, Klaus Hoeller of Harley-Davidson's Creative Direction Design Studios in Los Angeles designed this striking tartan for the company at its centenary in 2003.

Harley-Davidson　5816　　*Coigach*　6570

COIGACH 6570

One of the very few new district tartans to have appeared in recent years – the Coigach tartan – covers part of MacKenzie country and shows the potential for plucking design elements from the past and weaving them into a modern tartan.

Coigach (pronounced *coo-yach* or *coy-yach* [*ch* as in loch]) is the Gaelic for 'fifth', signifying that this large peninsula in Wester Ross, north of Ullapool, was one fifth of the Earl of Cromarty's landholdings. This huge land mass shelters the most fantastic scenery and mountains, beloved of generations of climbers – Stac Pollaidh, Cul Beag, Cul Mor, Beinn an Eoin, the Fiddler and Ben Mor Coigach.

Traditionally the clans and tartans that would have held sway in this area were MacKenzie, MacLeod of Lewis and Ross but almost of equal antiquity was the Coigach Tweed – one of the oldest of Scotland's estate tweeds, which appeared around 1847. It proved very popular in shooting circles and – because of people's difficulty in pronouncing *Coigach* – became universally known as the gun club check.

The dominant design feature in the Coigach District tartan is therefore the rust, white and black check of the estate tweed which is set against a backdrop of the blue and green bands of the MacKenzie tartan. The MacLeod of Lewis connection is represented by the yellow and black and the Ross by the blue, green and red. The five black lines on the green represent the Coigach 'fifth'.

The main settlement in Coigach is Achiltibuie (pronounced *ach-ill-tee-boo-ee*) on the south-west tip of the peninsula and opposite this 100-strong crofting community is the 310-hectare, privately owned island of Tanera Mor which attracts many thousands of seaborne visitors in the summer months. It boasts its own post office and even its own legal stamps – used to pay for the one-mile sea trip to the mainland. Those stamps have long been favourites of the philatelic world and recent issues have featured the Coigach tartan and MacKenzie, MacLeod, MacDonnell, Sutherland, Sinclair, Gunn, Ross and Oliphant – a Gathering of the Tartan Stamps!

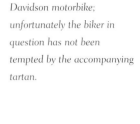

Left: An iconic Harley-Davidson motorbike; unfortunately the biker in question has not been tempted by the accompanying tartan.

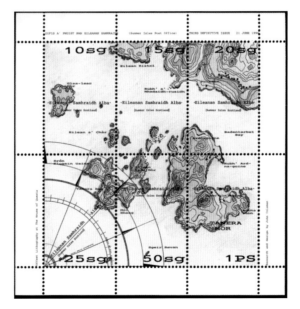

Left: A map of Tanera Mor, made from its famous stamps

MacKenzie

The MacKenzie clan motto is *Cuidich 'n Righ*, Gaelic for 'Help the King'. The clan history tells us that in 1266 Alexander III of Scotland was charged by a stag while hunting. The MacKenzie Chief, Colin of Kintail, raced to the King's aid yelling *Cuidich 'n Righ* and, with sword in hand, cleaved off the stag's head. The King, as a token of his gratitude, granted the MacKenzies the motto *Cuidich 'n Righ* and the stag's head or *Cabar Feidh* as their clan crest.

ONE of the most colourful stories of the MacKenzies concerns the Brahan Seer – a Highland labourer called Kenneth MacKenzie who was regarded as the Scottish Nostradamus. Born around 1650 on the Isle of Lewis, Kenneth MacKenzie worked from about 1675 on the Brahan estate, seat of the Seaforth chieftains.

He was said to always carry a black and blue stone with a small hole in it (a hagstone), into which he peered to make his predictions. Those were many and varied and uncannily accurate in many cases. He foretold the Battle of Culloden: 'Thy bleak wilderness will be stained by the best blood of the Highlands. Glad I am that I will not live to see that day where heads will be lopped off in the heather and no lives spared.' He is also said to have predicted the Caledonian canal some 200 years before it was built and foresaw the advent of the steam train – 'great black, bridleless horses, belching fire and steam, drawing lines of carriages through the glens'.

He looked over 300 years ahead and seemed to see a Scottish Parliament . . . but only when 'men could walk dry-shod from England to France'. The Scottish Parliament opened in 1999 – five years after the opening of the Channel Tunnel between England and France.

Kenneth MacKenzie came to a very grisly end after telling Isabella, wife of the Earl of Seaforth and one of the ugliest women in Scotland, that her absent husband 'is this moment with another who is fairer than yourself'. Tacked on to that rather unfortunate announcement was the frighteningly accurate prediction of the fall of the Seaforths. This enraged Isabella and she had him

Left: An elegant MacKenzie woman on the tennis court

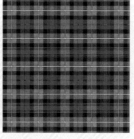

MacKenzie 267

dragged out and thrown head-first into a barrel of boiling tar.

MacKenzie may well have known the clan's early tartan – said to be red – but it disappeared from ken, probably lost in the post-Culloden ban. The replacement tartan was that of the 78th Ross-shire Regiment, raised by the Earl of Seaforth in 1778 and later to become the Seaforth Highlanders. It was only natural that since the Earl was the MacKenzie Chief and the bulk of the men were from the clan, the 78th adopted the stag head clan crest as its own regimental badge and the 18th-century pipe tune 'Cabar Feidh' as its regimental charge.

Another colourful and inspiring MacKenzie was Roderick, an Edinburgh goldsmith who together with some other Jacobite fugitives was surrounded by Redcoats when travelling in Glen Moriston (west of the southern end of Loch Ness). He had a close resemblance to Bonnie Prince Charlie and, Jacobite to the end, cried out as he lay dying: 'Alas, you have killed your Prince.'

The delighted Redcoats took his head back to Fort Augustus from where it was sent to London. Although the Hanoverians later learned that Charles was still alive, the temporary relaxation of the hue and cry allowed the Prince to escape from his Glen Moriston cave to the coast and thence to France. There is a memorial cairn to Roderick MacKenzie close to the bridge crossing the River Moriston. His grave is nearby and is said to be tended to this day by a direct descendant.

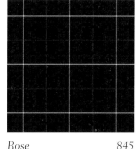

Rose Hunting   1226   Rose   845

Ross and Rose

It's sometimes difficult to see the wood for the trees when dealing with Clan Ross and Clan Rose. Geographically they were close – the Rosses are connected with Balnagown about 12 miles north of Inverness and the Roses (said to be pronounced *Ross*) are 10 miles east of the same city at Kilravock (pronounced *Kilrock*), the only Scottish castle of its era to have been continuously inhabited since it was built, in 1460.

Clan Rose was described by one historian as 'Men of Peace from Nairn'; over 25 generations, successive chiefs acted as peacemakers in the area. However, they were not slow to take up arms when they considered the cause was just. Colonel Hugh Rose, the 24th Chief, commanded the Black Watch for many years and his son and Chief apparent lost his life with the regiment in North Africa in the Second World War.

On the mantelpiece in the old Dining Hall of Kilravock Castle are these words:

Religion-Justice-Truth-Mercie
And-The-Exercise-Of-The-Fear-Of-God
Are-Surer-Preservers-Of-A-Familie
Than-Al-The-Other-Methods-And
Measures-In-The-World

Right: Stac Pollaidh (pronounced 'stack polly') means 'peak of the peat moss' and lies just north of the single-track A835 road to Achiltibuie in the Coigach peninsula deep in MacKenzie country.

ROSE HUNTING   1226
This Rose tartan was first mentioned in Logan's 1831 work but didn't get a mention in the Sobieskis' 1842 *Vestiarium Scoticum*. Either they didn't know about it or it was too dull for their liking because they produced a new and brighter clan tartan (845), and the 1831 design later became known as the Rose Hunting. Since Logan obtained the majority of his woven samples from Wilsons of Bannockburn it's quite likely that this sett is older than 1831.

ROSE   845
This *Vestiarium* offering is regarded as showing a little more imagination than was usual from the Sobieskis and proved popular until the latter part of the 19th century when predominantly red tartans were replaced in popularity by the blue and green hunting types.

Above: McIan's depiction of the Rose tartan shows an inappropriately well-dressed farmer using the 'cas-crom' – an ancient foot-plough.

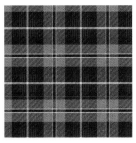

New York Fire Department   060

Ross   883

Ross Hunting   757

Balnagown – the Harrods Tartan   5824

The Chisholm   532

NEW YORK FIRE DEPARTMENT   060

In 1964 Grainger & Campbell of Argyll Street, Glasgow, replaced the red line of Rose Hunting (or the black line of Melville) with an azure one and the New York Fire Department tartan was born. What prompted their use of this sett is not known – perhaps there was a connection with the fire chief.

ROSS   883

The Ross tartans give rise to confusion and errors, too – the many variations open the way for misinterpretation.

ROSS HUNTING   757

The *Vestiarium Scoticum* version of the Ross clan tartan didn't gain currency but was said to be the basis for this hunting tartan which was first published in the 1880 *Clans Originaux*. Whether the Sobieskis based their clan tartan on this hunting design from Wilsons of Bannockburn or whether Wilsons based their hunting on the Sobieskis' earlier manuscript version of the clan design will probably never be known.

BALNAGOWN – THE HARRODS TARTAN   5824

The Balnagown (sometimes written Balnagowan) Estate was bought in 1972 by Mohamed Al-Fayed, the Chairman of Harrods, and he commissioned Kinloch Anderson of Edinburgh to design a tartan, which was based on the Ross Hunting.

THE CHISHOLM   532

The Chisholm is the traditional title of the Chief of Clan Chisholm and one old holder of that office reportedly boasted that only two other people could be addressed in such grand terms – the Pope and the King!

The Chisholm tartan shown here is without doubt the oldest of the tartans associated with the clan and is said to feature in an 1800 portrait of the clan heroine Mary Chisholm, who apparently sided with the clansmen during the Clearances. This didn't deter her uncle William, the 24th Chisholm, from evicting over half of them to make way for sheep. Time softens painful memories – in 1832 it was reported that despite the fact that he had evicted them, exiled members of Clan Chisholm who had settled overseas still swore allegiance to the chief back in Scotland. An early example of the tartan, woven by Wilsons, survives in Glasgow's Cockburn

The exterior of Harrods; its owner Mohamed Al-Fayed commissioned a tartan to suit its grandeur.

William Ross

William Ross was Her Majesty's Piper at the time MacLeay painted this portrait in 1866. He's shown wearing not his own tartan but the Royal Stewart and is holding a banner embroidered with the Royal Arms of England. In the background is a view of the East Terrace of Windsor Castle where all these original MacLeay watercolours reside in the Queen's collection.

Aɴ expert of pipe music, Ross often adjudicated at Highland Gatherings in Scotland and abroad. He ran a bagpipe business in London and had special permission to live outside Buckingham Palace. In 1876 he published a collection of pipe music, the result of 30 years of research. It contained nearly 400 tunes collected from Scottish and Irish pipers and opens with his own 'Prince Consort's Lament'. Ross was still in Queen Victoria's employment at the time of his death in 1891 at the age of 68.

Evidence of Tartan

Their [the Celts'] aspect is terrifying . . . They are very tall in stature, with rippling muscles under clear white skin. Their hair is blond, but not naturally so: they bleach it artificially, washing it in lime and combing it back from their foreheads. They look like wood-demons, their hair thick and shaggy like a horse's mane . . . The way they dress is astonishing: they wear brightly coloured and embroidered shirts, with trousers called bracae and cloaks fastened at the shoulder with a brooch. These cloaks are striped or chequered in design, with the separate checks close together and in various colours.

Diodorus Siculus, Greek historian, 50 BC

The common people of the Highland Scots rush into battle, having their body clothed with a linen garment manifoldly sewed and painted or daubed with pitch, with a covering of deerskin.

John Major, *History of Britain*, 1521

They delight in marled clothes, especially that have long stripes of sundry colours; they love chiefly purple and blew. Their predecessors used short mantles or plaids of divers colours sundry waies divided; and amongst some, the same costume is observed to this day; but for the most part now they are browne, more near to the colour of the hadder [heather]; to the effect when they lie amongst the hadder the bright colour of their plaids shall not betray them.

George Buchanan, 1582

The plad wore only by the men, is made of fine wool, the thread as fine as can be made of that kind; it consists of divers colours, and there is a great deal of ingenuity requir'd in sorting the colours, and so as to be agreeable to the nicest fancy . . . every isle differs from each other in their fancy of making plaids, as to the stripes in breadth and colours. This humour is as different thro' the main land of the Highlands, insofar that they who have seen those places, is able at first view of a man's plaid, to guess the place of his residence.

Martin Martin, *Western Isles of Scotland*, 1703

Their habute is shooes with but one sole apiece; stockings (which they call short hose) made of a warme stuff of divers colours which they call tartane . . . jerkin of the same stuff as their hose is of . . . with a plaed about their shoulders, which is a mantle of divers colours, much finer and lighter stuffe than their hose.

John Taylor, 'The Water Poet', 1618

Galgacus or Calgacus, pictured here in an imaginative reconstruction by a 19th-century artist, was a chief of the northern tribe the Caledonii who conducted a determined campaign of resistance against the Roman legions of Agricola as they advanced up the east coast of Scotland. Galgacus was eventually defeated by the Romans at the AD 84 battle of Mons Graupius, thought to have been at Bennachie near Inverurie, about 17 miles north-west of Aberdeen. The artist has dressed some of Galgacus' men in tartan, which they may have worn in reality. However, the fetching checked boxer shorts are probably a guess too far.

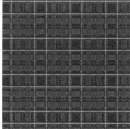
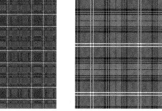

Chisholm   1454   *Chisholm Hunting*   1458

Collection and is a fine example of the weavers' art of the period with the white lines woven in silk, producing a beautiful vibrant cloth.

Three Chisholm brothers were among the Seven Men of Glen Moriston who gave aid to Bonnie Prince Charlie and one of them, Hugh Chisholm, recounted: 'when Charles came near they knew him and fell upon their knees and Charles was then in great distress. He had a bonnet on his head, a wretched yellow wig, and a clouted hand kerchief about his neck. He had a coat of coarse dark-coloured cloth, a Stirling tartan waistcoat much worn, a pretty good belted plaid, tartan hose, and Highland brogues tied up with thongs, so much worn that they would scarcely stick upon his feet. His shirt (and he had not another) was of the colour of saffron.'

When they conveyed the Prince to the coast at Arisaig, Hugh shook hands with him and vowed never to shake hands with another man. Towards the end of the century, Hugh lived in Edinburgh at the same time as the young Walter Scott attended college there. Scott wrote of him: 'He was a noble, commanding figure of six feet and upwards, had a very stately demeanour, and always wore the Highland garb . . . he kept his right hand usually in his bosom, as if worthy of more care than the rest of his person, because Charles Edward had shaken hands with him when they separated.'

Enthusiasts for the 'Wild West' will know that a few years after this, the merchant and slave trader Ignatius Chisholm married a Cherokee woman in Tennessee and they had a son called Jesse who became famous for the trail he scouted to supply his various trading posts among the Plains Indians. In its time, the Chisholm Trail was considered to be one of the wonders of the Western world with cattle herds as large as ten thousand strong being driven the 800

McIan here paints the Chisholm chief in what he describes as 'the court dress of a Highlander'.

miles from south Texas over the trail to Abilene in Kansas.

CHISHOLM   1454
This is today's accepted clan tartan, from the stable of the Sobieski Stuarts.

CHISHOLM HUNTING   1458
This sett illustrates what happened after the new aniline dyes were introduced in the 1860s, transforming most tartans into bright (some might say 'garish') versions of their originals. Subtler forms of the tartan were then produced that often replaced the brilliant reds with green or brown, as happened here with the red of the 1842 *Vestiarium* pattern.

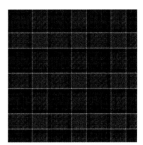

MacDonald

MacDonald was one of Scotland's largest clans, with nine branches in multiple territories, the main seat being in the Islands. The clan is dealt with more fully in that section (see page 68), but here are some of the branches with mainland roots.

MacDonald of Clanranald   427

One way of producing a distinctive new tartan is to modify an existing one and that process uses a self-explanatory heraldic term – differencing. To produce the Clanranald version of the MacDonald tartan, a white line has been inserted between the green band and the blue of the clan sett, which differences it enough to be a separate tartan.

The Smiths in their 1850 publication *The Authenticated Tartans of the Clans and Families of Scotland* had this to say: 'The MacDonell of Glengarry differs very little from the Clanranald, and we had some little difficulty in ascertaining the respective Tartans of each family; but at last we obtained a specimen from a gentleman who had it from Miss MacDonell of Glengarry, which removed the doubts, and enabled us to assign to each its proper Tartan.'

Sited on the tidal island of Eilean Tioram in the sea loch Moidart, the ruined Castle Tioram (pronounced Cheerum) is the former seat of the MacDonalds of Clan Ranald. The castle was torched during the 1715 Jacobite Rising to keep it out of the hands of the Hanoverian forces and has been an unoccupied ruin ever since.

MacDonnell of Glengarry
473

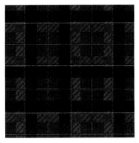

MacDonald of Glenaladale
79

MacDonald Dress   1997

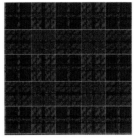

MacDonnell of Keppoch
(Clan)   6387

MacDonnell of Glengarry   473

Glen Garry runs east from Invergarry on the Great Glen about 16 miles (25 km) north of Fort William. It was here that this branch of the MacDonalds settled – MacDonnell being an alternative spelling for MacDonald. The 15th Chief, Alasdair Ranaldson MacDonnell of Glengarry, invented the famous Scottish military hat the Glengarry, a boat-shaped, peakless woollen cap that is creased lengthways and has short ribbons at the back.

Some more differencing takes place to produce this tartan from the basic MacDonald. Here a white line has been inserted between the inner red tramlines on the green band. The MacDonald tartans were clearly in a state of flux in the early 1800s since this one was called Clanranald in a collection of 1810, a name that the Sobieskis picked up and used in their *Vestiarium Scoticum*.

MacDonald of Glenaladale   79

A romantic mystery surrounds the MacDonald of Glenaladale tartan. This sett is said to have belonged to Alexander MacDonald of Glenaladale, one of Prince Charles's staunchest supporters at the time of Culloden, and shipped to Canada when he and his son emigrated in 1772.

Corroboration of this appeared in 1968 when a scrap of tartan was discovered in Canada by Ranald S.J. MacDonald. It had been owned by an elderly priest who claimed to be a descendant of Capt. John MacDonald of Glenaladale whose 'heroic' father was Major Alexander MacDonald.

There is a close association of the Glenaladale family with Glenfinnan – the rallying point for Prince Charles in August 1745 – and it was another Alexander MacDonald of Glenaladale who built the famous Glenfinnan Monument some 70 years later.

The tower is now in the care of the National Trust for Scotland and it was the Trust's historian Lt. Col. Iain Cameron who arranged in 1968 for a version of this tartan to be woven and marketed by the Trust at the Glenfinnan Visitor Centre.

The name given to this version of the tartan was 'MacDonald of Glenaladale (Glenfinnan)' or 'Glenfinnan (MacDonald of Glenaladale)'.

MacDonald Dress   1997

Like many of the early dress tartans, this MacDonald is asymmetric and its first known appearance was in the 1880 *Clans Originaux* from Paris.

MacDonnell of Keppoch (Clan)   6387

The MacDonnells of Keppoch had royal blood in their veins, being descended from Alistair Carrach ('left-handed'), son of the 7th Lord of the Isles and Margaret, daughter of Robert II. The clan fought in the last inter-clan battle against the Frasers in 1544 – *Blar na Leine* (Battle of the Shirts), so called because the weather was hot and the combatants took off their plaids and fought in their shirts. This rather vividly illustrates the lack of uniform clan tartans at that date. Clan, or tribal, warfare was fought by relatively small groups that would have known everyone on their side and so would have probably killed anyone that they weren't sure of. There was no time to work out from the tartan which side someone was on once the swords were flying! The Keppoch tartan was first recorded in the mid-19th century and claimed to have been copied from a relic of the '45 given by the Keppoch of the time to Prince Charles Edward.

Above: *MacDonnell of Glengarry*

Above: *MacDonnell of Keppoch*

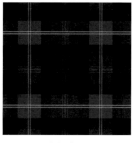

MacDonald of
Borrodale   2584

Matheson   860

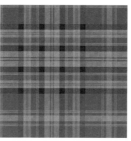

Matheson Hunting   693

MacDonald of Borrodale   2584

Another tartan closely associated with the story of Prince Charles Edward is the MacDonald of Borrodale. Following the Battle of Culloden on 16 April 1746 the Prince was a fugitive in the West Highlands until rescued by French ships in Arisaig on 20 September. His escape took him into the 'safe' Clanranald territory of Morar, Arisaig and Moidart where he was sheltered by Angus and Catriona MacDonald of Borrodale. As a later account told the story,

> Six days later the Prince, four companions, Donald MacLeod and seven Clanranalds sailed for the Outer Hebrides in an eight-oared boat of the Borrodales. As soon as they were clear of the sheltered waters of the sea loch at Arisaig, a violent storm arose. Driven by the gale through the night and in constant danger of capsizing, the boat reached Benbecula where the Prince, his companions and crew hid for two days. They then sailed to Scalpay off Harris where they were hospitably received by Donald Campbell, a tenant of MacLeod of Dunvegan, and where the Prince was given a change of clothes. On departure, he left the sea-soaked tartan lately given to him by Lady Borrodale with Donald Campbell and his family.

Three fragments of this tartan cloth are known to have survived. One in the West Highland Museum, Fort William, another among a collection of Stuart relics at Stonyhurst Jesuit College in Lancashire, and a third in the possession of the Royal Scottish Museum. The disparate pieces were brought together by tartan historian Peter MacDonald of Crieff and a length of his reconstructed tartan was presented to H.M. the Queen by Stonyhurst College.

It was at Glenfinnan at the head of Loch Shiel, on 19 August 1745, that Bonnie Prince Charles Edward raised his standard for the last attempt to reinstate the Stuarts on the British throne, an ill-fated occasion commemorated by the monument shown in this photograph. It's often assumed that Loch Shiel is a sea loch and paintings of Charles sometimes show an ocean-going sailing ship in the background. In fact the loch is a freshwater one which fails by a mere two miles to meet the sea and Charles was apparently rowed up the northern side to make his 'landing'.

Matheson   860

The name Matheson is not, as might be thought, short for 'Matthew's son' but is the Gaelic for 'son of the bear'.

History records that the Mathesons were once the equals of the MacKenzies, but backing the wrong side can bring disaster in Scottish power politics as they discovered when they ended up as tenants rather than in their traditional role as landlords. It was to be many years before they made any territorial gains again!

There can be very few in the clan who haven't heard of Jardine Matheson, the hugely successful mercantile company founded in Hong Kong in 1832 by William Jardine and James Matheson. So successful were their trading operations throughout the Far East that in 1844 – two years after he returned to Scotland – James Matheson was able to buy the island of Lewis. In 1851 he was created Baronet of Lewis for his great humanitarian efforts during a period of famine. Another Matheson – Alexander – had joined the Far Eastern family firm and when he returned to Scotland he started to buy land in Ross-shire and recovered the Lochalsh estate. For his efforts he was created Baronet of Lochalsh in 1882.

Both Sir James and Sir Alexander would probably have known their clan tartan and perhaps it was one of them who was referred to in William and Andrew Smith's *Authenticated Tartans of the Clans and Families of Scotland*. The Smiths were always very careful to ensure that they recorded the correct tartan for each clan and would make every effort to verify their findings. After suggesting that the Mathesons' power had greatly faded in the Highlands they added: 'There are, however, in Scotland, many respectable families of the name, and the Tartan from which we took our pattern, was manufactured for one of the wealthiest among them.'

Matheson Hunting   693

The Matheson hunting tartan first appeared in W. & A.K. Johnston's 1906 publication where readers are assured that 'in every case the tartans in the book have been taken thread by thread from the actual cloth, not from any previously printed work'. This is the normal clan tartan with blue in place of red and black in place of blue.

MacRae

The MacRaes have always been known as one of the Highlands' greatest fighting clans. In Kintail they supported the MacKenzies and fought so hard that they became known as 'MacKenzie's shirt of mail'. At the Battle of Killiecrankie they were in the second line with the MacKenzies of Seaforth and put up a desperate resistance which resulted in them dying 'almost to a man'. Their leader that day was Duncan Mhor of Torluish and before he was slain it was reported that he killed fifteen with his own hand – a hand that was so swollen on his claymore hilt that in death the sword was 'extricated with difficulty'.

MacRae, The Prince's Own   981

This and an almost identical tartan associated with the Lumsdens are both claimed as being some of the earliest surviving patterns associated with Prince Charles Edward. D.W. Stewart said in 1893 that it was undoubtedly the pattern of the old MacRaes and was certainly worn by the Prince when in their territory. But whether it was previously used by members of the clan or whether it was adopted by them afterwards – as a compliment to the wearer – can't be determined. Tradition indicates that the Prince was a great diplomat and always endeavoured to wear the local colours of the various clans during his stays in their respective areas. The Lumsden specimen survives but the MacRae one hasn't been found so there is still no answer to who had the tartan first – the MacRaes or the Lumsdens!

MacRae   859

The clan tartan appeared in the Smiths' 1850 work where they said of it: 'Our specimen . . . besides being approved by the manufacturers and dealers, has had the concurrence of a gentleman of the name, who has bestowed a good deal of attention on Clan matters.' The reader can see that this pattern is a simplified version of The Prince's Own, but by design or error no one knows.

MacRae of Conchra   1683

This is a popular contender for the MacRae of Conchra title. In 1904 Major John MacRae-Gilstrap of Otter Ferry explained this particular sett:

> When my great-great-grandfather, John MacRae of Conchra, Lochalsh, was on his way to Sherrifmuir from Kintail, some of his followers being without stockings, the occupants of a shieling in which some of them lodged, spent the night in cutting out stockings for them from a web of cloth which they had in the place. A piece of this web was in the possession of my grand-aunt Miss Flora MacRa [*sic*] of Ardintoul, from which she knitted the accompanying hose when a girl at the turn of the last century . . . Unfortunately the original piece of cloth has been lost.

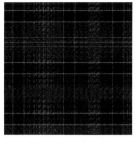

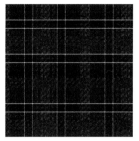

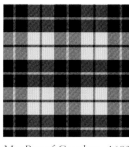

MacRae, The Prince's
Own   981

MacRae   859

MacRae of Conchra   1683

Cameron

The Cameron of Locheil tartan, illustrated by William Stewart in his 1928 book Clanland

Of all the Highland clans, the illustrious Camerons – always staunch Jacobites – have one of the most convoluted and intriguing histories. Over a period of almost 450 years the clan participated in no fewer than 39 battles, many of them household names in the history of Scotland – Bannockburn, Harlaw, Flodden, Killiecrankie, Sherrifmuir, Prestonpans, Falkirk and Culloden – not to mention the huge sacrifices in two world wars of the famous Cameron Highlanders. Traditionally the Laird of Locheil has always been the Cameron Chief.

CAMERON OF LOCHEIL   1398
This is the oldest of the Cameron tartans. It was first recorded in 1850 by the Smiths of Mauchline, who were sent a sample 'by Locheil, the undoubted Chief of the Clan, who says it is what he has always considered the Tartan of the Camerons, and is the same as represented upon a portrait of one of his ancestors' – the portrait being of 'the Gentle Locheil' by George Chalmers from 1764.

Locheil was badly wounded at Culloden and was carried off with two broken ankles shattered by grapeshot. He fled to France from where he continued to lead the clan. The present Chief has a fine plaid in this tartan woven by Wilsons of Bannockburn *c.* 1800.

CAMERON   1528
The clan tartan was first shown in the 1842 *Vestiarium Scoticum* where the Sobieskis described it in their affected, quaint medieval English as 'fovr stryppis of grein upon ane scarlatt fyeld, and throuchovt ye redd sett ain strypp zello'. At least four other clan tartans (Fraser, MacKay, Mackeane and MacQueen) are all colour changes on a common sett: the Sobieskis were obviously adherents of the *one size fits all* school of design!

CAMERON HUNTING   1535
The clan tartan formed the basis for the hunting tartan that was launched in 1956 at the Cameron Gathering at Achnacarry, the traditional home of the chief.

CAMERON OF ERRACHT   993
Alan Cameron of Erracht raised the Cameron Volunteers in 1793, later famously known as the Cameron Highlanders, and it's claimed that this tartan was designed by his mother who created it by taking the MacDonald sett, omitting two red lines, and then adding a yellow line. In 1881 reorganizations were in the wind and the following message was sent by wire to the Regiment in

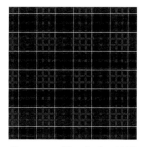
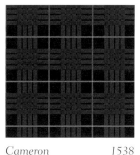
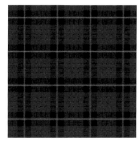
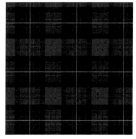
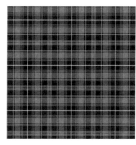

| Cameron of Locheil 1398 | Cameron 1538 | Cameron Hunting 1535 | Cameron of Erracht 993 | MacInnes 1464 |

Gibraltar: 'If 79th is linked to 42nd, will your regiment adopt tartan of the 42nd Regiment?' The immediate wired reply was: 'No. The Cameron Highlanders will not adopt 42nd tartan.'

MacInnes   1464

The Clan MacInnes of the West and the Clan Innes of Moray are two separate clans, but the similarity of their names has led to much confusion over the years as to their tartans, with the Innes wearing (to this day it is said) a MacInnes tartan under the impression that it is their own.

The design of this MacInnes green tartan has been attributed to John MacInnes, the 'Onich Grocer', said to have been born around 1851. Apparently he was the Registrar for Ballachulish and Corran of Ardgour between 1874 and 1920. By trade he was a tailor and weaver and ran a general merchant stores which doubled as his Registrar Office with his loom and workshop at the rear. When Edward VII was Prince of Wales, he called at John's 'Nether Lochaber Stores' to have an outfit made, after which it was said that the royal patronage went to his head, to the disdain of his neighbours.

Above: *A beleaguered MacInnes, as imagined by McIan*

Left: *Ballachulish Bridge with Beinn a Bheithir in the background*

Moray Firth

Lossiemouth

Elgin

MACDUFF

Forres

DUNBAR

INNES

BRODIE

CUMMING

CUMMING

KEITH

Inverness

Cawdor

Huntly

Culloden

Spey

LESLIE

HAY

MACBEAN

ANDERSON

MACINTOSH

GRANT

GORDON

Loch Ness

FRASER

MACGILLIVRAY

Grantown-on-Spey

SHAW

FORBES

MACPHERSON

Aberdeen

FARQUHARSON

SKENE

Loch Lochy

CLAN CHATTAN

Dee

Loch
Laggan

Dalwhinnie

Fort William

Blair Atholl

0   10   20   30   40   50 kilometres

0   10   20   30 miles

36

THE NORTH-EAST

The Great Glen is a geological fault, a split in the earth that almost – but not quite – turns the north-west of Scotland into an island. Two of the great lochs that run for most of its length are Loch Ness (24 miles long) and Loch Lochy (10 miles long). Linking those lochs with each other, and with the sea, is the famous 22 miles of Caledonian Canal completed in 1847 by Thomas Telford to provide sailing ships with a safer passage than tacking around the extreme north of Scotland.

No mention of Loch Ness is complete without referring to the Monster. Pipers serenade it, tourists seek it, zoologists deny it, but in the last 40 years there have been 1,000 'sightings', and an inscription on a 14th-century map tells of 'waves without fish, fish without fins, islands that float' . . . scary stuff!

Loch Ness with Castle Urquhart in the foreground.

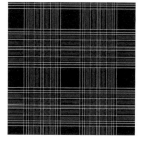

Loch Ness   5450   MacBean   952

LOCH NESS   5450

Designed in 1995 by Donald John MacKay of Luskentyre Harris Tweed for Mrs Rosemary Samios of Skye, this fashion tartan is also woven by Lochcarron of Scotland. Donald John first started weaving with his father at the age of twelve and has been doing so ever since. He was recently commissioned to weave 10,000 metres of special tweed for Nike shoes, which necessitated him calling on Harris Tweed weavers throughout the Outer Hebrides to meet the demand, because he could only produce so much in the loom shed behind his house.

Whilst this Loch Ness tartan is categorized as 'fashion' at the moment, it may soon, through use and wont, be regarded as a district tartan.

MACBEAN   952

Close to Loch Ness and Inverness (the mouth of the River Ness), MacBean or MacBain is one of the federated clans of Clan Chattan, on whose tartan vagaries there is no greater expert than Jamie Scarlett, author of *The Tartans of the Clan Chattan*. In his book he says:

> Ultimately we owe the MacBean tartan to the artist Robert McIan and to that artist's depiction of Gillies MacBean in his book, *The Clans of the Scottish Highlands*. Gillies, in conformity with the Victorian imagination, which always liked its Highlanders to go into battle in full evening dress, is wearing a kilt of the MacKintosh tartan and hose in a sett that appears to be the late 18th century Birrell tartan . . . the tartan trade has never missed a chance to proliferate tartans, and so it was an interpretation of McIan's interpretation of Birrell that became the MacBean.

Major Gillies MacBean, by the way, was a 6ft 4½in. combatant at the Battle of Culloden who, filling a breach in a wall, cut down and killed thirteen of the Hanoverian enemy before being killed himself. So great was his bravery that a Hanoverian officer is said to have called out 'Save that brave man!' but in the heat of battle he was slain. His widow is said to have composed a lament to his memory and a set of verses attributed to Lord Byron later appeared in a northern periodical, the last verse of which read:

> With thy back to the wall and thy breast to the targe,
> Full flashed thy claymore in the face of their charge;
> The blood of their boldest that barren turf stain,
> But alas! thine is reddest there, Gillies MacBain!

The famous Gillies MacBean at Culloden McIan

Clan Chattan   1851

Shaw   768

Weavers' proliferation or not, 200 years have passed and if the MacBean tartan is based on Major Gillies MacBean's hose, then it is a fitting and lasting tribute to just one of the many great warriors that came from Clan MacBean.

Extract from the *Clan Chattan Journal* written 14 September 1969 by Hughston McBain of McBain: 'I have just learned that one of our MacBean Clansmen, Com. Alan Bean, has been assigned the position of Explorer on the next flight to the moon on Apollo 12! . . . Commander Bean has agreed to take a half yard of MacBean Tartan with him, leave half of it on the moon as a flag, and bring back the other half for deposit in our Archives.'

CLAN CHATTAN   1851

Clan Chattan (pronounced *Hattan*) was the name of a group or confederation of individual clans which came together for mutual security. Its principal clans were MacIntosh, MacPherson, MacBean, Shaw, MacThomas, MacLeans of Dochgarroch, MacGillivray, Farquharson, Davidson, MacPhail, MacQueens of Strathdearn and the MacIntyres of Badenoch. Together those clans also had an amazing total of 153 septs – smaller dependent clans who looked to the 'parents' for security in return for their sworn allegiance in time of peace and war.

The story behind the Clan Chattan tartan is so long and convoluted that an illustration of this beautiful tartan – woven by Wilsons of Bannockburn in the early 1800s – will have to suffice.

SHAW   768

When the Victorian actor-cum-artist Ronald McIan (1803–56) painted Farquhar Shaw the Black Watch mutineer, he had no tartan to study but depended

Commander Alan Bean walks on the moon during the Apollo 12 landing of November 1969.
Unfortunately the tartan flag is not visible here.

on his friend and collaborator James Logan to describe the pattern to him. That description was faulty and so was born a completely false Shaw tartan which in reality had been the Black Watch coarse kilt sett from which, it's suggested, Logan had missed a red line – perhaps because it was hidden in the pleats of the kilt.

This Shaw tartan, shown here, was to remain in circulation until the 1970s, when Major C.J. Shaw of Tordarroch was recognised as Chief of all the Highland Shaws. All Shaws had always enjoyed the right to wear the MacKintosh tartan but as a result of a decree by the Lord Lyon of the day to the effect that only those who bore the name could wear the tartan, the Shaws were suddenly disenfranchised. Major Shaw had the option of continuing to wear the erroneous Shaw or having a new Shaw designed.

Shaw of Tordarroch Red 352   Farquharson   1957

Right: *The unfortunate Farquhar Shaw McIan*

Far right: *A Farquharson of 1715 from William Stewart's 1928 book* Clanland. *Stewart wrote of his subject that he was evidently lying in wait for a Lowlander!*

along most of the River Dee; the estate now covers about 200,000 acres of forest and moor in the region.

Of similar structure to the Gordon clan tartan, the Farquharson made its first public appearance in early-19th-century collections and Wilsons' 1819 Key Pattern Book.

One most unfortunate chief of the clan was Finlay Mòr, who was the Royal Standard Bearer. On his way to the Battle of Pinkie in 1547, aged 60, he was killed by a cannon ball fired from an offshore enemy ship. His body was interred in the Inveresk churchyard where his resting place is known to this day as the 'Lang Highlandman's Grave' – Finlay Mòr meaning 'Big Finlay'.

SHAW OF TORDARROCH RED   352
Major Shaw turned to D.C. Stewart (author of *The Setts of the Scottish Tartans*) for help and Donald created this design, called the Shaw of Tordarroch Red or Dress.

FARQUHARSON   1957
One imagines the Farquharsons must have had a plentiful supply of salmon since their lands stretched

MacGillivray

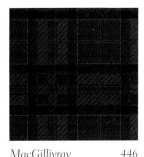

MacGillivray 446

MacGillivray Hunting 3371

The lands to the north of the Shaws belonged to the MacGillivrays, who were sandwiched between the Frasers and the MacIntoshes. The clan stood at the forefront of Scottish historical events for almost a thousand years and is one of the leading septs of Clan Chattan, an alliance which has prospered and endured to today.

The clan played a prominent part in the 1715 and 1745 risings and it was Chief Alexander MacGillivray – a tall, blond and handsome warrior – who perished when he led the Clan Chattan Regiment at Culloden, nearly wiping out the left wing of the Hanoverian army.

Another very colourful MacGillivray, according to Marion Elisha Tarvin's history of the family, was 'Lachlan McGillivray, a Scotch boy of sixteen summers, [who] had read of the wonders of America. He ran away from his parents at Dunmanglass, Scotland, and took passage for Charleston, S.C., arriving there safely in 1735, with no property but a shilling in his pocket, a suit of clothes, a stout frame, an honest heart, a fearless disposition and cheerful spirits.' Lachlan became an Indian trader, married a French Indian girl called Sehoy, made his fortune and attained great position and influence. His son Alexander (Hoboi-Hili-Miko – 'Good Child King') became a chief of the Creek Indians.

Lachlan returned to Scotland in 1782 and died on the Isle of Skye.

MacGillivray 446

This sett comes from the MacKintosh and is a good example of how existing tartans were manipulated to produce a new pattern – this one has had light and dark blue overchecks added. The first known date for this is 1819 when Wilsons of Bannockburn first wove it. That doesn't mean of course that it wasn't known before that date – Wilsons had their agents scouring the countryside for authentic tartans, so it could have been in existence for many years.

MacGillivray Hunting 3371

How this became MacGillivray Hunting is not clear. Jamie Scarlett also found it named MacAllister of Glenbarr and MacAllister of Glenbarr Hunting. He suggested that speculation was fruitless however, since the tartan trade had decided it was MacGillivray Hunting and that was what was printed

A MacGillivray, ready for battle McIan

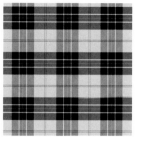

| MacPherson 1410 | MacPherson of Cluny 906 | MacPherson Hunting 547 | MacPherson Dress 1872 | Loch Laggan 796 |

in their sample books! He also commented, 'The early collectors [of tartan] played their cards pretty close to their chests. They were willing to enter into all kinds of pointless arguments with their rivals but remained cagey when it came to revealing the sources of their unusual specimens.' Thus, as with so many other tartans, we will probably never know how this design came into being and which clan had it first.

A cigarette card of the MacPherson tartan

MacPherson 1410

In 1816 when the Highland Society of London solicited samples of clan tartans for their records, the MacPherson chief of the day, Duncan, sent them this pattern which Wilsons of Bannockburn listed as No. 43 or Kidd or Caledonia. Why Duncan chose this fashion tartan to pass off as the clan tartan is hard to explain, especially when Wilsons already had a MacPherson tartan of impeccable provenance – the MacPherson of Cluny.

Scarlett suggested that since the Cluny tartan was a MacIntosh type favoured by the Jacobite clans, Duncan may have been sensitive about using it. Alternatively, it could be that Duncan regarded the MacPherson of Cluny as being his own private sett.

MacPherson of Cluny 906

Wilsons of Bannockburn included this in their 1819 Key Pattern book and it may be that they named it after the romantic Cluny MacPherson of '45 fame. It was certainly very popular, as shown by the number of letters that Wilsons received in the 1830s ordering lengths of it.

MacPherson Hunting 547

This tartan is claimed to be the earliest known to have been worn by the clan. It first appeared in the Smiths' 1850 *Authenticated Tartans of the Clans and*

Families of Scotland, which said of it: 'This pattern, which, upon the Chief's authority, we give as the Hunting MacPherson was made . . . for the grandmother of the present representative of the family, from an old shawl or plaid, which had been preserved in Cluny Castle for some generations.'

Jamie Scarlett in his 2003 *The Tartans of the Clan Chattan* explains that the shawl in question was

probably that given by Lord Lovat to his daughter when she married Ewen Macpherson of Cluny before the 1745 rebellion.

MacPherson Dress 1872

This first appeared in *Vestiarium Scoticum*. At the same time as the Sobieskis were selling it to Cluny MacPherson (the traditional name for the chief of the clan) Wilsons of Bannockburn were also making it under the name of 'Maggie Lauder', possibly named after Sir Dick Lauder's daughter – he being a great supporter of the two Sobieski brothers. When the Smith brothers asked Cluny MacPherson about it prior to 1850, he replied: 'The light one enclosed by you and now returned was known as "Breacan Glas" long before John Stuart [one of the Sobieski brothers]) was heard of in this country, although I rather think the addition of the yellow stripe was introduced by him, or rather taken from his MS; but at all events the Tartan is an old MacPherson.' 'Breacan Glas' is the Gaelic for Pied Wagtail.

This dress version with the yellow is said to have been worn by Duncan, the Chief in 1829, he having been supplied with the sett well in advance of the *Vestiarium* publication date of 1842.

Loch Laggan 796

Loch Laggan is a beautiful inland loch in MacPherson territory that forms the historic route south-west to Lochaber. The only reason this tartan seems to have been saved for posterity is that it was one of many deposited with the Highland Society of London in the early 1800s. Why, when the HSL had requested *clan* tartans, someone should include a district tartan, remains to be discovered.

Loch Laggan, the beautiful location for the television series Monarch of the Glen

Fraser

The Frasers were a hugely powerful family in Scotland whose influence and achievements spread around the globe. Their tartans are almost as confusing as their genealogy. The Frasers of Philorth, Lords Saltoun, although a Lowland family, are the senior line descended from Sir Alexander Fraser, who took part in the victory at Bannockburn in 1314. Their Chief today is Lady Saltoun, whose official title is Chief of the Name of Fraser.

FRASER   1424

Above: Castle Fraser, a magnificent 16th-century edifice

This is from the *Vestiarium Scoticum* and it has been claimed that the Sobieskis may have taken it from an earlier portrait of Robert Grant of Lurg. However, in 1850 the Smiths of Mauchline confirmed the choice with the following: 'We addressed Lord Lovat on the subject of the Frazer Tartan, who writes us, – "I many years ago took a great deal of trouble to find out the old set, and I ascertained, beyond all doubt, from the evidence of old people and old plaids, that the Frazer Tartan, previous to the year 1745, was the same pattern I now send you."' The Smiths were fastidious in their research and there is no reason to doubt this statement but it does cut across the assertion that the Fraser of Lovat was regarded as the Fraser clan tartan until the *Vestiarium* in 1842.

Fraser 1424

Fraser of Lovat 391

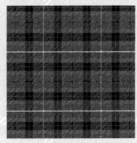

Fraser Hunting 1659

Fraser of Altyre 528

FRASER OF LOVAT 391

The Frasers of Lovat are descended from Sir Simon Fraser, the younger brother of Sir Alexander Fraser, Chamberlain of Scotland in Bruce's time. Their Chief today is Simon Fraser, 25th MacShimidh and 16th Lord Lovat. *MacShimidh* is the Gaelic for 'Son of Simon' and traditionally all chiefs on the Lovat side have held this title.

The Lovat side seem to have had more than their fair share of inspirational derring-do, and in 1900 the 14th Lord Lovat formed the Lovat Scouts for service in the Boer War. The Scouts went on to win honours in the First World War, and during the Second World War his son Simon,

15th Lord Lovat, along with his piper Bill Millen, led the Scouts' D-Day landing on the Normandy beaches under heavy fire. Lord Lovat died much respected and decorated in 1996 and was buried to the accompaniment of his brave and trusted piper – the same Bill Millen from the Normandy beaches.

FRASER HUNTING 1659

This tartan is something of a rarity in that it was said to have been designed by the Sobieski Stuarts at the request of Lord Lovat, rather than being one of their skilful but fanciful inventions from the *Vestiarium Scoticum*. They appear to have produced this by taking their Fraser tartan, and exchanging brown for red and then making some minor adjustments to the overstripes.

Apparently Lord Lovat wanted this tartan for the Inverness and Nairn Militia and it's reported that this was confirmed by a letter to Lord Lovat from the War Office, *circa* 1855, authorising its use for the corps.

FRASER OF ALTYRE 528

Another major branch of the Fraser clan was that of Altyre – a parish near Forres in Morayshire where Altyre House is now the home of the Gordon-Cumming family.

The way this pattern came to light is typical of many tartan finds. The thread count was apparently taken from a silk sample from Andersons of Edinburgh – a leading Highland dress 'purveyor' of the day – and an early researcher, MacGregor-Hastie, aged it to about 1850 on the basis of an old lady who said (c.1938) that a kilt of this pattern had been in the family for about 100 years.

Left: Highland pipers have been urging troops into battle since time immemorial, and these are the pipes of Bill Millen who, in June 1944, scorned withering enemy fire to stand on Sword Beach in Normandy playing 'Highland Laddie' to pipe ashore Simon Fraser, the 15th Lord Lovat, and his brigade of commandos. The faded tartan on Bill's pipes is in fact MacKenzie.

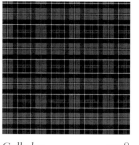

Culloden   1328

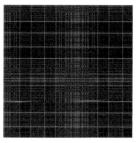

Lumsden   931

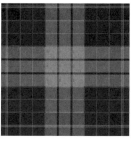

Lumsden Hunting   2366

The memorial cairn found on the Culloden Battlefield was erected by Duncan Forbes of Culloden in 1881, in memory of the fallen Jacobites.

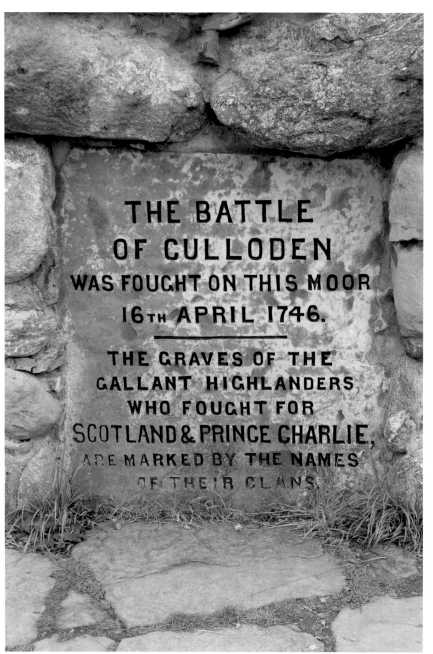

CULLODEN   1328

Culloden was the last great land battle fought on British soil and despite the fact that it pitted brother against brother and precipitated the most shameful slaughter of combatants by the Hanoverian forces, there remains a strange fascination with the event as evidenced by the many tartans it has spawned.

This one is the original, said to have been worn by a member of Prince Charles's staff during the battle, but which family or district it was associated with is not known. It was first illustrated in the 1893 *Old and Rare Scottish Tartans* by D.W. Stewart, whose son wrote in his own work *The Setts of the Scottish Tartans*:

'We have seen that highly complex tartans were in vogue at the time of the final crash of Jacobite hopes, and here we have one which shows that the Highland love of exuberant colour could express itself with admirable taste.'

This has now become the de facto district tartan for the Culloden area, although what we see now is probably not what it looked like originally and it is very likely that the purple and yellow were formerly blue and green respectively.

LUMSDEN   931

Another connection with Culloden is this Lumsden tartan, a shortened version of the more complicated sett found in a waistcoat said to have belonged to Andrew Lumsden, Prince Charles Edward's secretary. Attainted after Culloden, he fled to Rome and became secretary and then Secretary of State to Charles's father, James VIII the 'Old Pretender'. He returned to Scotland in 1773 and was fully pardoned in 1778. The tartan waistcoat is preserved at Pitcaple Castle, south-east of Huntly on the A96 road to Aberdeen.

Campbell of Cawdor   002   *MacIntosh   521*

LUMSDEN HUNTING   2366

Commissioned in 1997 by David Lumsden of Cushnie as a quieter alternative to the bright clan tartan. Designed by Peter MacDonald and based on the Old Stewart sett, this can be worn by all Lumsdens.

CAMPBELL OF CAWDOR   002

Eight miles from Culloden lies Cawdor Castle, the 15th-century home of one of the northern branches of the Campbells. The Smith brothers were quite loquacious in 1850 about this sett: 'Finding amongst the Tartan Manufacturers a pattern known by this name, we took the freedom to address the Earl of Cawdor on the subject, and we have his Lordship's authority for giving the adjoining pattern as the Tartan of his family.'

They continued by explaining the difference between this and other Campbell tartans but didn't go into its humble beginnings. It was originally a Wilsons' numbered pattern, acquiring the name 'Argyle' in 1798 and 'Argylle' in 1819, but it was not until the Smiths' work of 1850 that the full title was given of 'Campbell of Cawdor'.

MACINTOSH   521

The largest and most senior clan in the federation was that of MacIntosh and this clan tartan was the one signed, sealed and deposited in the Highland Society of London's collection around 1817. The design is known from older specimens and appears to have been the basis for a range of tartans from the 18th century to the present.

The Fiery Cross

IT'S said that the tradition of rallying one's clansmen with a flaming cross was the Scottish equivalent of the Old Norse fire arrow. Such a call to arms as the Fiery Cross was the direst of summons, which a clansman would ignore at his peril and subsequent ostracism.

The cross, shaped like the conventional Christian cross, was said to have been made of yew or hazel and small enough to be carried in one hand. The 'fiery' aspect of it seems to have varied:

A MacGregor bears the Fiery Cross.
Clanland

sometimes the ends of the horizontal bar were set alight and then extinguished in the blood of a goat 'slain for the purpose'; at other times, one of the ends would be set alight and a piece of white cloth stained in blood attached to the other as shown in this illustration by William Stewart from his 1928 book *Clanland*.

Two or more men, each with a fiery cross, would be dispatched by the chief in opposite directions and would run at full speed shouting the clan's war cry and naming the place and time of rendezvous. As they tired they would pass the 'baton' to a fresh runner and in this manner, huge swathes of territory could be covered in a short time. One of the last instances it was used in earnest – in 1745 by Lord Breadalbane – it went round Loch Tay, a distance of 32 miles, in three hours, to raise his people and prevent their joining the rebels.

Unfortunately the symbol was appropriated by America's notorious Ku Klux Klan and it became their most potent icon. Even today they try to justify its use with the cynically misleading claim that in Scotland 'it was utilized as a sign of opposition to tyranny from government and obedience to God'.

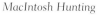

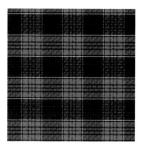

| MacIntosh Hunting | 544 | Anderson | 1394 | Royal Canadian Air Force 1343 |

MacIntosh Hunting 544

Despite this tartan being a figment of the imagination of someone in the weaving industry, how it ended up being accepted by the Chief as the clan's hunting tartan makes for rather hilarious reading as author Jamie Scarlett recorded.

An aunt of the late Chief apparently came across it for the first time in a tartan shop, thought it so awful that it should be suppressed and to that end bought up the entire stock. Unfortunately, this huge surge in demand only convinced the weavers how popular their new tartan was and galvanized them into further production. Lachlan the Chief was eventually forced to recognize it.

Above: A bewigged MacIntosh

Right: Archibald MacIntosh (left) demonstrates the origins of 'putting the shot', against the background of Strathnairn in Inverness-shire.

Carrying on south-west, MacDonnell and Cameron territory occupies both sides of the Great Glen – those clans were covered in the North-West section.

Anderson 1394

St Andrew is the patron saint of Scotland so it's not surprising that over many centuries Andrew has been one of the country's most popular first names. In its surname form 'Andrew's son' became Anderson in the Anglicized Lowlands of Scotland. The Highland form MacAndrews ('son of Andrew') owed its origin to its Gaelic root *Mac Ghille Andreis*, 'son of the servant of Saint Andrew'. Note the *Ghille* portion of the name meaning 'servant' – a word with which we are very familiar in modern times when thinking of grouse moors, stalking or salmon fishing expertly mentored by today's ghillies.

The MacAndrews first appeared around AD 1400 in the area called Badenoch – on either side of today's A9 trunk road stretching from Dalwhinnie in the south to Grantown on Spey in the north. The origins of their distinctive and elaborate tartan – it has seven colours instead of the normal maximum of six – can be found in many minor variations dating back to its first known 'outing' in a Paris merchant's sample book of 1880. The Highland Society of London began to collect specimens of tartans in 1815, but since the Anderson was not included it's assumed it was designed between then and its appearance in the J. Claude Frère et Cie's pattern book in Paris.

It's probable that it had its basis in one of the 'fancy' types of design that were becoming popular in those heady times after the 1822 Edinburgh visit of George IV. There was a ready sale for such patterns in the days when they could be worn for reasons of preference, and several of them, the Anderson among them, passed to posterity as clan tartans.

Clans, families and tartans grow more and more intriguing the further you look beneath the surface. A cursory Web search brings up a thousand references to the Anderson tartan but one of them just catches the eye:

Traditionally the Anderson family were farmers from the Perthshire region of Scotland. Daniel McLaggan Anderson migrated to Queensland, Australia on the 'Gulf of Carpentaria' when aged 19 in 1885, and began mixed farming in the Farnborough area near Yeppoon on the Central Queensland coast. Daniel would not have known that his wife-to-be, Isabella Kerr, had arrived in Queensland from Scotland in that same year aboard the 'Waroonga'. Isabella was 9 years old. Daniel and Isabella married in 1895 and continued farming in the area until moving to Rockhampton in 1926.

If Daniel was anything like so many other emigrating Scots, no doubt there was a length of Anderson tartan in the hold of the SS *Gulf of Carpentaria* on that voyage to the New World. That emigrant ship can still be seen today as part of Victoria's maritime history – as a shipwreck visited by scuba divers in one of the state's most popular national parks.

ROYAL CANADIAN AIR FORCE   1343

In the early 1940s the idea of a Royal Canadian Air Force tartan was sparked off by Group Captain E.G. Fullerton AFC, Commanding Officer of RCAF Station Trenton, Ontario. He completed preliminary sketches and the Loomcrofters of Gagetown, New Brunswick, were commissioned to produce a woven sample. After their modifying the design by adding a white line, the woven sample was sent to the Air Council, who made some minor changes to the shades of the blues.

Mystery enters the story here because after it was finally approved, submitted to the Lord Lyon of the day and then woven by Peter MacArthur, the resultant tartan was an exact copy of the Anderson with just three colour changes. This gives credence to the long-held belief that Wm. Anderson's of Edinburgh – whose weavers were Peter MacArthur and who were tartan and Highland dress suppliers to the Canadian forces in the 1940s – were involved in the design.

The next chapter in the life of the RCAF tartan is related by the Canadian Forces Base (CFB) Trenton Pipe Band website:

With the amalgamation of Canada's three military services in 1968, the distinctive blue Air Force uniform and the RCAF tartan was lost for over 20 years . . . This was a time of profound change for Canada's military, when unit titles, insignia, and all distinguishing

hallmarks of the Army, Navy, and Air Force were officially proscribed in favour of a singular, generic-looking force. In hindsight, it is incredible that the RCAF Tartan survived, for amid the post-integration haste for uniformity, precious swatches of the original tartan samples were incinerated, and its official documentation hung in oblivion. Thanks to the prudence of the RCAF Association, a piece of Air Force – indeed national – heritage was carefully preserved. Today, as much as ever, its colours reflect the mettle of a proud, professional Service.

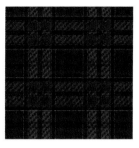

Grant   1384

An interesting tailpiece came to light in 2005 from John Bain, 83-year-old retired director of tartan weavers Peter MacArthur. He well remembers watching an old Hollywood 'cowboy and Indian' film set in the 19th century and seeing a close-up of an Indian squaw seated outside a tepee wrapped in a blanket of the unmistakable Royal Canadian Air Force tartan!

GRANT   1384

Twenty miles inland from the coast lies Grantown on Spey. As can be surmised from the name, it's on the River Spey and its founder was a Grant! Sir James Grant was the local laird and he established the town in 1766 on a 'greenfield site' at a road

Above: The Royal Canadian Air Force tartan, worn here by the Canadian Forces Base Pipe Band

Gordon

The Gordons were an ancient and distinguished family from Normandy that at one time was considered the most powerful clan in the north with its Chief, the Duke of Gordon, known as the Cock o' the North. Branches of the family acquired territory throughout the north-east and beyond, and many of the famous castles in the region were clan seats.

GORDON 223

The Gordon tartan is the regimental tartan of the famous Gordon Highlanders, whose formation is described on the regimental website as follows:

> Raised on the 10th February 1794 by the 4th Duke of Gordon and assisted by his wife the Duchess Jean, who rode to the country fairs in highland bonnet and regimental jacket, it is told how she would place a golden guinea between her lips and offer a kiss to any man who would take the king's shilling. On one occasion, a certain blacksmith, renowned for his strength and good looks and who had turned down other offers of recruitment, took the kiss and the guinea; but to show it was not the guinea that had tempted him, threw the guinea into the crowd.

This tartan was selected by Alexander, the 4th Duke, from a choice of three submitted by William Forsyth, a weaver and outfitter from the town of Huntly. Forsyth took the basic Black Watch or Government tartan (the 42nd Regiment plaid) and modified it. He wrote on 15 April 1793: 'When I had the honour of communing with His Grace the Duke of Gordon, he was desirous to have patterns of the 42nd Regiment plaid with a small yellow stripe

Left: *In this MacLeay portrait, Donald Gordon is wearing a kilt and plaid of Gordon tartan. His sword is inscribed Andrea de Ferrara, the name of a sword maker from Belluno in Italy, many of whose swords came to Scotland. In the background is a view of the hills above Abergeldie, just east of Balmoral.*

Above: *The main square of Huntly, in the Gordon heartland*

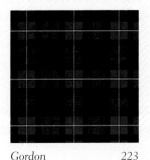

Gordon 223

Gordon Dress 3592

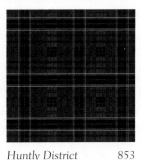

Huntly District 853

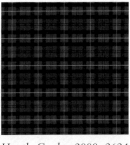

Huntly Gordon 2000 2624

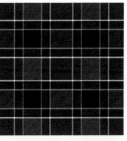

Gordon of Abergeldie 955

properly placed . . . I imagine the yellow stripes will appear very lively.'

A Gordon website suggests that the Duke offered the other two Forsyth samples to other Gordon families and that the Gordons of Hallhead and Esslemont selected the tartan with three yellow lines and the Gordon-Cummings of Altyre and Gordonstoun chose the one with two yellow lines. Some academics view this with suspicion and think the story is based on the Sobieski brothers' misinterpretation of the Forsyth letter.

GORDON DRESS 3592

The Gordon Dress tartan seems to have suffered more than most from the whims of individual weavers and fashion designers and there are over a dozen different versions. An amusing historical note relates to one particular fashion version: 'The Marquis of Huntly did NOT approve of this trade fancy but could do little about it when his American wife insisted on dressing the children in it.' The sett shown here is the most commonly accepted Gordon Dress available today.

HUNTLY DISTRICT 853

A very different Huntly tartan from Wilsons was their Marchioness of Huntly, which was claimed to have been worn at the time of the '45 rebellion by Brodies, Forbeses, Gordons, MacRaes, Munros and Rosses. That gives a strong indication of the greater antiquity of the district setts compared to the clan tartans. Jamie Scarlett suggests that this tartan was the personal tartan of the Marchioness, thus the Wilsons' name, but over time, because it contained the name 'Huntly' it became accepted and used as the district tartan for Huntly.

HUNTLY GORDON 2000 2624

A method of bringing democracy into the world of district tartans was this celebratory design from Claire Donaldson of the Perth weavers the House of Edgar. It was chosen by the local people of Huntly from a number of trial designs to celebrate the Gordon Millennium Gathering held there in August 2000.

GORDON OF ABERGELDIE 955

South of Huntly at Ballater and just a couple of miles from Balmoral Castle is the family seat of the Abergeldie Gordons. This tartan was taken from a portrait of Rachael Gordon of Abergeldie, painted in 1723. The author D.C. Stewart played down the importance of this and attributed it to a fashion tartan of the day into which more should not be read just because it appeared in the portrait. He may have been right, but tartan as an industrial fashion cloth was still nearly 100 years away and this could equally have been locally produced around the Ballater area.

Like many of these ancient buildings, the castle is host to its own ghost – a servant called French Kate or Kitty Ranke who was suspected of practising black magic. Her spirit is said to inhabit the castle in protest at her being burnt at the stake for her supposed crimes.

GORDON OF ESSLEMONT 1064

The ruins of Esslemont Castle are near the town of Ellon, north of Aberdeen. This tartan was previously called 'Ancient Gordon' and the claim has been made – as mentioned earlier – that it was one of the 'also-rans' offered to the Duke of Gordon by Huntly weaver William Forsyth. Whether or not the story is accurate, the Gordons of Esslemont now have this three-striped version of the regimental sett as their clan tartan.

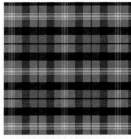

Gordon of Esslemont 1064

The Duke of Gordon monument in Elgin

51

Above: Grant of Glenmorrison McIan

Opposite: Craigievar's Great Tower has changed very little since it was first built by Master William Forbes in the early 17th century. His family continued to live in the castle for the next 350 years and when a group of benefactors (including members of the family) bought the castle and presented it to The National Trust for Scotland in 1963, it came complete with the vast majority of the contents, collected and lovingly preserved over centuries by the Forbes-Sempill family.

junction on the north side of the Spey. Whilst it was not the prime reason for his act, he did rehouse his tenants displaced by the agricultural reforms that he introduced in his considerable estates.

The imprecise history of tartan is exemplified by the existence at one time of ten Grant portraits at Cullen House, on the Moray Firth a few miles east of Buckie. In those, each brother wore a different tartan, and where a coat or plaid was worn, those also differed!

The tartan shown here was originally called 'New Bruce' and in the 1819 Key Pattern Book of Wilsons of Bannockburn is this hand-written note: 'How this pattern was named Bruce cannot be found out. In 1819 Patrick Grant of Redcastle, Ross-shire, head of a great branch of the Clan Grant ordered 200 yards of this Pattern as the tartan of his own Clan.' Thus did this pattern become the accepted clan tartan which was later – much later in 1946 – recorded in the Lord Lyon Public Register of all Arms and Bearings in Scotland. To muddy the water even more, it's said that this was also worn by the Drummonds when they met George IV in 1822 and it is still sold as Drummond to this day.

In 1820 the Chief of the Grants is said to have called out his clansmen by sending round the Fiery Cross – the last time this was ever done – to defend his brother who was trying to be elected as the Member of Parliament for Elgin and had been attacked and locked in his house by supporters of the other candidate. Eight hundred clansmen rallied to the Cross and 'the townspeople fled at their coming'.

FORBES 211
In the 14th and 15th centuries the Forbes clan was the leading power in Aberdeenshire but became embroiled in a long and murderous struggle with the Gordons. At the Reformation, religion was added to the equation, with the Gordons remaining defiantly Catholic and joined by the Forbeses' traditional enemies, the Leslies, plus the Irvines and Setons. Ranged against them were the Protestant Forbeses and their allies including the Frasers and Crichtons. Eventually, two Acts of Parliament were enacted to force the clans to lay down their arms but for the Forbeses it was too late and much of their land had to be sold to cover accrued debts.

Forbes 211 Skene 516

This is the Forbes tartan in use today, which first appeared in the Wilsons' 1819 pattern book. In William and Andrew Smith's 1850 *Authenticated Tartans of the Clans and Families of Scotland* they write: 'The correctness of the Forbes Tartan here given, seems to be, in the opinion of the Trade, a matter beyond the slightest doubt: it was once worn by the 74th regiment, but that corps now wear the Lamont in use today.'

SKENE 516
The Skene armorial bearings contain, amongst other elements, wolves' heads, daggers, a laurel wreath and the motto *Virtutis Regia Merces*, 'A Palace the Reward of Bravery'. These all encapsulate the legend of the origin of the clan, which, according to 'tradition and old chronicle' as related by the Smith brothers in their 1850 book, is that, in 1014, King Malcolm II, travelling south near Aberdeen, was attacked by a ravenous wolf. Fortunately, a younger son of Donald of the Isles 'rushed in between His Majesty and the wolf, thrust his left hand, which he had wrapped in his plaid, into the beast's mouth, and then dispatched him with his skean [*sgian*, pronounced *skee-an*, Gaelic for dirk or knife]'.

For that brave act the King 'gave him lands extending about five miles in length, conferred on him and the lands, the name of Skene of Skene'. Interestingly, the arms, which date to 1604, contain possibly the earliest example of the little kilt.

Some confusion surrounds their tartan however and prior to the Smiths' naming of it as Skene, it had been known as Logan. The Smiths' accompanying comment was: 'we must confess that it is a pattern about the antiquity of which we entertain some doubts'. The clan also uses a second tartan which they refer to as the Skene Ancient.

The 'Right' to Wear a Tartan

Often over the years one has heard people explaining how they have 'the right' or that they are 'entitled' to wear this or that tartan. In fact no such right, in any legal sense, exists for them or for anyone else. The only considerations which govern the wearing of a particular sett are usage and good taste.

P ERHAPS somewhat surprisingly there is no legal definition of what is or what is not the tartan of a particular clan. It is now accepted that the arbiter of what the clan should wear is its chief but his decision has no legal force behind it.

The general idea of using tartan for identification is of relatively modern origin; it gained ground swiftly in the early 1800s, when surviving correspondence shows chiefs (heads of major clans) and chieftains (heads of minor clans) writing to ask the manufacturers what their tartan was. They received a ready response.

The Officers of Arms in procession at the Thistle Installation Service at St Giles Cathedral, Edinburgh, in 2003

Prior to this, for centuries, the pattern of a man's plaid depended on what was available locally and which pattern took his fancy. By the end of the eighteenth century the manufacture of tartan had moved from being a local cottage industry down into the Lowlands and into the hands of such large firms as Wilsons of Bannockburn whose marketing skill was of a high order by the standards of any age. The steady production of new patterns given attractive names coincided with the great growth of romanticisation of all things Highland and the boom in clan tartans was on.

People who asked for a particular clan tartan were readily obliged and in the pattern books of the day it is possible to see the change of title as, for instance, in the case of Wilsons' pattern No. 250 which becomes successively 'Argyll' and then 'Campbell of Cawdor'. Sometimes the attribution was duplicated, a pattern is shown under several different clan names, and minute differences in a basic sett sufficed to produce a new clan tartan.

To sum up then, the whole subject of wearing a tartan with a particular significance is open to interpretation. For my own part – and I would stress again that this is only a personal opinion – I see nothing very wrong in people wearing any particular tartan which takes their fancy; such, after all, was the original use. I can sympathise with those who seek any relation however distant whose tartan they may wear, although I believe it wrong to claim that such a relationship confers any sort of right.

So the answer to the question 'What tartan am I entitled to wear?' is – 'Any tartan you fancy.' The sole considerations are good taste – some tartans are appalling clashes of colour! Highland attire looks smart and feels great to wear. Perhaps Cary Grant's advice for choosing a tie – always dress to go with your eyes – is also the best criterion for choosing a tartan.

Alastair Campbell of Airds
Unicorn Pursuivant of Arms
The Court of the Lord Lyon

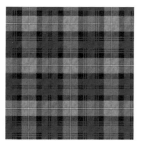
Sempill   2420

Leslie   1113

Leslie Red   1142

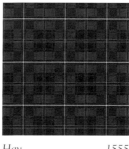
Hay   1555

SEMPILL 2420

The Sempills originally came from Renfrewshire and were awarded land in the Largs area in gratitude for their support of Robert the Bruce. In 1884 the Chief died without issue and the title passed to her great-nephew Sir William Forbes of Craigievar in Aberdeenshire. The National Trust for Scotland now owns Craigievar, commenting: 'This perfect Scottish castle remains as unspoiled as it was when lived in by the Forbes-Sempill family.'

The historic connection between the Forbeses and the Sempills can be seen in the similarity of the tartans. Sir Thomas Innes of Learney, GCVO, Lord Lyon 1945–69, suggested that red should be used in the tartan because that colour was in the Sempill chevron. The white in the Forbes was adjusted to light blue as a late change and a further difference.

LESLIE 1113

When Edward the Atheling, the Saxon claimant to the throne of England, was defeated by William the Conqueror, he fled to Scotland with his Hungarian mother – herself a princess – and his two sisters. One of them, Margaret, married King Malcolm III of Scotland. Her Chamberlain was a Hungarian nobleman called Bartholf whose abilities soon impressed the King, and the Barony of Leslie near Aberdeen was granted to the family. The Leslies excelled as soldiers of fortune – mercenaries – and many served with great distinction on the Continent. No doubt their long-standing strife with their traditional enemies and neighbours, the Forbeses, honed these military skills.

This tartan – also called Leslie Hunting and Green Leslie – is thought to have been designed around 1810 and in 1850 the Smiths wrote: 'The present possessor of this ancient title is George William Evelyn Leslie, fourteenth Earl; and we know that the Tartan here given is worn by his Lordship.'

The tartan also became that of the King's Own Scottish Borderers – see page 175 in the Border Lands section.

LESLIE RED 1142

In their 1842 *Vestiarium Scoticum* the Sobieskis unveiled the red dress tartan for the Leslies, which is similar to another of their inventions – the Red Brodie. Many of the Sobieskis' contemporaries were completely taken in by them and their use of supposed quaint old Scots helped to maintain the illusion. This is how they described the Red Leslie: 'Leslye heth fovr stryppis vpon ane reidd fyld, of ye quhilk stryppis ye ynnermaist be blak, and ye tua vtterward blew, and throuch ye ylk blak ane spraing zello, and throuch ye scarlat ane spraing blak.'

HAY 1555

The Hays – or de la Hayes – first came to Scotland from France about 1160, the name being a place name in Normandy. The falcon featured in their arms, together with the two country men holding oxen yokes and the clan motto of *serva jugum* ('keep the yoke'), either lends credence to a clan myth or prompted the invention of the myth in the first place! Here's how Alexander Nisbet told the tale in 1722:

In the reign of King Kenneth III, about the year 980, when the Danes invaded Scotland, and prevailing in the Battle of Luncarty, a country Scotsman with his two sons, of great strength and courage, having rural weapons, as the yokes of their plough and such plough furniture, stopped the Scots in their flight in a certain defile, and upbraiding them with cowardice, obliged them to rally, who with them renewed the battle and gave a total overthrow to the victorious Danes; and it is said by some, after the victory was obtained, the old man, lying on the ground, wounded and fatigued, cried 'Hay, Hay,' which word became a surname to his posterity. The King gave them as much land in the Carse of Gowrie as a falcon did fly over without lighting, which having flown a great way she lighted on a stone there called the Falcon Stone to this day.

Over the centuries the Hays acquired more land and honours through marriage and royal patronage and their influence spread to many other parts of Scotland as far south as Stranraer.

Hay was the real name of the Sobieski brothers, and if this tartan was pure invention rather than a copy of a contemporary sett, it does indeed show the great design skills of John Sobieski Hay.

HAY & LEITH   1215

This beautiful tartan has been variously named Hay & Leith, Leith & Hay, Hay of Leith, Hay/Leith, Hay and, in Wilsons' 1819 pattern book, Leith – perhaps another of their old town tartans like Crieff or Glasgow. The Hay & Leith label suggests that it was perhaps adopted or recycled as a family tartan through marriage – the Hays' home was the uniquely Scottish Delgatie Castle in Turriff whilst 26 miles away in Rhynie lay Leith Hall, now operated by the National Trust for Scotland.

Leith Hall, a typical Scottish laird's residence, was built over three centuries, starting in 1650, and remained the home of the Leith-Hay family until the mid-20th century. The family line was tragically brought to an end by a motor cycle accident in 1939 which killed the young 23rd Chief of the House of Leith, Charles Leith-Hay of Rannes. Six years later Charles' mother passed the property to the National Trust for Scotland.

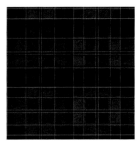
Hay & Leith 1215

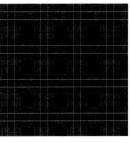
Cumming 1157

Cumming Hunting 4636

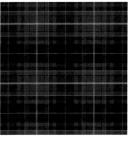
Gordonstoun School 362

CUMMING 1157

To the west of Hay territory lay the Cumins, Comyns or Cummings who were at the height of their power and influence in the early 13th century when it's reported that they had amongst their number one lord, four earls and 32 knights. 'Black Comyn' was one of the six guardians of Scotland during the minority of the Maid of Norway and his son was the famous 'Red Comyn' whose intrigues and shifting loyalties resulted in his murder by King-to-be Robert Bruce and two of his followers.

The surname is thought to come from Comines, a village near Lille in northern France, and to have been brought over with the Norman Conquest in 1066. There were Cumins in Scotland before that but those names are said to have been associated with the spice cumin. A rather fanciful explanation of the origin of the name comes from Andrew Wyntoun (c.1350–1420) in his *Orygynale Cronykil of Scotland*. In that eight-volume manuscript he suggests that there was at the court of Malcolm III a young foreigner whose task was that of door-ward or usher of the royal apartment. In his early days he only knew two words of the Scottish language, 'Cum in,' and accordingly became known by that name!

Sir Thomas Dick Lauder, writing to Sir Walter Scott in 1829 about the forthcoming *Vestiarium Scoticum*, said: 'Comyn, who was quite ignorant of his tartan, has now worn [it] more than ever at the Caledonian Balls in London his "twa wyd strypis of greine upon ain scarlatt field", &c.; and so of many more whom the Messrs Hay have enlightened as being their particular friends.'

In 1849, a different version had been accepted according to William and Andrew Smith, who wrote: 'Sir W.G. Gordon Cumming is now the head of this family, and from him we received the pattern here given as "The Cumyn Tartan".'

CUMMING HUNTING 4636

It has been suggested that this is a misrepresentation of an early Wilsons of Bannockburn pattern called Cumming and Glenorchy. It was possibly chosen as a hunting tartan because of the name association and the fact that it was quieter than the clan tartan.

GORDONSTOUN SCHOOL 362

Clearly based on the Cumming Hunting tartan is that of the famous Gordonstoun School in Morayshire, founded by Dr Kurt Hahn who left Germany to escape Nazi aggression. Its most famous modern ex-pupil is Charles, HRH The Prince of Wales. Dr Hahn settled on two historic 17th-century buildings, Gordonstoun House and Round Square, in Morayshire, that had been built by the famed eccentric Sir Robert Gordon, the Wizard of Gordonstoun. With a handful of boys he opened the school in 1933.

The tartan, designed *circa* 1956 by Gilbert Duncan Macleod Bullard, is a marriage of the three families who have owned Gordonstoun Estate over the centuries – Innes (1535–1616), Gordon (1616–1805) and Cumming (1805 1934). The Hunting Cumming dominates as it was the most recent family to own the estate. The single black stripe of 12 threads was replaced by the pale blue from the Innes and the yellow stripe derives from the military Gordon. It took over a year to develop and several attempts to get the right balance. The original samples were woven by Campbells of Highland Tweed House, Beauly, but the actual production went to the Border firm of D.C. Dalgliesh. It is now produced in two weights by the Morayshire weavers Johnstons of Elgin.

The Cumming tartan McIan

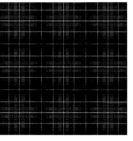

Innes   361

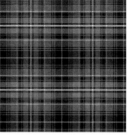

Innes of Learney   367

MacDuff   2455

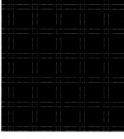

Red Brodie   1192

Dunbar of Pitgaveny   1634

The commentary to this McIan portrait explains that this is not only a MacDuff but the Duff himself! It explains that he wears 'mogans' or knitted stockings without feet, 'by no means an uncommon covering, which is used more for the purpose of protecting the legs from the prickly shrubs, than as an appurtenances of dress'.

INNES   361

Just west of the Hays' north-eastern territory lie the Innes lands. Understandably, confusion arose with the tartans of the Inneses and MacInneses and it wasn't until 1951 that a record of the accepted clan tartan was made in the Lord Lyon Public Register of all Arms and Bearings in Scotland.

The root of Innes is *Innis*, the Gaelic for 'meadow' or 'island', which is descriptive of the six-mile stretch along the south shore of the Moray Firth between the River Spey and the River Lossie that was gifted to the family in 1160 by King Malcolm IV. MacInnes on the other hand means 'Son of Angus' and that clan comes from quite a different area of Scotland – Morven in the west around Fort William.

Traditionally this tartan had seven colours, which made life awkward for weavers who, conventionally, were only used to weaving a maximum of six. That problem was solved by replacing the azure (light blue) shown here, with black.

Through service to the Crown and profitable marriages the Inneses grew to be one of the most powerful families in the province and left behind a rich legacy of castles and houses including, 4 miles east of Elgin at Coxton, the archetypal Scottish tower house with its five-feet-thick walls, built in 1644.

Elgin Cathedral, 'the Lantern of the North', is another monument to the family, rebuilt by John Innes, Bishop of Moray, in 1407–14 after it was sacked and burned by the Wolf of Badenoch.

INNES OF LEARNEY   367

This version was worn by Innes of Learney (a former Lord Lyon) and was reputed to be his personal tartan. It was designed by making colour changes to the Innes tartan at 361.

MACDUFF   2455

Right on the coast of the Moray Firth were the MacDuffs, whose dynasty started in Fife in the 12th century but moved north to Banffshire after the southern line died out.

The very positive confirmation of their tartan seems to come from Andrew and William Smith in their 1850 *Authenticated Tartans of the Clans and Families of Scotland*. Of this they say: 'Our authority for this Tartan is "use and wont". It is universally worn in the North as MacDuff, it has always been known by the "Trade" as such; and upon a late occasion, when, in honour of Her Majesty, there was one of those grand fetes given at Braemar, called a "Gathering," the numerous retainers of General Duff and many others were attired in this Tartan.' 'Her Majesty' was of course Queen Victoria.

RED BRODIE   1192

The origin of the name is the lands of Brodie, close to Forres in Morayshire, and the 16th-century Brodie Castle near Forres is now owned by the National Trust for Scotland. Distinguished members of this ancient 12th-century clan range from the Lord Lyon King of Arms during the Jacobite rebellion to the colourful Deacon William Brodie – Edinburgh councillor by day and burglar by night.

He was a skilful cabinet maker but would copy the door keys of his clients and return at leisure with an accomplice to rob them. He was said to have been the inspiration for Robert Louis Stevenson's *Dr Jekyll and Mr Hyde*, and although the Deacon Brodie public house in Edinburgh's Royal Mile is said to have been named after his father Francis, it tends to be looked upon as commemorating the notorious son.

The tartan worn by Brodies at the time of William's trial and death in 1788 – despite wearing a special steel collar and bribing the hangman, he couldn't be revived – was said to have been the Huntly. A few decades later, however, the Brodies adopted this new Red Brodie tartan which was yet another product of the inventive minds and skilful pens of the Sobieski brothers.

Left: The Deacon Brodie public house in Edinburgh's old High Street

DUNBAR OF PITGAVENY   1634

Near neighbours to the Brodies were the Dunbars of Pitgaveny in the Elgin area of Morayshire – just one of the five branches of the once great Dunbar dynasty. The Earldom of Murray was acquired through a marriage to Black Agnes Randolph, a famous character mentioned later in the Borders section. A 17th-century historian remarked: 'Second only to the Cummings, and of course, the Royal family, the Dunbars are the greatest family of Scotland.'

In 1815 members of the Highland Society of London resolved to request of each of the Highland chiefs a sample of their clan tartan. The swatches were to be signed and sealed in the chief's own hand. This most unusual sett – hardly recognizable as a tartan – is said to be one of those delivered to the Society between 1815 and 1822.

Below: The 16th-century Brodie Castle

MORRISON

MACLEOD

Lewis

MACAULAY

MACLEOD

Harris

North
Uist

MACDONALD

MACNICOL

MACLEOD
Portree

Raasay

Skye

MACKINNON

South
Uist

MACDONALD

Soay

MACNEIL
Barra

MACDONALD
Rum

Eigg

Mull
Ulva

MACQUARRIE

MACLEAN

Iona

MACNEIL
Colonsay

MACFIE

Jura

MACGILL

CURRIE

Islay

Gigha

0   10   20   30   40   50 kilometres

0   10   20   30 miles

THE ISLANDS

What better way to introduce the tartans of the Isles than with that classic and evocative marching song written by the famous Minister Bard of Gigha, the Revd Kenneth MacLeod (1871–1955)? There must hardly be a Scot anywhere who, on hearing the names Loch Tummel, Loch Rannoch, Lochaber or the Cuillins, can resist humming or breaking into silent song with the chorus from 'The Road to the Isles'.

Sure by Tummel and Loch Rannoch
And Lochaber I will go
By heather tracks wi' heaven in their wiles.
If it's thinkin' in your inner heart
The braggart's in my step,
You've never smelled the tangle o' the Isles.
Oh the far Coolins are puttin' love on me
As step I wi' my cromack to the Isles.

Luskentyre, Isle of Harris

Red MacLeod   496   MacLeod Yellow   1272

Skye

The Coolins, or Cuillins to give them their correct name, are the black basalt mountain range in the south of Skye beloved of climbers that history says got its name from the legendary Irish hunter Cu Chulainn, said to have come from Ireland to Skye in two great strides! The Cuillins form the heart of MacLeod country, and one of the great glens running due south through them to the sea and the island of Soay is Sligachan, pictured on Raphael Tuck's 1906 postcard shown here that features the Dress MacLeod tartan – also known as MacLeod of Lewis and, jokingly, as the 'Loud MacLeod'.

In 1906 W. & A.K. Johnston's *The Tartans of the Clans and Septs of Scotland* remarked upon the widespread distribution of the MacLeods: 'In modern times the most famous members of the clan have been the scions of the MacLeods of Morven . . . but all over the world are to be found cadets [families of younger sons] – MacLeods of Gesto, of Meidle and Glendale, of Drynoch, of Talisker, of Bernera, of Hamer, of Greshornish, of Ulinish, Dalvey, Orbost, Rigg, Assynt, Geanies, and many others.'

Fortunately they don't all have their own tartans since the situation is complicated enough. Many 19th-century portrait painters threw the cat amongst the tartan pigeons by draping their sitters in whatever piece of tartan they had lying around in the studio. Similarly they often painted the sitter's features from life and then clothed them at a later date – sometimes after the sitter's death. This frequently led later researchers astray and resulted in false attributions and obfuscation! The classic example of this can be seen in the Red MacLeod.

RED MACLEOD   496

This tartan has a fascinating history. Many years ago a researcher reconstructed it from a plaid in a portrait of Norman MacLeod, 22nd Chief of the Clan, painted by Allan Ramsay in 1747 – the year following the prohibition of tartan. Following publication of the information, members of the Clan MacLeod Society expressed a desire to use this 'new' red tartan in addition to the commonly seen Green or Hunting, and the Yellow or 'Loud' MacLeod. They assumed, as had the researcher initially, that the sett was a MacLeod and adopted it enthusiastically. It was only later discovered that the tartan was in fact Murray of Tullibardine whose home ground was some 100 miles to the south. To regularize the situation, 'in 1982 the Clan Chief, John MacLeod of MacLeod, agreed at a Clan Parliament that a new modified version of the misattributed tartan should be officially adopted as the Red MacLeod and the yellow lines were introduced to enhance the family resemblance to other MacLeod tartans.

MACLEOD YELLOW   1272

This first appeared from the Sobieski brothers in 1829 – a good few years before its inclusion in their 1842 publication *Vestiarium Scoticum*. Sir Thomas Dick Lauder was a friend of theirs and of Sir Walter Scott and wrote to Scott saying, 'MacLeod has got a sketch of this splendid tartan, three black stryps upon ain yellow fylde.' MacLeod was apparently a 'particular friend' of the brothers, one of whom gave him the yellow design which had never been seen before. An early researcher D.C. Stewart commented that the choice of colour was very brave of the 'inventive' Sobieskis, whilst a critic of the two

Above: A postcard from the 1906 Raphael Tuck clan series featuring the 'Loud Macleod' tartan and Glen Sligachan – Gaelic for 'shelly place' – on Skye.

Left: Standing at the Sligachan Hotel and looking south, the dramatic glen separates the jagged Black Cuillin to the west from the smooth-topped Red Cuillin hills to the east and runs down to the sea at Camasunary near the tiny settlement of Elgol.

The Fairy Flag

Dunvegan Castle is the MacLeod family seat and it was said, in 1906,
to combine the romance of the ninth century with the comfort of the twentieth.
Most famous of its countless relics is the Fairy Flag.

Dunvegan Castle, ancient home to Clan MacLeod

Once upon a time . . . many, many years ago, the Chief of Clan MacLeod was a handsome, intelligent man, and all the young ladies in the area were very attracted to him, but none suited his fancy. One day, he met a fairy princess, a bean shìth, one of the Shining Folk. Like all the other females he met, she fell madly in love with him, and he with her as well. When the princess appealed to the King of the Fairies for permission to marry the handsome Chief, he refused, saying that it would only break her heart, as humans soon age and die, and the Shining Folk live forever. She cried and wept so bitterly that even the great King relented, and agreed that she and the Chief could be hand-fasted for a year and a day. But, at the end of that time, she must return to the land of Fairie and leave behind everything from the human world. She agreed, and soon she and the young MacLeod were married with great ceremony.

No happier time ever existed before or since for the Clan MacLeod, for the Chief and Lady MacLeod were enraptured of each other. As you might expect, soon a strapping and handsome son was born to the happy couple, and the rejoicing and celebration by the Clan went on for days. However, the days soon passed and a year and a day were gone in a heartbeat. The King led the Fairie Raide down from the clouds to the end of the great causeway of Dunvegan Castle, and there they waited in all their glamourie and finery for the Lady MacLeod to keep her promise.

Lady MacLeod knew that she had no choice, so she held her son to her, hugged him tightly, and at last ran from the castle tower to join the Fairie Raide, and returned with them to the land of Fairie. Before she left, however, she made her husband promise that her child would never be left alone, and never be allowed to cry, for she could not bear the sound of her son's cries.

The Chief was brokenhearted with the loss of his wife, but he knew, as did she, that the day would come when she would return. He kept his promise, and never was the young MacLeod allowed to cry and never was he left unattended. However, the Laird of MacLeod remained depressed, and grieved for the loss of his lady. The folk of the clan decided that something must be done, and on his birthday a great feast was proclaimed with revelry and dancing until dawn. The Laird had always been a grand dancer, and at long last he agreed to dance to the pipers' tunes. So great was the celebration that the young maid assigned to watch the infant Laird left his nursery and crept to the top of the stairs to watch the folk dancing in all their finery and to listen to the wonderful music. So enraptured was she that she did not hear the young Laird awaken and begin to cry.

So pitiful was his crying that it was heard all the way in the Land of Fairie, and when his mother heard it, she immediately appeared at his crib, took him in her arms, and comforted him, drying his tears and wrapping him in her fairy shawl. She whispered magic words in his ears, laid her now-sleeping son in his crib, kissed him once more on the forehead, and was gone.

Years later when the young lad grew older, he told his father of his mother's late-night visit, and that her shawl was a magic talisman. It was to be kept in a safe place, and if anyone not of the Clan MacLeod touched it, they would vanish in a puff of smoke. If ever the Clan MacLeod faced mortal danger, the Fairy Flag was to be waved three times, and the hosts of Fairie, the Knights of the Fairie Raide, would ride to the defence of the Clan MacLeod.

There were to be three such blessings, and only in the most dire consequences should the Fairie magic be used. The Chief placed the Fairy Flag in a special locked box, and it was carried with the Chief wherever he went.

Hundreds of years later, the fierce Clan Donald of the Lord of the Isles had besieged the MacLeods in battle, and the MacLeods were outnumbered three to one. Just before the Donalds' last charge, the Chief opened the box, and placing the Fairy Flag on a pole, waved it once, twice, and three times. As the third wave was completed, the Fairy magic caused the MacLeods to appear to be ten times their number! Thinking that the MacLeods had been reinforced, the Donalds turned and ran, never to threaten the MacLeods to this very day.

On another occasion, a terrible plague had killed nearly all the MacLeods' cattle, and the Chief faced the prospect of a winter of starvation for all his people. Having no alternative, he went to the tallest tower of Dunvegan Castle, attached the Fairy Flag to a pole, and waved it once, twice, three times. The Hosts of Fairie rode down from the clouds, swords drawn, and rode like the wind over the dead and dying cattle. They touched each cow with their swords, and where there once had been dead and dying cows, now stood huge, healthy, and well-fattened cattle, more than enough to feed the Clan for the winter to come.

There remains one more waving of the Fairy Flag, and the Flag is on display at Dunvegan Castle, there awaiting the next threat to the Clan MacLeod.

It is said during World War II that young men from the Clan MacLeod carried pictures of the Flag in their wallets while flying in the Battle of Britain, and not one of them was lost to the German flyers. In fact, the Chief of Clan MacLeod had agreed to bring the Fairy Flag to England and wave it from the Cliffs of Dover should the Germans attempt to invade Great Britain.

(Reproduced from www.dianaduncan.homestead.com/Scots.html.)

Sir Reginald MacLeod of MacLeod (1847–1935), the 27th Chief and Under-Secretary for Scotland, had the Fairy Flag mounted in a specially sealed frame. An expert from the Victoria and Albert Museum in London apparently discussed with Sir Reginald the possible origins of the flag, but avoided any reference to the supernatural. The chief listened politely, and at the conclusion of the thesis, simply said, 'You may believe that, but I know that it was given to my ancestor by the fairies.'

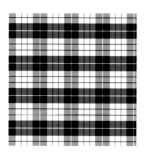

MacLeod Black & White
1828

compared it to a horse blanket! It's also called MacLeod of Lewis and elsewhere MacLeod of Lewis and Raasay. John Macleod of Raasay, 13th Chief, was painted wearing this pattern in about 1840.

MacLeod Black & White   1828
Apparently a colour variation of the MacLeod of Lewis, the MacLeod Black & White or 'Mourning' tartan first appeared in a work of 1906. The introduction of mourning tartans was part of the Victorian love of pomp and ceremony which was, as can be imagined, readily embraced by the weavers of the day.

Green MacLeod   1583
This simple design is the one most usually worn by MacLeods across the world. Although it was first described in Logan's 1831 book it was not generally used until authorised by the Chief in 1909. The origins of the design are obscure but, without the black guards on the yellow, the design was worn by Loudoun's Highlanders (1745–8). Its basic format is therefore very old.

MacKenzie   267
In 1777, the 73rd Regiment was raised by John, eldest son of the Earl of Cromartie, and was known as Lord MacLeod's Highlanders because his courtesy title was Lord MacLeod, even though his family name was MacKenzie. Because of this, and for about 100 years, the MacLeods wore the MacKenzie tartan as their own. It was worn by Neil MacLeod of Dunvegan in the MacLeay portrait of 1868 shown opposite.

MacLeod of Gesto   1258
Not a great deal is known of this beautiful tartan, which bears a striking similarity to the MacFarlane and Clan Chattan designs, except that it was woven by the famous weavers Wilsons of Bannockburn before 1850. The MacLeods of Gesto occupied land on Loch Harport – a sea loch on the west coast of Skye. Their ruined family home is said to be one of the oldest houses on the island.

R.R. McIan's The Clans of the Scottish Highlands (1845) shows a MacLeod during the period when the clan wore the MacKenzie tartan

Though scorned by some, the Victorian penchant for 'mourning tartans' amongst those who could afford them must have presented a very sombre and evocative sight, although the only two tartans documented as 'funeral' are the MacLeod and the Stewart.

By the very nature of their use, since one had to kit out a large retinue of kilted followers, mourning tartans could not be a spur-of-the-moment production. The 'morning dress' which doubled as 'mourning dress' had no equivalent in tartan and it takes a strong imagination to accept with equanimity the idea of the average clansman possessing the several outfits described by Victorian outfitters. The Sobieski brothers dreamed up a few black and white sets but even they didn't suggest that these were anything but 'clanne' tartans.

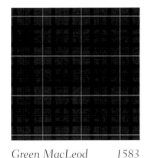

Green MacLeod　　1583

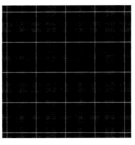

MacKenzie　　267

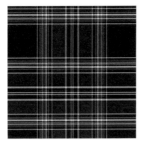

MacLeod of Gesto　　1258

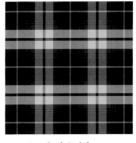

MacLeod of California
1623

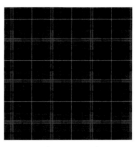

MacLeod Society of
Scotland, Clan　　2375

MACLEOD OF CALIFORNIA　　1623

Based on the Hunting MacLeod and the Baillie Fencible tartans, this sett was designed in 1988 by Dr. Frank B. Cannonito of California, whose wife's grandmother came from Dunvegan in Skye. Frank was co-designer of the official Washington State tartan and this new one was accepted and approved by John MacLeod of MacLeod, the 29th Chief.

The MacLeod presence in the United States typifies the unbridled enthusiasm of overseas Scots descendants to celebrate their heritage. The American MacLeod Society was founded in 1954 as a result of the tremendous surge of interest generated by the visits of John MacLeod's mother, the 28th Chief, Dame Flora MacLeod of MacLeod, and today there is a national council and members in all 50 states, organized into geographical regions.

Historically, Skye was also the domain of two other major clans, the MacDonalds and the MacKinnons, but it is probably best known to the Scottish world at large for its lilting Skye Boat Song:

> Speed bonny boat like a bird on the wing,
> 'Onward' the sailors cry,
> Carry the lad that's born to be king,
> Over the sea to Skye.

The subject matter is, of course, Bonnie Prince Charlie's sea journey with Flora MacDonald from Benbecula in the Outer Hebrides, across the Little Minch to the Isle of Skye. Thanks to the song, that epic journey became a legend which imprinted the island's name on generations of Scots and their absent kith and kin. It seems very appropriate that had it not been for a MacLeod, the composition would never have seen the light of day.

It was in the 1870s that Miss Annie MacLeod – on a visit to Skye – was being rowed across Loch Coruisk in the Cuillins when the boatmen gave voice to what was referred to as 'an old Highland measure used in rowing' – an old Gaelic rowing song, *'Cuchag nan Craobh'* ('The Cuckoo in the Grove'). Miss MacLeod took note of the tune, which was later put to words in 1884 by Sir Harold Boulton (1859–1935).

MACLEOD SOCIETY OF SCOTLAND, CLAN　　2375

The MacLeod Society of Scotland celebrated its centenary in 1991 and the designer Trudi Mann of Wick was invited to design a tartan for the occasion, which was accepted by the Chief as an official Society sett.

To confuse the unwary, Neil Macleod is shown (left) in this 1868 MacLeay portrait wearing the MacKenzie of Seaforth tartan which, at that date, was the correct form of MacLeod tartan – see MacKenzie ITI 267 opposite. Murdoch MacNeill is wearing the newly designed MacNeill of Colonsay tartan (discussed later in the Colonsay section). MacNeill is wearing a badger sporran and in the foreground lie two mallard and a curlew. The background shows the Cuillins looking south-east from Dunvegan.

MacDonald

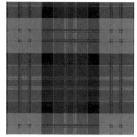

MacDonald 419

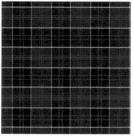

MacDonald of Kingsburgh
1562

Below: William Mosman's The
MacDonald Boys (c. 1749)

Of all the Highland clans the MacDonalds are unique in having so many tartans associated with them that can be dated to the period of the last Jacobite rising or earlier and which are still commonly worn. Among the nine independent branches of the Clan Donald there are at least 27 different tartans, which made for a very confusing situation. In 1947 however the MacDonalds again had a High Chief, *MacDhomhnuill*, who by tradition has the final word on the tartans of the clan. That *MacDhomhnuill* was Alexander MacDonald of MacDonald whose son Godfrey, Lord MacDonald of MacDonald, is now the 8th Lord and 34th Chief.

Godfrey lives in Skye and runs – with his wife Clare – the very prestigious Kinloch Lodge, noted for its luxury accommodation and, more importantly, its prize-winning cuisine – Lady MacDonald is a leading food writer.

MacDonald   419

Often simply called the Clan Donald tartan, this is the oldest recorded version of the sett, dating back to at least the beginning of the nineteenth century, and the one most commonly seen. A weaver's description of the period raises the possibility that this was originally a military tartan, perhaps for a Fencible (Home Guard) Regiment.

MacDonald of Kingsburgh   1562

MacDonald of Kingsburgh was a tackman (tenant) whose title came from the small farm that he possessed near Broadford in Skye. This pattern was reconstructed from a small piece of a waistcoat that Kingsburgh (whose son later married Flora MacDonald) gave to Bonnie Prince Charlie. Since it

MacDonald of Sleat   904

MacDonald, Lord of the
Isles (Red)   873

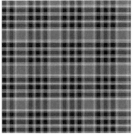

MacDonald, Lord of the
Isles Hunting   3267

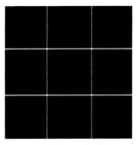

MacDonald, Lord of the
Isles   1366

was too bright for his use, Charles exchanged it with one Malcolm MacLeod who, before his capture by government forces, hid it in a rock cleft. After his release a year later he retrieved it but only a small scrap had survived undamaged. A piece was eventually preserved by Bishop Robert Forbes for his 1747 *The Lyon in Mourning*, one of the best records of the Jacobite rising of 1745, which includes accounts of battles and of the cruelties of Jacobite persecution. He also acquired relics of the time, one of the more fascinating being pieces of the dress worn by Bonnie Prince Charlie when disguised as 'Betty Burke', Flora MacDonald's maid.

Other relics included a pair of Prince Charles Edward's brogues, from which, it's said, honoured guests in the Bishop's home were allowed to drink champagne. If however these were the original brogues kept by Kingsburgh which were 'so much worn that the Prince's toes protruded through them', the guests would not have had very much champagne.

D.W. Stewart's recording is that which is usually seen, however, and the colours of the original are in fact those shown here as 'artefact'; the discrepancy has never been explained.

MacDonald of Sleat   904
The area of Sleat (pronounced Slate and often written as that) is the southernmost landmass of Skye that stretches from the Skye road bridge south-west to the Point of Sleat, overlooking the islands of Rhum and Eigg. This pattern differs from, but seems to have been based on, an old MacDonald tartan, Lord of the Isles (Red). A Wilsons' sample in the 1810 Cockburn Collection is labelled *Lord MacDonald*. As can be seen, the original (873 above) has an additional black line that didn't

appear in the later specimen. Whether this was an intended 'differencing' or a mistake is not known.

MacDonald, Lord of the Isles (Red)   873
The chiefs of the MacDonalds held the title Lord of the Isles until it was annexed by the Crown in 1493. The title is nowadays held by the heir to the throne.

In William Mosman's portrait known as 'The MacDonald Boys' (opposite), the two subjects wear a total of four different red-based tartans. This sett, taken from the jacket of the younger son, is the only one seen today and appears to have been the original version of the MacDonald of Sleat described previously. The portrait is an excellent example of the style of the dress of the period.

MacDonald, Lord of the Isles Hunting   3267
In a portrait of Sir Alexander MacDonald of Sleat *c*.1775 – he was the elder of the two MacDonald Boys referred to above – he wears a completely different tartan. The design appears to be blue and green in the original version which is that worn by Godfrey Macdonald, High Chief of the MacDonalds. D.W. Stewart's woven silk sample in *Old and Rare Scottish Tartans* (1893) erroneously employs two shades of green, dark and light, and it is that version that is worn today by Prince Charles as titular Lord of the Isles.

MacDonald, Lord of the Isles 1366
This is undoubtedly the most commonly seen of the Lord of the Isles tartans. In fact, it has no historical links with the clan and was an invention of the Sobieski Stuarts.

Over the Sea to Skye

Mention was made earlier of Flora MacDonald and Bonnie Prince Charlie's epic voyage to Skye and this contemporary report, reproduced in John Keltie's *History of the Scottish Highlands* (1874), adds fascinating flesh to the bones of the legendary journey.

ON the evening prior to his departure from the Outer Hebridean island of Benbecula a small party joined Charles. On entering the hovel, they found Charles employed in roasting, for dinner, the heart, liver, and kidneys of a sheep upon a wooden spit. The ladies began to compassionate the prince upon his unfortunate situation; but he diverted their attention from this melancholy subject by some facetious observations. He remarked that the wretched to-day may be happy to-morrow, and that all great men would be better by suffering as he was doing. The party dined in the hut, Miss Macdonald sitting on the right and Lady Clanranald on the left of the prince.

After dinner, Charles put on the female attire, which had been provided for him by the ladies. It was coarse and homely, and consisted of a flowered linen gown, a light-coloured quilted petticoat, a white apron, and a mantle of dun camlet made after the Irish fashion with a hood. Whilst Charles was putting on this extraordinary dress, several jokes were passed on the singularity of the prince's appearance.

The Prince left the island the following evening on a clear and calm sea in the six-oared boat hired by Flora MacDonald. Shortly after their departure the weather deteriorated rapidly and 'a tempest ensued'.

Miss Macdonald and the boatmen grew alarmed but Charles showed the greatest composure and, to revive their drooping spirits, alternately related some amusing stories and sang several songs . . . when day-light appeared next morning, they found themselves out of sight of land without knowing where they were

In his publication Clanland, *William Stewart shows a MacDonald of Sleat cornered in a wood by English soldiers after Culloden.*

. . . but they had not sailed far when they perceived some of the headlands of Skye. Favoured by the wind, they soon gained the point of Waternish, on the west of the island. In passing along this point they were fired upon by a party of Macleod militia, who called upon them to land; but they continued their course, and, to prevent suspicion, plied their oars very slowly. Charles told the boatmen 'not to fear the villains' but they assured him that they did not care for themselves: their only fear was for him. 'No fear of me!' was Charlie's reply . . . whilst the bullets were falling about the boat. Charles, it is said, requested Miss Macdonald to lie down in the bottom of the boat in order to avoid them; but she heroically declined the proposal, and declared that, as she was endeavouring to preserve the life of her prince, she would never degrade herself by attending to the safety of her own person while that of her master was in jeopardy. She even solicited Charles to occupy the place he had assigned for her. The prince, as the danger increased, became more urgent; but no entreaties could prevail upon Miss Macdonald to abandon her intrepid resolution, till Charles offered to lie down also. Both accordingly lay down in the bottom of the boat, till out of reach of the bullets of the militia.

After landing in the northern peninsula of Skye and suffering the vicissitudes of the fugitive, Charles and his small party ended up at the home of Macdonald of Kingsburgh, factor for Sir Alexander Macdonald, where he enjoyed 'a hearty supper, and drank a bumper of brandy to the health and prosperity of Kingsburgh and his wife'.

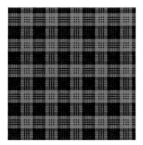

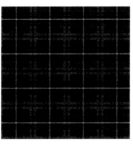

Flora MacDonald   1404

Prince Charles Edward
1170

MacCrimmon of Skye
2610

FLORA MACDONALD   1404

This is said to be an interpretation of a tartan illustrated in a portrait of Flora MacDonald at the Fort William Museum.

PRINCE CHARLES EDWARD   1170

There exists a profusion of tartans associated with Prince Charles Edward, as a result of his diplomatic habit of honouring whatever hosts he was staying with by wearing their tartan. Those hosts were many and varied during the '45 but were doubtless all very honoured to present one of their plaids to their royal guest.

This particular sett, which doesn't appear to have any clan connections at all, may be a reversal of that habit in that Charles presented it to one of his hosts. In his 1893 *Old and Rare Scottish Tartans* D.W. Stewart included one of his meticulously woven silk samples and explained the background:

The fragments employed in the preparation of this illustration are portions of a plaid worn by Prince Charles Edward during his brief sojourn in Edinburgh in 1745. On his departure he presented the garment to Susanna, Countess of Eglinton, a belle of the day, at whose house in Cannongate he was a frequent visitor. Divided by her amongst her seven daughters, a portion was given by one of them – Lady Frances Montgomerie – to her grand-niece, the late Mrs Erskine of Torrie, who bequeathed it to the Rev. Henry Bruce, Dunimarle. Mr Bruce mentions that Mrs Erskine, who assured him of the genuineness of the relic, spoke of Lady Frances as having often conversed with the Prince. Well-nigh a century back the tartan was cut up for slippers by the daughters of Sir William Erskine

of Torrie. It was thus greatly mutilated, but enough remained intact to permit the rendering of the design here given. Sir Arthur Halkett, Bart., in whose collection are some small pieces of the plaid, lent these to ensure the reproduction of the precise tints of the original.

MACCRIMMON OF SKYE   2610

The famous MacCrimmons were hereditary pipers to the Chiefs of Macleod and one fascinating claim suggests that the founder of the clan was an Italian priest from Cremona named Giuseppe Bruno whose son Petrus (born 1475) travelled to Ulster in 1510. Once there, he used the name Cremona, and on his marriage to a daughter of the famous piping family of MacKinnon he altered it to MacCrimmon to bring it nearer to that of his wife. Professor George Black, the noted bibliographer and historical scholar of the New York Public Library, dismisses the story as 'too silly for belief'.

Another interesting claim (on a MacCrimmon website) is that the MacCrimmons 'from earliest times were known to have worn a plain blue kilt, which is still worn to this day'. Although the wearing of plain-coloured kilts in Ireland was popularized in the early 1900s by the Irish antiquarian writer P.W. Joyce as a type of national uniform, the idea was founded on very imprecise early documents. The Irish historian Henry McClintock, in his 1958 work *Handbook on the Traditional Old Irish Dress*, concluded: 'the fact remains that there is no evidence that kilts were ever worn in Ireland till modern times'. So . . . another myth 'too silly for belief'!

Ronald McIan, in his 1845 book *The Clans of the Scottish Highlands*, painted a MacCrimmon piper (right) in an indeterminate green and red tartan

| MacKinnon | 5684 | MacKinnon Hunting | 1641 | MacNicols and Nicolsons | 1004 | Isle of Skye | 2155 |

which *could* be construed as a MacLeod of Assynt. Then at some time in the 1990s a MacCrimmon tartan knee rug was discovered with a label saying 'Angus Macleod of Dunvegan Skye'. Angus proved untraceable but might be the same Angus Macleod who designed the Isle of Skye tartan in 1997. This 'new' MacCrimmon tartan now seems to have been widely accepted by clan members.

MacKinnon   5684

A MacKinnon tartan was first recorded in the Cockburn Collection of 1810. Subsequent publications gave rise to a very confusing situation with different versions documented in five major works. However in 1959 the clan chief, MacKinnon of MacKinnon, deposited details of the correct setts for the clan and hunting tartans of the Clan MacKinnon with the Office of the Lord Lyon.

MacKinnon Hunting   1641

This uninspiring design of twentieth-century origin has no connection with the older pattern; it followed the tradition of duller brown- and green-based tartans. A letter to all its manufacturing members from the National Association of Scottish Woollen Manufacturers dated 17 September 1959 advises that 'The Mackinnon of Mackinnon has this year recorded with the Lord Lyon . . . the correct setts for the Clan and Hunting Tartans of the Clan Mackinnon.'

According to James Logan, this MacNicol girl (pictured by McIan) is a dairy maid 'who bears in her hand the vessel called cuman, which receives the milky tribute of the fold'! He also comments on her dress as that usually seen among young persons, especially the tartan tonag or shawl being worn around the shoulders and fastened by a silver brooch – often a family heirloom handed down through the generations.

MacNicols and Nicolsons   1004

It is difficult at times to clearly separate the MacNicols and Nicolsons. It's said that the MacNicols originally came from Assynt, that great promontory in the north-west of Scotland stretching from Kylesku down to Ullapool, and moved to Skye when the heiress of the last MacNicol chief married Torquil, a son of the MacLeod of Lewis.

In the 19th century the Nicolsons were badly affected by the Highland Clearances and the Chief was forced to abandon Scorrybreac, near Portree in the north of Skye, in favour of faraway Tasmania, where the present Chief was born. Many Nicolson clansmen were evicted from their crofts and also emigrated – mostly to Prince Edward Island in Canada.

The name was anglicized to Nicholson/Nicolson in the 17th century and in 1980 the Nicolsons and the MacNicols became separate clans. Confusion still seems to pervade the clan tartans however, with early weavers translating the McIan illustration into at least two different tartans that still seem to hold sway with today's mills.

This now seems to be the most widely accepted version of the MacNicol/Nicolson.

Isle of Skye   2155

This very popular fashion tartan was initiated in 1992 by Mrs Rosemary Nicolson Samios, an Australian of Skye descent. It was selected through a worldwide competition won by weaver Angus MacLeod from Lewis, who also produced the first commercial quantities in traditional kilt weight in 1993 at Lochcarron Weavers in North Strome, within view of the Cuillin Mountains. The colours of the tartan depict those of the island, often called the 'Misty Isle'.

Raasay

MacLeod of Raasay   1172

MacLeod of Raasay   1172

Raasay is from the Gaelic *Ratharsair* which means Isle of Roe. It's the birthplace and home to the poet Sorley Maclean – one of the principals of the 20th-century Scottish Renaissance.

There is a temptation to assume that every clan occupied vast swathes of Highland territory, but that wasn't always the case. The ruggedly beautiful island of Raasay, a few miles off the eastern coast of Skye, is just 13 miles long and 3 miles wide. Sparsely populated by a small crofting community of about 200, it offers a flavour of real island life, with a general store, a post office and an abundance of wildlife, including otters, red deer, the unique Raasay Vole and some 60 species of birds, including golden eagles.

Those that are sharp of eye will notice that this tartan is the Dress Macleod (MacLeod of Lewis) with the yellow changed to red; it dates to around 1845.

Within sight of Skye to the south are the islands of Rhum and Eigg where the MacDonalds held sway. The next major island is Mull, which offers a cornucopia of tartans.

Isle of Man

Manx National   185

The Isle of Man is that large (221 square miles) island in the Irish Sea which is at the geographical centre of the United Kingdom – equidistant from Ireland, Scotland and England. Strangely, it's not part of the UK but is a self-governing Crown dependency with a population of about 70,000. The inhabitants are of Celtic origin and the island – part of the Viking empire as far back as ad 700 – was ceded to Scotland by Norway's King Magnus VI in 1266, coming under English control in the 14th century.

With its Celtic and Norse origins it's not surprising that there is a revival of the Gaelic Manx language, which is closely related to Scottish Gaelic. The island's Celtic roots are also demonstrated by its liking for tartan and there are over a dozen associated with the island,

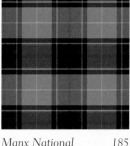

Manx National   185

the favourite probably being the Manx National.

This seven-colour tartan was designed in 1957 by a well-known hand weaver on the Isle of Man, Miss Patricia McQuaid, at, it is reported, the instigation of the Rt. Hon. the Lord Sempill (probably John, the 18th Lord Sempill), although why he was involved is not recorded.

In the early days of modern tartan design, the true potential of tartan to encompass a really interesting range of design elements hadn't been fully appreciated and practitioners frequently chose what could be regarded nowadays as the mundane. This tartan uses light blue for the sky; dark blue for the sea; green for the hills and valleys, white for the cottages and the purple for the heather.

Mull

Britain is known for its great ecological diversity and richness, but nowhere can match the Island of Mull with its 1,000ft-high sea cliffs, white sand beaches, towering mountain range with the 3,000ft Ben More as its summit and crystal-clear blue seas around its 300 miles of coastline. And yet its population is a mere 2,700!

The Island of Eagles, as it is often referred to, shows a similar diversity when it comes to tartans. The MacLeans have been located in Mull since the 14th century, and their ancestral home, overlooking the Sound of Mull, is Duart Castle, which was reduced to rubble by the Campbells and the ravages of time. In 1911 the present Chief's great-grandfather, Sir Fitzroy Maclean, bought and restored it; he lived to enjoy it, dying at the age of 101.

In addition to Mull, the clan's extensive lands included the islands of Tiree, Coll and Islay, as well as mainland Morvern and Lochaber. As the clan expanded, it split into a number of different branches, including the MacLeans of Coll and the MacLeans of Ardgour.

Mull – the 'Island of Eagles'

When the Reformation reached Mull, people were very reluctant to abandon their old religion of Catholicism and the MacLean laird was initially unwilling to interfere. Eventually however he decided to take a hand and, as shown here, stood one Sunday on the path that led to the Catholic Church. As his clanspeople approached he drove them back with his cane until they obediently made their way to the Protestant Church. From this 'persuasive method of conversion, the people ever after called Presbyterianism the religion of the gold-headed stick'. McIan

MacLean of Duart 2125

There is a similarity between this and the Royal Stewart tartan in which the number of threads and colours are reversed. Wilsons of Bannockburn were weaving several versions of MacLean in the early 1800s. In their 1850 book *The Authenticated Tartans of the Clans and Families of Scotland* William and Andrew Smith of Mauchline wrote: 'This Tartan is sometimes woven with only one shade of blue, but this is done merely to save trouble; the oldest pattern which we have been able to procure has two shades of that colour, as we have given it.'

MacLean of Duart 2125

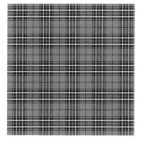

MacLean of Duart Hunting 824

MacLaine of Lochbuie 1462

MacLean of Duart Hunting 824

Some references suggest that this tartan dates back as far as 1587 but the historical evidence for that is slender and requires a major leap of faith. The suggestion is based on a Gaelic charter granted to Hector MacLean, Heir of Duart, in the lands of Islay, stipulating that the feu duty (annual payment to the feudal landlord) was to be in the form of 60 ells of cloth of white, black and green colours. It may be that the Sobieski Stuarts got hold of this information and translated it into the tartan that they displayed in their *Vestiarium Scoticum*.

MacLaine of Lochbuie 1462

The progenitor of the MacLeans was Gilleann-na-Taughe, whose great-grandson Iain Dubh (Black John) granted charters of land in the 14th century to his two sons Lachlan and Hector – Lachlan at Duart and Hector at Lochbuie on the shore of the sea loch of the same name in the south of the island. It was around 1600 that the 8th Chief, another Hector, initiated the spelling of 'MacLaine' in preference to 'MacLean'.

Despite their familial closeness, the MacLaines of Lochbuie occasionally feuded with the MacLeans of Duart but, like most families, they joined forces when threatened from outside. It's related that one particular feud was put to bed when the Lochbuie Chief and his followers came upon the Duarts deep in exhausted sleep after another armed skirmish. Lochbuie's followers were all in favour of an instant attack but the Chief held them back. Instead, he crept up on the sleeping Duart Chief and twisted his hair around his dirk before sticking it into the earth. When the Duart Chief awoke to find his hair pinned to the ground, he recognized the dagger as that of the MacLaine

This 1927 Mitchell's cigarette card features Sir Harry Aubrey de Vere Maclean (1848–1920), who resigned his army commission in 1876 to take up an appointment in the Sultan of Morocco's army, of which he eventually became commander. The British government recognized his many achievements and he was created KCMG in 1907 (Knight Commander of St. Michael and St. George). It's said that he maintained his Scottish personality and expert bagpipe skill but adopted Moorish costume.

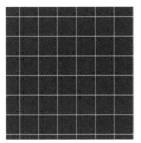

MacLaine of Lochbuie
Hunting   491

Mull   162

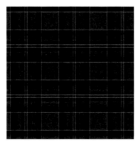

Mull Millennium   2573

Mull Rugby Club   5648

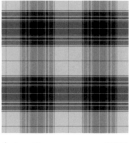

Antarctic   2701

Chief and was so moved by the act of mercy that he decided to end the feud immediately.

This distinctive and ancient tartan exists in the Cockburn Collection in the Mitchell Library in Glasgow and dates to before 1810 when the collection was put together.

MacLaine of Lochbuie Hunting 491
This was first documented in 1906 in the W. & A.K. Johnston *The Tartans of the Clans and Septs of Scotland*. It was shown there with black guards to the yellow line but today's weavers seem to omit those since the dark blue ground is often so dark as to render the black guards invisible.

Mull 162
The Mull District tartan dates from 1819 and is an example of the confusion that the famous weavers Wilsons of Bannockburn caused by their marketing methods. Almost all of their early tartans started life as a numbered pattern and this one shown here was No. 53, a simple textile design that is referred to as a 'fancy pattern'. Frequently in their record books, Wilsons would subsequently attach unofficial names to tartans – possibly that of the locality in which they had sold well. Whether or not that happened with the Mull tartan, or whether it was just a random geographical name given for marketing purposes, will never be known. Confusion arose for later tartan-watchers as the same tartan was also known as Glenlyon, a long narrow glen in Perthshire some 100 miles to the south-east.

Mull Millennium 2573
For geologists, the substrata and landscapes of Mull and its nearby island of Iona are of great fascination and the Mull Millennium tartan celebrates the diversity of its 2,800-million-year geological history. Green and white marble, Mull granite, basalt lava, shale, dolerites and gabbros are all represented in this tartan, the sales of which help to raise funds for various Isle of Mull charities.

Mull Rugby Club 5648
From hard rocks to hard men: the tartan of the Mull Rugby Club, worn, no doubt, for their club ceilidhs and not on the field in place of conventional shorts.

Antarctic 2701
Two most unusual tartans from Mull designer Ros Jones, the first of which is the Antarctic: this was authorized by the British Antarctic Survey and designed to raise funds for the UK Antarctic Heritage Trust. It enjoys the distinction of being sold in the most southerly outlet on the globe, Port Lockroy on the Antarctic Peninsula – 10,000 miles south of Mull. It has a beautiful natural harbour where the scientific base was renovated in 1996 and turned into a 'living museum'. Since then, it has been opened during the summer months by the British Antarctic Survey under the guidance of the Trust and is now one of Antarctica's top tourist destinations. The operation of Port Lockroy is self-financing; profits from the small gift shop at the base where the tartan is sold are used to pay the staff, shipping and logistical costs and for the maintenance of the buildings.

The tartan encompasses many complex design elements but in simple terms, white represents the ice-covered continent; grey is for outcropping rocks,

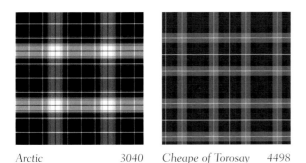

Arctic	3040	Cheape of Torosay	4498

ARCTIC   3040

Using almost identical colours, the Arctic is the second of the snowy tartan twins that are – as Ros Jones says – '"poles apart" in geography and wildlife and yet "poles together" in what they symbolize and the conservation issues that they're designed to help'. This tartan was authorized by the WWF (World Wide Fund for Nature).

CHEAPE OF TOROSAY   4498

Souvenirs of one family's Antarctic adventures in the early 20th century can be seen at Torosay Castle – a Victorian mansion built in the Scottish baronial style in 1858 by the Scottish architect David Bryce. The castle and the 12 acres of ornamental gardens are open to the public but the property is still very much a family home with the upper floors still lived in. This tartan was designed for the Cheapes of Torosay in 1934.

seals and birds; orange and yellow are for the head plumage of the Emperor and King penguins; black and white together depict penguins and whales; pale blue symbolizes the crevasses in the ice and shallow waters on the ice shelves; whilst dark midnight blue represents the deep Antarctic Ocean and the darkness of the Antarctic winter.

Restored by the UK Antarctic Heritage Trust in 1996, Port Lockroy is the globe's most southerly outlet for the Antarctic Tartan – sold to the increasing number of cruise-ship passengers spellbound by the beauty and isolation of this polar outpost.

Tartan: the Fabric of Fashion

Until recently in some Scottish quarters, tartan has been regarded a little like the biblical prophet – 'not without honour, save in his own country …'. This attitude may have been instigated by the Scots' Calvinist dislike for showiness or the remnants of the lowland belt's envy of 'they rich folk' in the Highlands, whose use of tartan was often taken as a class statement. Add to these tartan's indiscriminate use in cheap 'tartan tat', and tartan, as an art form, has been done a great disservice, and presented the press with a defenceless victim at which it can sneer with impunity.

Above: Three Vivienne Westwood outfits stride down the catwalk at the 2006 Dressed to Kilt fashion show in Los Angeles, sponsored by Johnnie Walker whisky.

Not so in the world of fashion, however, where tartan is rarely out of the runway spotlights. One great fan since her early designing days has been Vivienne Westwood who has embraced many tartans in her collections, pushing the boundaries and using the fabric in ways never seen before for everything from bondage trousers to ball-gowns. A faithful client of the Lochcarron mill in the Scottish Borders, she has created many new tartans in conjunction with their design team and greatly influenced other major designers such as Alexander MacQueen, Tommy Hilfiger, Jean-Paul Gaultier, Jimmy Choo and many more.

Unlike so many fashions that never make the transition from the rarefied atmosphere of the catwalk to the high-street stores and chains, tartan has had no trouble bridging the gap between high and popular culture, infiltrating outlets such as Miss Selfridge, Topshop, Next, Debenhams, Jenners, John Lewis and even George at Asda to name but a few.

One of the consistent proponents of tartan has been Burberry, whose world-famous trade-marked check is said to have first appeared in the 1930s as a raincoat lining. It occupies a strange place in the fashion world in that it graces – in various forms – many expensive luxury products, while being, at the other end of the market, the most copied tartan in existence. Bootleg and counterfeit versions are bought at street markets up and down the country and enthusiastically sported by 'chavs' – young people favouring ostentatious jewellery ('bling'), tracksuits, sports gear and baseball hats. Strangely, this hasn't proved to be the 'kiss of death' for the Burberry Check and the company continues to use it very successfully for branding in the most innovative of ways.

As might be expected in the fashion sector, tartan is not normally chosen for any of its traditional connections with people, places or events but purely for its visual appeal. If a conventional clan tartan doesn't have that season's colours, then designers will often have a special weave produced. Some designers will even eschew tartan altogether – Edinburgh's Howie Nicholsby of 21st Century Kilts is an excellent example where kilts can be produced in leather, denim, hessian, canvas and any other material that's likely to catch on with the 'young set'. For the young businessman there's even a pinstripe kilt suit.

The 'man skirt' idea has also been enthusiastically taken up in the United States with the invention of the 'Utilikilt' in red corduroy, army camouflage and even tie-dyed, and the addition of internal or external pockets and loops for artisans' tools nudges even more at the boundaries of traditional Highland dress. Some weavers may throw up their arms in horror at this trend but it helps to initiate a new generation of kilt wearers who will doubtless come back to the 'tartan fold' for their wedding ensemble.

For many decades, the wedding-day spotlight has been on the bride in shimmering white and colourful flowers, while the comparatively drab groom has tagged along in her fashion wake – a reversal of nature's conventional order of things! Tartan's popularity in redressing that imbalance grows daily with many more grooms, both north and south of the border, opting for Highland dress and vying with the bride for the appreciative murmurs.

Tartan also exercises the minds and talents of designers outside the world of fashion, and many are intrigued by the strict geometric rules surrounding the designs. Jill Kinnear of Toowoomba in Australia has recently enjoyed arts funding and great success with her extremely imaginative tartan-style designs in metal which she has then translated into colour by passing them through an airport baggage X-ray machine. Anything further from the traditional 'shortbread tin' stereotype is hard to imagine.

Above: One of Vivienne Westwood's more restrained but still inimitable creations

Top: Jimmy Choo shoes: Tartan shoes from Jimmy Choo, a couture shoe-maker based in the East End of London

Left: Stylish kilt suits at home in the snooker room

Iona

Just a five-minute ferry crossing from the southern Mull port of Fionnphort lies the tiny but legendary island of Iona. With its stunning landscape of sandy beaches and dramatic changing light, Iona is one of the most sacred sites in Britain. It was here in AD 563 that St Columba and his disciples arrived from Ireland in a hide-covered boat to spread the gospel throughout Scotland and northern England. Iona is still a centre for Christian pilgrimage, and its atmosphere of spirituality and serenity continues to inspire visitors and those who live and work on the island.

The island – excluding the buildings – is owned by the National Trust for Scotland and is only three miles long and a mile wide, with a population of under 200. It's said to be the last resting place of 48 Scottish, 4 Irish and 8 Norwegian kings. It's also home to 16 American sailors who perished in an 1865 shipwreck. Legend suggests that Iona was a desirable burial place because of the following prophecy:

> *Seachd bliadhna 'n blr'ath*
> *Thig muir air Eirinn re aon tr'ath*
> *'S thar Ile ghuirm ghlais*
> *Ach sn'amhaidh I Choluim Chl'eirich*

This tells that seven years before the day of judgement the ocean will sweep over both Ireland and Islay. Yet the Isle of St Columba will swim above the waves!

St Columba   2383

To commemorate the 1,400th anniversary of St Columba's death, the St Columba tartan was designed in 1997 by Peter Eslea MacDonald of Crieff. The original version with seven colours and two shades of green is shown here and its design reflects all the natural colours of Iona: from the grey and purple of the Abbey through the green pastures to the golden sands and finally the white surf before the surrounding blue Atlantic. Its purpose was to raise funds to restore the roof of St Columba's Church on Mull.

Iona fashion   6858

Since the days of Wilsons of Bannockburn, weavers have always had an eye for the marketing benefits of using romantic Scottish names for their tartans and this fashion tartan woven in Vancouver, British Columbia, is no exception.

Gaelic College of St Ann   4942

Due west from Iona stretch over 2,000 miles of wild Atlantic ocean and at the end of that lies another Iona . . . in Cape Breton, Nova Scotia. Celebrated by Condé Nast Traveler as the most beautiful island in the world, it has also been described as the most recent and far-flung outpost of Gaelic Scotland and is the only area in the world – outside of Scotland itself – where Gaelic continues as a living language and culture. Not surprisingly, the island has a thriving Gaelic College and Marie MacDonald, a teacher there and Iona resident, designed this tartan for the college in 1997.

Right: Iona Abbey

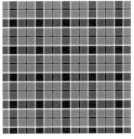

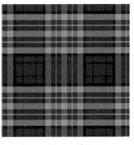

St Columba   2383   *Iona Fashion*   6858   *Gaelic College of St Ann*
4942

Ulva

Clerke of Ulva   168   MacQuarrie   892

Nestling in the huge western bay of Mull is the tiny, privately owned island of Ulva with – according to the island's website – 'a thriving population of approximately 16 people who are involved variously in traditional sheep and cattle farming, fish farming, oyster farming and tourism'.

There are no conventional roads on Ulva, so transport for all is four-wheeled cross-country bikes 'used by all inhabitants, young and old. The proprietors (the Howard family) are dedicated to creating a balance between the needs of the community and the preservation of one of Scotland's most unique, beautiful and accessible islands.'

CLERKE OF ULVA   168

The first record of this design appeared in a Wilsons' pattern book of 1847, after which it seems to have disappeared from commercial production. In February 2005 the Tartans Authority was asked to identify a kilt made *circa* 1930 for Francis William Clark who was an officer in the Argyll and Sutherland Highlanders – killed with the Commandos at Gallipoli. At that time the Clarks owned the island of Ulva. It was therefore no surprise to discover that the kilt was a very well-worn Clerke of Ulva with the black faded to brown, the light blue to light grey and with orange lines on the blue rather than the crimson suggested in the original historical notes.

MACQUARRIE   892

The drive and ability of so many 18th- and 19th-century Scots is exemplified by 'the Father of Australia' Lachlan MacQuarrie who was born in 1761 on Ulva. He came from farming stock and rose through the ranks to become Governor General of New South Wales – taking over from Captain Bligh of *Bounty* mutiny fame. After a long and distinguished career in Australia he finished his service in 1821 by laying out the city of Sydney before returning to Mull where he died in 1824.

The 16th and last Chief of the tiny clan was another Lachlan MacQuarrie who, forced to sell the island in 1778 to settle debts, joined the army at the remarkable age of 63 and served as an officer in the American War of Independence. He died in Mull at the even more remarkable age of 103.

The clan's motto and pipe tune is 'The Red Tartan Army' and for a small clan they certainly had their share of red tartans – four in all with this one being the accepted clan tartan from about 1886.

Ulva being approached by a small passenger craft from Mull

Colonsay

MacFie/MacPhee 1847

MacNeil of Colonsay 196

Below: *In his commentary on McIan's illustrations, his colleague James Logan provided the following description of MacNeil:*

The simple caparison[1] of the horse betokens its antiquity, but the same rude style is yet to be seen in many secluded districts: . . . the harness is composed of withies[2], or twisted rods of hazel; a 'rung' is used for a crupper[3], and the rein is a rope of hair; the covering, instead of a saddle, is a fine goat skin! We have heard that a Highland gentleman of some eccentricity astonished the Auld reekie[4] (sic) Athenians[5], when George IV visited Scotland, by appearing in a similar costume!

1 Decorated covering, formerly for a warhorse
2 Flexible twigs
3 Strap under the horse's tail
4 Edinburgh – from the amount of smoke generated by domestic fires
5 inhabitants of Edinburgh, the 'Athens of the North'

One of the very many tombs on Iona bears the inscription *Hic jacet Malcolumbus MacDuffie de Colonsay*. MacDuffie was just one of the alternative names for MacFie or MacPhie and the island of Colonsay lies about 10 miles (15 km) due south of Mull. Until the middle of the 17th century the MacFies held lands here, but after their chief Malcolm MacFie was murdered it appears that they were scattered by the Clearances. Their lands were possessed firstly by the Duke of Argyll, then by the MacDonalds and finally by the MacNeils.

Thus the MacFies became what's known as a 'broken clan' – dispossessed of their lands and destined to follow a more powerful neighbour. Most of those that remained pledged their allegiance to the MacDonalds of Islay whilst the rest settled in Cameron country on the mainland. Many of them emigrated, and a large number that didn't became so completely homeless that even today the name MacPhee is equated with the profession of itinerant tinsmiths who were known as 'tinkers'. In this age of zealous political correctness, the historical name is being eschewed in favour of the misleading term 'travelling people', which is more accurately applied to Romany Gypsies.

MacFie/MacPhee 1847
First seen in the 1880 *Clans Originaux*, this is the tartan that was officially approved in 1991 by Commander A.C. 'Sandy' McPhie, and included in the records by the Court of Lord Lyon in that year. The resemblance of this tartan to that of both the MacDonalds and Camerons may denote the MacFies' allegiance to those clans after they were dispersed from Colonsay.

There are a few other tartans reputed to be MacFies/MacPhees – a black and white, a hunting and a dress version but no reliable provenance can be found for those.

Apparently the MacNeils were traditionally known for three things: arrogance, lawlessness and piracy. History certainly confirms the last two and legend seems to confirm the first. The 35th Chief, Rory the Turbulent, is reputed to have sent, each evening, a herald and a trumpeter to the battlements of Kisimul Castle on the Hebridean island of Barra, their standard routine being to announce to the four corners of the world: 'Hear, oh ye people, and listen oh ye nations! The Great MacNeil of Barra having finished his meal, the princes of the world may dine!'

Another example was the MacNeil boast that they didn't need to avail themselves of Noah's Ark because they had a boat of their own. The last and most outrageous claim was that a clansman had huge landholdings in Egypt and that the River Nile was a corruption of 'Neil'. Bare-faced cheek or devilment, one has to admire it!

MacNeil of Colonsay 196
This sett is the usual modern form that appeared in *Clans Originaux* and the Johnstons' publication of 1906. The 46th clan chief, Ian Roderick MacNeil of Barra, had this to say on the Colonsay tartan in 1997: 'The tartan of the MacNeils of Colonsay, which has also been in use for a very long period is somewhat similar [to the Barra MacNeil], but has two white stripes quite close together rather than alternating yellow and white equidistant stripes.'

Jura

MacGill   1487

Just across the water from Colonsay lies the Island of Jura, whose ownership has changed hands a bewildering number of times over the centuries – MacLeans … Darrochs … Campbells … MacDougalls … Buies … MacDonnells. 30 miles long and 8 miles wide, Jura is one of Scotland's wildest inhabited islands, with only 190 humans compared to over 6,000 deer. It obviously agreed with George Orwell for it was here that he wrote his seminal novel *Nineteen Eighty-Four*. If he was partial to a drop of malt he would have had quite a walk from his Barnhill farmhouse – a six-mile track before he reached the single-track road that would take him to the Isle of Jura single malt distillery at Craighouse in the south of the island.

MacGill   1487

The only tartan uniquely associated with the island is that of the MacGills of Jura, which was said to have been in use before 1745. When tartan was proscribed, the sett seemed to have been lost … until a piece was discovered in Kintyre. That piece was reported as having been kept in the Museum of Antiquities in Edinburgh. The current version, which first appeared in 1930, is known as the MacGill Society tartan.

Jura

Islay

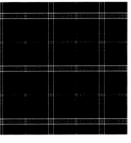

| Currie | 778 | Bunnahabhain | 6685 |

Just across a narrow strait from Jura lies the island of Islay – the Queen of the Hebrides. In the 1830s the population was around 15,000 but thanks to natural emigration and the Highland Clearances, today it's only 3,000. Most who left settled in Ontario, North and South Carolina and Australia.

One of the very early immigrants to Islay was the founder of the Curries – Muiredach O'Daly (1180–1222), an outstanding Irish poet of his time who fled his homeland after killing a royal servant. He arrived in Scotland in 1213 and settled in Islay, the stronghold home of Donald, Lord of the Isles, where – to Donald's great additional prestige – he became an integral part of his court and his descendants became hereditary bards to the Lord of the Isles.

CURRIE   778
Originally the private family tartan of William Currie of Balilone and Garrochoran granted by charter in 1822 by MacDonald, Lord of the Isles, the sett is based on the Lord of the Isles tartan and the design is attributed to the Chief, William Currie.

This grant was reconfirmed on 22 August 1971 to the last of the Balilone line of Curries, Col. William McMurdo Currie, by Lord MacDonald, the Right Honourable Godfrey James Macdonald of Macdonald, High Chief of Clan Donald. The grant states:

I Godfrey James Macdonald of Macdonald, Lord, Macdonald, take pleasure in granting to you the right to use the Lord of the Isles Tartan, with certain heraldic differences, as your own Family Tartan. The difference to consist of two tinctures from your own Coat-of-Arms, namely Black and Gold, the same to constitute a guard to the darker green square of the basic Lord of

the Isles Tartan. This is done in recognition of you as the present Representer of the Highland Family or Clan of Currie, anciently Clan MacMhuirich, who of old were the Historians to the Lords of the Isles. This confirms an earlier grant of August 1822 made by Sir Alexander of Sleat, 10th Bart and 2nd Lord Macdonald giving to your great-great-grandfather, James Currie of Balilone and Garrochoran the right to this aforesaid Tartan.

The tartan remained in a restricted state (solely for the use of the Balilone and Garrachoran line of Curries) until it was de-restricted on 27 December 1991 by Major General Sir William McMurdo Currie, Bart., the last hereditary descendant of the Curries of Balilone. It was then adopted as the official tartan for the entire clan in 1992.

Islay seems awash with malt whisky and to connoisseurs of the *uisge beatha* ('water of life') the Islay malts are in a very distinctive class all of their own – Bunnahabhain, Ardbeg, Caol Ila, Bowmore, Bruichladdich, Lagavulin and Laphroaig.

BUNNAHABHAIN   6685
Built in 1881, the distillery is on the sheltered north-eastern coast of Islay and enjoys magnificent views out to the Paps – two prominent hills on the neighbouring Isle of Jura.

Bunnahabhain (pronounced *Boon-a-ha-ven* and meaning 'mouth of the river') is a rich and peaty single malt and this tartan was designed by Kirsty Anderson of the House of Edgar for use in promotional items for the brand. Colours are from the labelling and the sett is based on the tartan bonnet worn by 'The Helmsman' on the label.

Isle of Gigha   3085

Gigha

Due east of Islay and just 3 miles offshore from the Kintyre peninsula lies the tiny island of Gigha – 6 miles long and 1½ miles wide. Pronounced *Gee-a* (as in 'gear'), it was once the province of the MacNeils, who had to continually defend their ownership against the powerful MacDonalds. To quote from Wikipedia:

> In recent times the island has gone through numerous owners, which caused various problems in developing the area. This came to an end in March 2002 when the islanders managed, with help from grants from the National Lottery and Highlands and Islands Enterprise, to purchase the island and they now own it through a trust. As a result, the day when the purchase went through is celebrated as the island's independence day.

ISLE OF GIGHA   3085

As befits any newly independent island, less than three months later, Gigha was presented with its own tartan. Janette Ker – a Gighach herself – got together with her employers Johnstons of Elgin, and designed and wove a new tartan that forms the backbone of Gigha mementoes for visitors to buy and boost the island economy.

An oystercatcher; this handsome bird is a common sight on all Scotland's coasts and islands

Lewis

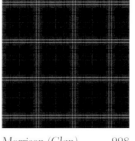
MacAulay of Lewis   6286

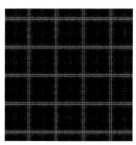
Morrison (Clan)   998

Morrison (Original)   933

MACAULAY OF LEWIS   6286

There are two clans of the name, associated with districts as far apart as Dumbarton on the mainland and Lewis in the Outer Hebrides, and they have no family connection with each other. They are the MacAulays of Ardincaple associated with the MacGregors and the MacAulays of Lewis who are associated with the MacLeods. This sett was designed by Dr Phil Smith of the United States in 1992, at the request of some MacAulays of Lewis who wanted to create a different identity from their mainland namesakes. This is the MacAulay Hunting with the white and red overchecks reversed and a slight change of proportions.

MORRISON   998, 933

There appear to have been three distinct and unconnected branches of the Morrison clan. One was descended from the natural son of the King of Norway who was shipwrecked off the shores of Lewis. Another was descended from the O'Muirgheasain bards from County Donegal in Ireland who settled in Harris; and the third from the Aberdeen and central Highlands areas of Scotland were the 'sons of Maurice'.

There are two stories surrounding the Morrison clan tartans:

1. The official Morrison clan tartan was recorded by Lord Lyon on 3 January 1968, from the tartan cover of an old Morrison family bible found in 1935 during the demolition of a Black House – a traditional single-storey cottage, so called because the walls and roof were blackened by the smoke from the central fireplace. The bible was said to be dated 1747 and to contain a hand-written reference to the tartan.

When the discovery was made, Lord Lyon was convinced that it represented the most authentic pattern of what the Morrisons wore in those days and he based the new tartan on the relic. A woven sample from Lochcarron dated 16 March 1972 states: 'Enclosed pattern of the new Clan Morrison tartan woven from the sett provided by the Clan Secretary about the end of 1968.' The note goes on to say: 'The Green one (ITI 1083) is now officially known as the Society Morrison.'

2. An alternative explanation is that ITI 933 shown above is actually the *real* Morrison clan tartan but Colonel Morrison (presumably John Morrison, the

St Kilda is the remotest part of the British Isles, 40 miles west of the Outer Hebrides. Its last permanent inhabitants left in 1930.

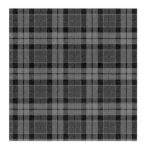

Morrison Society   1083

Stornoway on Lewis, the main port of the Outer Hebrides

Chief), wishing to re-establish his tartan – his old pre-1939 kilt had been destroyed in a London air raid – made an error by centring one green line instead of two on the red band when he gave the details to Lord Lyon. When this was later brought to the attention of Sir Thomas Innes of Learney (Lord Lyon) by tartan researcher Stuart Davidson in 1967, Lyon refused to alter what had been registered in the Lyon Court Books and remarked that the Morrisons would just have to accept it. This needn't necessarily have been as autocratic as it may sound: Lyon would have been aware than very many hundreds of kilts and other articles would have been made in the 'wrong' tartan, so common sense dictated that the status quo should be maintained.

MORRISON SOCIETY   1083

In the 16th century there was a falling out between the Morrisons of Lewis and the MacLeods, and about 60 Morrison families fled the island and sought refuge on the mainland in the vicinity of Durness in MacKay country. This explains the similarity between the MacKay tartan and this Morrison, which appeared in the 1880 *Clans Originaux* as 'Morrisson'.

When the 'new' clan tartan appeared (ITI 998), this old one was relegated to being the Society tartan, although it's also known as the Hunting Morrison and the Green Morrison.

Harris

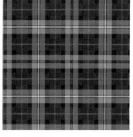

Isle of Harris   6198   Smith (Hebridean)   488

ISLE OF HARRIS   6198

This tartan was designed by a group of sixth-year pupils of the Sir E. Scott School at Tarbert on the Isle of Harris as a project to develop, market and sell the Isle of Harris tartan as part of the Young Enterprise Scotland (YES) Company Programme.

Their project won the 2003 Young Enterprise UK Award at the Savoy Hotel in London in July 2003. Various items have been made in the tartan and these can be seen and purchased on the pupils' website at www.beartas.co.uk

SMITH (HEBRIDEAN)   488

This is a variation of MacLeod of Harris and said to have been designed for a General Robert Smith in 1886 as a sett for those Smiths of Hebridean descent. Over time, however, that condition seems to have faded away and it has long been sold for all of the name, regardless of their origin. Its great similarity to the Smith of Pennylands (ITI 3957) suggests that the designer Harry Lindley modelled that Pennylands tartan on this 1886 sett by simply reversing the blues.

The Green MacLeod tartan is often called MacLeod of Harris, and this photograph shows the most spectacular sandy beach on the remote Island of Harris in the Outer Hebrides. By coincidence, the tiny settlement of the same name is home to Donald John MacKay and his Harris Tweed Company which still weaves Harris Tweed and tartan in the timeless tradition of hand weaving.

Uist

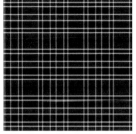

MacDonald of Lochmaddy
971

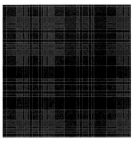

MacDonald of Boisdale
1668

MacDonald of Lochmaddy 971

Lochmaddy is a sea loch and settlement in the north-east corner of North Uist in the Outer Hebrides. It's the North Uist terminus for the ferry to Uig on Skye and to Tarbert on Harris, though since 1996 much of the traffic between North Uist and Harris has used the Sound of Harris Ferry.

Some sources give Captain MacDonald of Lochmaddy as the source of this tartan but nothing concrete is known about its origins and it may possibly be one of a number of smaller family patterns that were designed in the 1930s to '50s.

MacDonald of Boisdale 1668

The MacDonalds of Boisdale were a cadet branch of the MacDonalds of Clanranald that came from the area around Loch Boisdale in North Uist. In the 1770s, South Uist was owned by Colin MacDonald of Boisdale and his cousin MacDonald of Clanranald but it was Boisdale, a Catholic turned Protestant, who was responsible for the infamous religious persecution of his tenants. Another MacDonald – John MacDonald of Glenaladale on the mainland – liaised with the Catholic Bishop and mortgaged his estate to buy land on Prince Edward Island in Canada. He and the Church authorities then set about persuading the persecuted Catholics to consider mass emigration which they embarked on two years later and founded their settlement of Scotchfort.

Nothing is known of the origins of this striking design, which was first recorded just as 'Boisdale' in the Cockburn Collection of 1810.

Barra

MacNeil of Barra 1767

The MacNeils were hereditary pipers to the MacLeans of Duart; this tartan dates back to the early 19th century and the records of William Wilson and Sons, and possibly started life as one of their numbered patterns. In their 1850 book *The Authenticated Tartans of the Clans and Families of Scotland* William and Andrew Smith of Mauchline wrote: 'The Specimen here given, is what has always been known as "The MacNeill Tartan".'

The 46th Chief had this to say on the Barra tartan in 1997: 'The tartan of the Macneils of Barra is the familiar black, green, and blue tartan with narrow alternating white and yellow (encased in black) stripes . . . This has been that standard Macneil of Barra tartan for well over a century.' This tartan has also been called MacNeil Hunting at times.

MacNeil 'Chief's' Tartan 1839

In the same letter, the Chief also wrote that in the 1930s the 45th Chief of the clan, Robert Lister MacNeil of Barra, adopted this tartan for himself and his family. It's the same as the MacNeil of Barra with a slight change of proportion and red guard lines added to the white. He also condemned the unofficial use of this tartan by clansmen and said that he had no intention of recognizing this red-stripe version as a Clan MacNeil tartan, *except* for use by the chief and his family. However, he added that he did not intend to wear it himself since he believed that the chief should wear the same tartan as the clan.

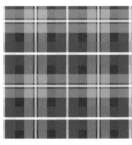

MacNeil of Barra 1767

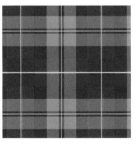

MacNeil 'Chief's' Tartan
1839

Highland Flings

Together with their tartans and their memories, emigrating Scots of all generations have taken with them their traditional dances – the wild whooping and hollering ones from local ceilidhs; the more sedate and structured ones from Highland balls and the individual ones that developed into competition pieces performed around the world.

THE traditional country dances have as their 'Mither Kirk' the long-established Royal Scottish Country Dance Society, which has almost 400 branches and affiliated groups. From Stockholm to Sydney, Tokyo to Tuscon and Newcastle to Nairobi around 25,000 members get together to learn the form and movements of the 'authorized' versions of a range of social dances, which, like tartans, are being continually added to with a reported staggering total to date of 10,000.

Royal Scottish Country Dance Society 6975

has always been very buoyant – competitors believing that a really outstanding tartan will catch the judges' eyes and swing marks, as well as kilts, in their favour. Some weavers and dance clothing suppliers have therefore tended to play fast and loose with long-established clan tartans by producing 'unauthorized' dress versions in a multitude of different colour ways. Although this practice keeps the looms and wheels of commerce turning, it does confuse many poor innocent clan members and adds to the profusion of spurious tartans.

Those formal dances usually involve combinations of up to five couples moving through a set routine of prescribed steps which eventually brings them back to their starting positions. The tartans they wear will invariably be of their own individual choice and there's no suggestion of any team tartan as such – although the recently designed RSCDS tartan, hot off the House of Edgar looms, will probably be enthusiastically adopted by many dancers with no tartan of their own.

Scottish Highland dancing originated in the very early days of folk dance and was said to be a highly athletic form of celebratory dance performed by Highland 'warriors'. Today's version of the art form is a familiar sight at almost all Highland games, and 'weel kent' dances include the Highland Fling, the Sword Dance, Seann Truibhs, the Irish Jig and the Sailor's Hornpipe. The individual dances are the domain of the Scottish Official Board of Highland Dancing, the umbrella authority for all competition dancing organizations and associations throughout the world.

Such are the huge numbers of devotees and young performers that the market for special dance tartans

As an exuberant social and musical pursuit, Scottish Country Dancing attracts lifelong devotees – some of whom are seen here living it up in Bell's Sports Centre in Perth, Scotland.

0 10 20 30 40 50 kilometres
0 10 20 30 miles

LINDSAY

GRAHAM

Stonehaven

OGILVIE

Montrose

Blair Atholl Bruar
MENZIES STEWART Pitlochry

ROBERTSON Forfar

STEWART CARNEGIE

CAMPBELL FERGUSON

Loch Tay

MACGREGOR MACNAB RUTHVEN
MACTHOMAS

Oban FERGUSON Loch Earn MURRAY Perth Tay

MACDOUGALL Balquhidder MACNEISH Crieff Earn St Andrews
MACLAREN

MACNAUGHTON DRUMMOND LINDSAY

MACCALLUM MACFARLANE
Inveraray GRAHAM
CAMPBELL MACAULAY BUCHANAN
COLQUHOUN Loch Lomond Stirling

MACLACHLAN Dunfermline Firth of Forth

MACTAVISH

MACMILLAN LAMONT

STUART
Bute

MACALISTER

Campbeltown

92

THE CENTRAL HIGHLANDS

From Stonehaven on the North Sea coast, south-west to the Island of Islay in the Atlantic, those lochs, glens and mountains have proved an almost impregnable barrier that helped to preserve the Highland way of life. They also channelled military incursions and excursions into one of a handful of access routes. The Romans tried forcing their way through the centre but gave up and built a watchtower to warn them of approaching Picts. A thousand years later the Danish Earl Siward and his Northumbrian army marched north through the same Sma' Glen in Perthshire to battle with Shakespeare's Macbeth. Another 700 years on, Bonnie Prince Charlie and his army saw the same steep, shale-covered slopes and heard the same tinkling river as *they* marched north to their Culloden fate.

Loch Lomond, perhaps the most iconic of all the lochs in Scotland

At the very same time as Charles was setting foot in the Sma' Glen to make the history that would elevate tartan to almost cult status, 35 miles south at Bannockburn, the wheels, cogs and shuttles of William Wilson's looms were clattering to fulfil their military contracts and the orders from the new world colonies.

LINDSAY 704

In the clan's early days the seat was Crawford in south Lanarkshire but they became most powerful in Angus and Fife where the principal seat became the now ruined Finavon Castle, a few miles north-east of Forfar. It was there that the infamously tyrannical 4th Earl of Crawford, known as the Tiger Earl for his legendary bad temper or Earl Beardie for his flaming red hair, was reputed to practise the Black Arts to further his causes.

His cruelty is typified by the tale of a messenger who cut a cudgel from a chestnut tree growing in the castle grounds. As punishment, Earl Beardie hanged him from the same tree. The messenger's ghost is said to still wander between Finavon and Cariston and a local rhyme refers to the incident:

Earl Beardie ne'er will dee,
Nor puir Jock Barefoot be set free,
As lang's there grows a chestnut tree.

The debut of the Lindsay tartan appears to be in the 1842 *Vestiarium Scoticum*, and its distinctive modern wine colouring is exactly that shown in the *Vestiarium*. This is unusual as the precise shade of a tartan's colours is usually left to the discretion of the weavers and all too frequently they would make do with whatever yarn they had in stock.

DUKE OF FIFE 790

This sett is now looked upon as the Fife District tartan but it was first noticed in the pattern book from Fraser Ross of Glasgow and was said to have been designed for the celebration of the wedding in 1889 of Alexander Duff, the 6th Earl of Fife, to Louise, the Princess Royal, daughter of Edward VII and granddaughter of Queen Victoria. Two days after the wedding the Queen elevated the new royal husband to Duke of Fife and Marquess of MacDuff.

The partner to this tartan was the Duchess of Fife, in which the red lines were changed to blue.

LERMONTOV 6493

MacDuff also features in this very modern tartan designed for a very old Russian family. In 1613 George Lermont, a 'Scotch Knight' of Fife, left his home county and emigrated to Russia to serve as a military instructor to Tsar Mikhail Romanov. In Russia the name quickly became Lermontov and the most famous of George's descendants, Mikhail – a much revered poet and dissident – was killed in a duel in 1841 aged only 27. His standing in Russia is almost akin to that of Robert Burns in Scotland.

This tartan is based upon the MacDuff because of Fife's literary connection with Shakespeare's *Macbeth* in which MacDuff was given the fictional title of Thane of Fife. The white lines on blue represent the Scottish flag, the St Andrew's Cross, St Andrew being the patron saint of both Russia and Scotland. The remaining colours are from the Lermontov coat of arms, registered in Russia in 1798. The significance of the diagonal cross of St Andrew is that he is believed to have been crucified by the Romans on a diagonal cross in Patmos, southern Greece.

EARL OF ST ANDREWS 85

Some 300 years after St Andrew's death, legend relates that Emperor Constantine decided to move the saint's bones, and a monk, possibly called St Rule, was warned of this in a dream by an angel, who told him to remove the saint's bones to 'the ends of the Earth' to keep them safe.

Apparently he managed to liberate a tooth, an arm bone, a kneecap and some fingers before setting out on an epic journey, ending in a shipwreck off what is now known as St Andrews. A chapel was built to house the relics and by 1160 St Andrews Cathedral was the religious capital of Scotland, and the goal of many pilgrims.

Earl of St Andrews was one of the titles held by Prince George, the Duke of Kent, and he first wore this tartan in 1939 to a Highland Society dinner in London three years before he was killed on active duty in the Second World War. It had been designed in 1930 by Arthur Bottomley, a director of Peter MacArthur Ltd, specifically for the use of Prince George.

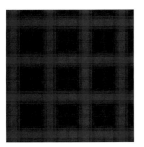

| Lindsay | 704 |

| Duke of Fife | 790 |

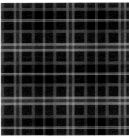

| Lermontov | 6493 |

| Earl of St Andrews | 85 |

Wilsons of Bannockburn

THERE is no doubt that had it not been for William Wilson, the clan and sartorial world would have been very much the poorer. Born in 1727 at Craigforth in the parish of St Ninians in the shadow of Stirling Castle, Wilson became a weaver and incorporated chapman (trader) and founded the firm of William Wilson and Son in which he was followed by four generations of his descendants.

The firm was remarkable in that it was weaving tartan during the period of the proscription of the Highland Garb Act (1746–82) and that it had a large civilian trade, which eventually sent tartan to North and South America, the West Indies, Europe and the Indian continent. It also supplied tartans to many of the Highland regiments from the last quarter of the 18th century until the end of the 19th. This two-pronged trade may be the reason why William Wilson and Son has been credited with (or blamed for) the 'invention' of clan tartans. Between 1765 and 1924, when it went out of business, the firm was known to have searched the Highlands for old patterns, then re-introduced them under names of their choosing if the original clan or district could not be determined.

The Wilson records are unique in the field of tartan and of inestimable value to the student. An estimated 10,000 letters, many legal documents, books of written patterns and samples of cloth have survived and are in the hands of various authorities such as the National Library of Scotland and the Royal Museum of Scotland. The letter reproduced here is evidence that tartan was frequently used for clothing slaves in the West Indies.

Messrs Wilson & Son

Gentlemen,

Send us 200 yd Linsey to The Inclosed pattern – the article is fr Negro wear and must be very low priced if possible not above 1/– or under if you can – It must also be had befr 1 January as a vessell sails early in the Year from Port Glasgow. You will forward the 42nd Clothing by your Carrier to Perth and send us Invoice to Morrow.

22 Decm 1797
Mason & Thomson

Pack the above well up & direct the Bale to W:W: Whitehill St Elizabeth, Parish Jamaica & forward the Bale to Mesr MLauchlan, to be shipped by them. Don't Send the 42nd Clothing to Perth till we ask you again as we believe the party are at Glasgow.

A surviving piece of 'Old Ross' tartan from Wilsons of Bannockburn, woven in the early 1800s or earlier

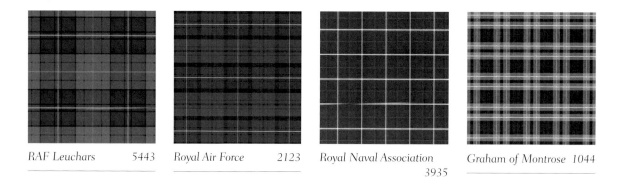

| RAF Leuchars | 5443 | Royal Air Force | 2123 | Royal Naval Association 3935 | Graham of Montrose 1044 |

Although it started life as a restricted royal tartan it's said that in 1973 a major UK store mounted a sales promotion with it and once they'd let the genie out of the bottle, it gradually became the district tartan for St Andrews and the surrounding area.

RAF LEUCHARS   5443

Regimental tartans have long been an accepted part of Scottish heritage, but with the sad passing of so many regiments, it seems appropriate that the mantle – in part – should be passed on to the other services.

Close to St Andrews in Fife lies Scotland's major Royal Air Force base at Leuchars and this tartan was designed in 1989 by Arthur Mackie of Strathmore Woollens in Forfar.

ROYAL AIR FORCE   2123

Another design from Arthur Mackie in 1989 was this sett which was originally called 'the Air Force tartan'. It was adopted by the Women's Auxiliary Air Force Association in 1990 and worn by its members as part of their uniform in the annual Remembrance

Right: A Tornado F3 Fighter from 56 (Reserve) Squadron based at RAF Leuchars in Fife

Parade past the Cenotaph in London. After quite a bit of lobbying of the Ministry of Defence (especially by the past Commanding Officer of RAF Leuchars, Air Commodore Jack Haines), the Air Force Board determined – in 2002 – that the tartan should be accepted and given its full title of the *Royal* Air Force tartan.

Royal Naval Association   3935

Moving out of Fife and across the Firth of Tay to Angus, naval man Granville Cooper designed this simple and very effective sett to be the official Royal Naval Association tartan. Woven by the House of Edgar in nearby Perth, the design is based on the Scottish national tartan with Fleet Air Arm colours.

Graham of Montrose   1044

As the writer René McOwan once wrote: 'The name Graham rings like a trumpet call in the pageant of Scottish history.' The two most outstanding individuals of the name were undoubtedly James Graham, First Marquis of Montrose (1612–50), who carried on the war in Scotland for Charles II, and John Graham of Claverhouse, Viscount Dundee (1648–89), the swashbuckling 'Bonnie Dundee' to

his friends and admirers and 'Bluidy Clavers' to his many enemies.

In the 1630s, James Graham was one of the Covenanters – the Presbyterian leaders who were intent on opposing English attempts under King Charles I to 'catholicise' Scotland. But when the Civil War began in 1642 Graham decided to support the King, thus finding himself in opposition to many of his former Covenanting allies, most of whom supported the Parliamentarian side. He conducted a series of brilliant campaigns in Scotland but was shamelessly betrayed by Neil MacLeod of Assynt for the huge sum of £25,000. He was taken to Edinburgh and, without trial, hanged as a traitor at the Grassmarket in 1650.

John Graham of Claverhouse was a distant relative of Montrose and carried on the fight of his kinsman for the Royalist cause, which after James II was deposed in 1685 became the Jacobite cause. He insisted on always fighting with his Highlanders and tragically died at the moment of victory at the head of the Jacobite army at the Battle of Killiecrankie when a musket ball entered beneath his breastplate. Legend had it that he was invulnerable to all bullets and what actually finished him was a silver button from his own coat. It was another Graham, the third Duke of Montrose, who in 1782 spearheaded the repeal of the ban on tartan.

This is a Wilsons of Bannockburn pattern from at least as far back as 1815 when they called it No. 64 or Abercrombie. It was a very practical design and

Above: Tartan takes to the skies: British Airways' late-1990s innovative ethnic livery for Scotland, which met with mixed reactions (Mrs Thatcher was famously appalled)

Left: James Graham, First Marquis of Montrose (1612–50), who led the Royalist cause in Scotland during the Civil War and was cruelly betrayed by a MacLeod

lent itself to many guises when the colour of the white overstripe was altered. Wilsons changed it to yellow and it became the Campbell of Breadalbane. In red it became the MacCallum. In alternate red and yellow it was Rollo. Changed back to white it magically became the MacLaggan! The entry in Andrew and William Smith's *Authenticated Tartans of the Clans and Families of Scotland* reads: 'Meyer and Mortimer of Edinburgh, for a period of at least nearly thirty years, have manufactured this pattern as The Graham Tartan, during which time they have supplied it to many distinguished families of that name.'

Killiecrankie, near Pitlochry, the scene of the great Jacobite victory of 1689

CARNEGIE 489

Carnegie is a geographical name, being an area around Carmyllie in the county of Angus. This tartan was a variant of the MacDonnell of Glengarry and was adopted by the head of the family Lord Southesk. The Glengarry white becomes yellow in the Carnegie but it's possible that this minor difference was caused by fading of the white with the passage of time.

Probably the most famous Carnegie of all was Andrew, son of a weaver, born in 1835 in Dunfermline a good few miles south of Carnegie country. When he was thirteen, his family emigrated to the United States. Fifty-two years later he sold

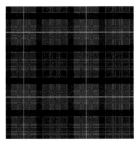

Carnegie 489

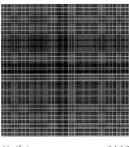

Ogilvie 2132

Scrymgeour 1627

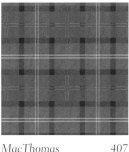

MacThomas 407

his steel company for $480 million and set about disposing of his fortune through innumerable personal gifts and the establishment of various trusts. His most notable contribution was the building of 2,509 libraries throughout the English-speaking world. It was said at one time there were more busts of Carnegie on public view than of any other human being.

OGILVIE 2132

Confusion surrounds the origins of this extremely complicated design (it has 79 colour changes before the pattern repeats) and the very similar Drummond of Strathallan tartan. In 1812 the Earl of Airlie (an Ogilvie) married Clementina Drummond and it is said that he adopted his new wife's family tartan but changed the green ground to blue.

However, at odds with that explanation is that two years prior to the 1812 wedding, the Cockburn Collection included two similar versions: this Ogilvie (blue ground with red lines) and Drummond (green ground with black lines). Whatever the origins, in 1816 the then Chief sealed a sample of this for the Highland Society of London as the tartan of the Ogilvys of Airlie.

The Smiths related a far more fetching explanation in 1850: 'There is a superstition among some of the Ogilvies, that the fairies, taking offence at the Clan for using so much of their own favourite colour in their Tartan, arrayed themselves as the auxiliaries of their antagonists in one of their feuds, and caused their defeat; and that the dread of this tiny and irritable race, has made some of this name substitute Blue for Green in their Tartan.'

SCRYMGEOUR 1627

The Scrymgeours (pronounced *scrim-jers*) were Hereditary Standard Bearers of Scotland but until 1971 had no tartan. It was at the Gathering of the Clans in that year that Inverness Chief Librarian Trudi Mann was chatting to Sir Ian Moncrieffe, his wife and his father-in-law. Sir Ian's wife – who was a Scrymgeour – was wearing an attractive checked blouse and her father said that he would like a tartan designed to include those colours.

Trudi Mann – who was also a tartan designer – obliged and had it vetted by Donald C. Stewart, author of *The Setts of the Scottish Tartans*. The finished design was displayed at a Scrymgeour gathering at their historical town residence of Dudhope Castle in Dundee and it was later adopted as the official clan tartan.

The family was closely connected with the city and until the 17th century retained the title of 'Constable of Dundee', and many descendants subsequently became provosts of the city.

MACTHOMAS 407

The establishment of the MacThomas clan is an excellent example of how new clans developed in Scotland. Its first chieftain was said to be Thomas, son of Angus, 6th Chief of the Clan MacIntosh, and in 1345 Thomas broke away and formed his own clan which later migrated from Badenoch – MacIntosh country – over the hills and down into Glenshee. The early chiefs settled on the east bank of the Shee Water at the Spittal of Glenshee.

A 16th-century tale shows how lawless such isolated areas could be. A group of tax collectors – they travelled in groups for safety – seized a newly widowed woman's livestock, valuables and furnishings in lieu of tax, and when the Chief of Clan

A McIan depiction of the Ogilvie tartan, with the dress style of 1745 and knee-breeches and stockings rather than trews

MacOmish (Gaelic pronunciation for MacThomas) heard of this he set off with a group of his men to intercept the tax collectors. This he did at the Finegand ford and in the ensuing argument, the chief collector was killed. One of his team shouted: 'MacCombie Mhor, we are the King's men and will bear witness against you.' That proved to be unwise because MacCombie's answer was: 'There will not be witnesses.' And he instructed his men to kill them all. When done he ordered them to be decapitated and the heads thrown in the burn. It's said that he then bellowed after the rapidly floating heads: 'Now swim back to your masters in Edinburgh and tell them what happens to thieves they send to Glenshee.' The long-term repercussions of this were that many of the MacOmishes had to flee and others had to start anglicizing the pronunciation of their surname.

One of the most photographed views in Scotland – Queen's View, overlooking Loch Tummel in Perthshire, in Robertson country

On to a more peaceable pursuit – tartan designing! The MacThomas clan didn't have a tartan until 1954 when David Thomas – at that time a director of the Strathmore Woollen Company of Forfar – designed this one, which the clan officially adopted in 1975.

ROBERTSON

Over the mountains to the west of Glenshee lay Robertson country and in 1837 the historian William Skene wrote that 'the Robertsons of Struan are unquestionably the oldest family in Scotland, being the sole remaining branch of that Royal House of Atholl which occupied the throne of Scotland during the 11th and 12th centuries'. Also known as Clan Donnachaidh (the Children of Duncan), the clan's territory stretched across some of Perthshire's most spectacular landscapes from the beautiful wilderness of loch-strewn Rannoch Moor to Bruar on today's north–south artery of the A9.

The 13th Chief, Alexander Robertson, fought with Bonnie Dundee at Killiecrankie. Known as 'the Poet Chief', he had the distinction of being 'out' in the risings of 1689, 1715 and 1745. It was reported that when he met Bonnie Prince Charlie at Perth he knelt before him and stated: 'Sir, I devoted my youth to the service of your grandsire and my manhood to that of your father. Now I have come to devote my old age to the cause of your Royal Highness.' The

clan's support for the Royal House proved to be its downfall and it lost much of its land to other clans, and whilst clansmen remained loyal to Struan in any dispute, they became part of the nearby Duke of Atholl's armed following. Whilst martial by necessity, the clan enjoyed a brilliant musical reputation and many of its compositions are still current today.

The clan tartan first appeared in Wilsons' 1819 Key Pattern Book and the Smith brothers had no doubts about it in 1850, it having 'been approved of by all the authorities to whom we have referred it'. Weavers now call this 'Robertson Red'.

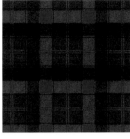

Robertson   1501   Menzies   894

MENZIES   894

The clan seat is the spectacular Menzies Castle near Aberfeldy in Perthshire which is an archetypal fortified mansion.

The simple two-colour design of the Menzies tartan has very pleasing proportions and has thus attracted the attentions of fashion and dance tartan designers over the years. This green and red version is now called the Hunting Menzies but confusingly tends to be used as a clan tartan rather than the red and white version which was originally certified by the Chief as the clan tartan in 1816.

The Menzies coat of arms features a severed Saracen head which relates to the 14th-century Battle of Teba de Ardales in Spain in which a group of Scottish knights found themselves involved. There was a call to 'Charge!' and the only Menzies in the group cried 'Vil God I Zal!' – 'With God's will I shall' – which became the clan's motto. Why he spoke in such a strange fashion is not revealed.

Menzies Castle

Murray of Atholl 281

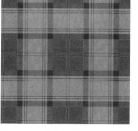
Stewart of Atholl 802

Murray

Just a few miles south of Bruar and the Clan Donnachaidh museum is one of Scotland's most inspiring and picturesque buildings rising up out of the Perthshire landscape – the Disneyesque, turreted and gleaming white Blair Castle, traditional home of the Dukes of Atholl – the Murrays.

Like so many powerful clans, their history is complicated and their branches many – Murray of Atholl, of Elibank, of Tullibardine, of Ochtertyre and of Polmaise. Of those, only the tartans of the first three survive to modern usage, joined by the very new Murray of Mansfield.

MURRAY OF ATHOLL 281

This was originally called the Atholl tartan and according to the 1906 Johnston publication was regarded as a district tartan which 'properly, belongs to no family but is purely a district or local tartan used by Atholl men generally, particularly Stewarts and Robertsons, who formed the bulk of the population'.

Blair Castle, the beautiful home of the Murray Dukes of Atholl

Murray of Tullibardine 441

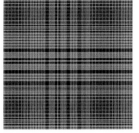
Mungo Murray   2173

Ruthven   1521

STEWART OF ATHOLL   802

This was prepared for the *Vestiarium Scoticum* but not included in the published version. It was, it is said (Johnstons, 1906), copied from 'a Highland dress worn by a Stewart from Atholl during the '45, and still in the possession of a descendant'. That Stewart from Atholl apparently had a 'remarkable resemblance to Prince Charles Edward and some time after Culloden was taken prisoner while at work on his farm under the belief that he was the hunted Prince himself. He obtained his release through his skill on the bagpipes (which of itself would have been sufficient to indicate the mistake), but which further led to his identification by an officer in Cumberland's army who recognised the music.'

MURRAY OF TULLIBARDINE   441

James Grant, in his book *The Tartans of the Clans of Scotland* (1886), says: 'That tartan called the Tullibardine is a red tartan, and was adopted and worn by Charles, the first Earl of Dunmore, second son of the first Marquis of Tullibardine.' The same sett is shown in the 1850 book from the Smith brothers in which they write: 'We found this very pretty pattern of Tartan in the market, but we can say nothing more anent it, than that the proprietors of the very respectable Tartan Warehouse from which we obtained it assured us it is the Tartan used by the Earl of Dunmore.'

This is the sett shown in the famous 1747 portrait of Norman, the 22nd Chief of the MacLeods, and it's also the one that's worn by the Transvaal Scottish Regiment.

MUNGO MURRAY   2173

This extraordinary tartan is from a 1670 portrait of Lord Mungo Murray (1668–1700) by John Michael Wright, the earliest known major portrait to show Highland dress.

Mungo Murray, the fifth son of the 2nd Earl of Atholl, was reputedly killed (possibly murdered) by the Spanish in about 1700 during Scotland's criminally inept and disastrous Darien Expedition to found an overseas trading company in Panama.

RUTHVEN   1521

Neighbours to the Murrays were the Ruthvens who were Norse in origin and had settled in the Perth area by the end of the 12th century. Their most famous – or infamous – appearance in the historical spotlight was in 1600 when John the 3rd Earl of Gowrie and his brother were killed in their Ruthven Castle home for allegedly trying to assassinate King

Huntingtower Castle, originally Ruthven Castle but renamed after James VI blacklisted the name of Ruthven following a seeming assassination attempt in 1600

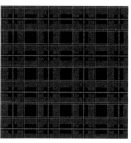

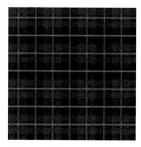

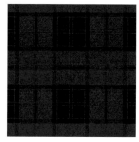

| Drummond | 457 | Drummond of Perth | 1711 | Moray of Abercairney | 51 | Crieff | 1636 | Crieff Hydro Hotel | 5166 |

James VI. The affair was known as the Gowrie Conspiracy and to this day, no one has fathomed the truth. James banished the name of Ruthven and the castle was renamed Huntingtower. Now just on the outskirts of Perth, it has a compensatory romantic tale to tell of Dorothea, the daughter of the first Earl of Gowrie. She happened to be visiting her lover in his chamber in one of the castle's twin towers when she heard her mother approaching. Dorothea apparently leapt the 9ft 4in gap to her own tower and was tucked up in bed when her mother found her. Since then the gap has become known as 'the Maiden's Leap'. Mary Queen of Scots and Lord Darnley stayed during their honeymoon and this unique time capsule is open to the public, courtesy of its guardians Historic Scotland.

The Ruthven tartan is another of the Sobieskis' confections but they slipped up with their quaint old Scots description when they omitted any mention of the white line.

DRUMMOND 457
To the west of Huntingtower Castle lies Strathearn – the broad valley of the River Earn which flows into the Firth of Tay just south-west of Perth. Here lay the lands of various branches of the Drummonds and the Morays that were frequently the scene of skirmishes between the two.

This tartan appears to be shared between the Grants and the Drummonds and it's certainly the one that the Drummonds wore to meet George IV in Edinburgh in 1822. Bearing in mind that in each of ten Grant portraits at Cullen House in Morayshire, each sitter is wearing a different tartan and where a coat or plaid is worn, they too are different, deciding who had first claim to this sett is weighted in the Drummonds' favour.

Jamie Scarlett relates the Drummonds' early progress: 'Sir Malcolm de Drymens was a local boy who made good at the Battle of Bannockburn, where he strewed the field with four-cornered spikes called caltrops, to the confusion of the English cavalry; the caltrop now figures in the chief's heraldic achievement and the motto "Gang Warily" is a reminder of the episode.'

In this MacLeay portrait, Duncan Drummond (seated) wears a plaid, waistcoat and kilt of his clan tartan. Andrew Murray wears a kilt of Murray of Tullibardine, a fox-skin sporran and an unusual tartan cockade in his bonnet. In the background is a view of Strathearn.

DRUMMOND OF PERTH 1711

Probably the earliest mention of this tartan is in a manuscript book in the National Museum of Antiquities in Edinburgh thought to date to around 1800, where it is called Drummond or Perth and before that, just Perth.

Tradition associates this tartan with the amiable, ill-fated James Drummond, 3rd Duke of Perth and Chief of Clan Drummond, who commanded the left wing of 900 men at the Battle of Culloden in 1746. He was severely wounded and had to be carried from the field. He died on board a French frigate while attempting to escape the following year. The battle also claimed the life of another senior Drummond, William Drummond of Machany, 4th Viscount of Strathallan. In fact this design appears to be a variant of the plaid said to have been left at nearby Fingask House by Prince Charles – the Stewart of Fingask tartan.

MORAY OF ABERCAIRNEY 51

Abercairney is close to Crieff and this sett is derived from the portrait of James, 14th Laird, painted about 1735. There are always dangers in trying to divine thread counts from portraits and many historians and observers have made different interpretations of this tartan.

CRIEFF 1636

Well known to Rob Roy MacGregor and many of his cattle-droving compatriots, Crieff was once the scene of the largest cattle markets (trysts) in Scotland. On the southern edge of the Highlands, it was very much a frontier town – as far north as fearful southern merchants dared venture and as far south as legally vulnerable Highlanders wished to go.

This tartan from Wilsons was probably just another one of their fashion setts given the name of a popular town to increase its sales.

CRIEFF HYDRO HOTEL 5166

The Crieff Hydropathic Establishment, to give its full name, is one of Scotland's great institutions, founded in 1868 and run by the same family to this day. A magnificent stone edifice on a hillside overlooking the town, it was part of the Victorian era's homage to clean living and rude health – a place where they put the water into the guests and the guests into the water with neither sullied by any trace of alcohol.

In Victorian times, families would make their annual pilgrimage and stay the summer at the Hydropathic with the husbands being taken daily by horse and carriage down to the railway station to commute to Edinburgh or Glasgow. The epitome of that holiday tradition was evidenced in recent years when five generations of the same family congregated there for their annual break.

The 'Hydro tartan' was instigated by the author in the 1990s and designed by the weaver/historian Peter MacDonald of Crieff.

STRATHEARN 1890

The Crieff Hydro tartan was based on this 1820 design from Wilsons of Bannockburn. Strathearn means the broad valley of the River Earn and that river flows from Loch Earn into the Firth of Tay. This tartan is said to have been worn by the father of Queen Victoria, HRH Edward, Duke of Kent, who was also Duke of Strathearn. As Colonel of the Royal Scots Regiment from 1801 to 1821, he apparently sent a sample to Wilsons with a view to 'dressing the gallant corps' with it.

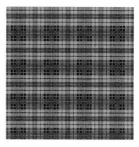

Strathearn 1890

The famous Crieff Hydropathic Establishment, which has offered guests wholesome relaxation for nearly 150 years

Heart of Strathearn   6844

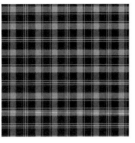

Scottish Tartans Authority
243

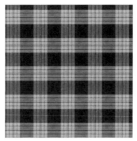

MacLaren   342

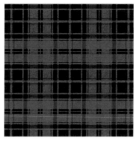

MacNeish   3509

MacNab   857

Scottish Tartans Authority

The arms of the Scottish Tartan Authority

The Scottish Tartans Authority is the world's leading information source on tartans and Highland dress and, as a registered Scottish charity, is supported by private, commercial and academic membership and industry patronage. It is the promotional body for the Scottish industry and maintains the de facto official register of historical and contemporary tartans and acts as Registrar for all new tartans. Its Perthshire headquarters houses the largest collection of woven samples in existence and a valuable archive of rare books.

The Authority is frequently commissioned to design new tartans and deals with many thousands of general enquiries from personal visits, telephone calls and letters and e-mails from around the globe. As the highly respected 'guardian' of Scotland's tartan and Highland dress heritage, the Authority is working towards facilitating the establishment of a National Tartan Centre to house and make publicly accessible the country's valuable artefacts that make up the 'fabric of the nation'

HEART OF STRATHEARN   6844

This tartan was just one output from a range of small business ventures established by a cluster of seven schools in Strathearn. It was part of a Scottish government campaign to encourage the next generation of young Scots (aged five to eleven) to acquire entrepreneurial skills and develop self-confidence, self-reliance and ambition to achieve their goals – in work and in life. This the kids certainly did!

A school-wide competition was organized and from the many hundreds of entries, youngsters voted on a winner. With help from the Tartans Authority the new tartan was taken through to the weaving stage and young representatives of each school – appointed as company directors with specific departmental responsibilities – visited the weavers and chose a wide range of tartan products to be sold at the schools, at local coffee mornings and many similar events. An imaginative project which taught the youngsters about their heritage, business and social skills *and* the process of democracy.

SCOTTISH TARTANS AUTHORITY   243

When the Perth-based Scottish Tartans Authority was founded in 1995 it was inconceivable that it should not have its own tartan and opinions were sought by its guiding light Blair C. Macnaughton, head of one of Scotland's leading weaving dynasties.

The consensus reached was that rather than add to the profusion of modern tartans, the Authority should blow the dust off one of the many unnamed historical patterns from the prolific output of Bannockburn weavers William Wilson & Sons (c.1750–1925). The handloom weaver and historian Peter MacDonald recommended Wilsons No. 060 – a fashion tartan included in their records up to 1819.

It's not known if it was one of their own in-house designs or a traditional sett discovered by one of their 'scouts'. Regardless of its origin, it has seen the useful light of day after almost two centuries of languishing in the shadows. Wilsons would no doubt be delighted to see it being used to commemorate their industry of the 18th and 19th centuries and to promote so many of their designs in the 21st.

MacLaren   342

Wilsons of Bannockburn originally produced this tartan as the 'Regent', but when George IV ascended the throne, the Regency was of course at an end and the name became outdated. Production of the sett continued, however, and the MacLarens appeared to come to Wilsons' rescue by adopting the sett as their clan tartan in time for George IV's visit to Edinburgh in 1822.

The MacLarens were a predominant clan in the 12th century and occupied lands in Balquhidder and Strathearn.

MacNeish   3509

A sept of the MacGregors was a small clan called Neish who occupied the east end of Loch Earn in Perthshire – the MacGregors occupied the other. As the power of both clans diminished they grew to rely on plundering the surrounding countryside and then retreating – in the case of the Neish clan – to a small crannog (a man-made island) at the eastern end. In December 1612 the Neishes waylaid and robbed a MacNab servant returning from Crieff with Christmas supplies to the clan base on Loch Tay in the next glen. The MacNab Chief was furious and dropped a broad hint to his sons that he would like something done about it. The Neishes considered themselves safe on their island home because they had destroyed all boats on the loch except their own. So the MacNab lads carried their own boat from Loch Tay up over the intervening mountain range and down Glen Tarken and into Loch Earn. The Neishes were totally surprised and all but one young lad and a man – who hid under a table – were killed. The MacNabs set out to carry the boat back to Loch Tay but ran out of stamina part-way up Glen Tarken and left it there. Over the decades it slowly rotted away with the locals raiding it now and again for firewood. What the MacNab boys *did* take back with

them, in a sack, was the Neish Chief's head. The occasion was commemorated by that severed head being incorporated into the MacNab coat of arms.

MacNab   857

The MacNab tartan is identical in structure with that of the Black Watch and shows how, with just a change of colours, the most subdued of tartans becomes one of the most striking. James Logan recorded this pattern in his book *The Scottish Gael* in 1831, despite receiving a different sett from Wilsons. Logan recorded the thread counts of 32 tartans including the MacNab but gave no justification for any of them. In Robert McIan's illustration of MacNab, his informant – none other than Logan – cited the source of the tartan as his own book. A fine example of circular provenance!

MacNab country originally stretched from Tyndrum west into Argyll, and then to the east down Glendochart to Killin at the western end of Loch Tay. Gradually over the centuries the landholdings and

Robert MacNab is standing in this MacLeay portrait and his boots seem out of place with his otherwise formal outfit. The Macnaughton pictured was later identified as a John McNaghton who was apparently robbed and murdered in Glasgow in 1868, and his body found four months later in the River Clyde.

McIan shows a Ferguson in the old 'lein-croich' form of dress in the 16th century. His fellow author James Logan wrote: 'The target (shield) is from one of the very oldest pattern, composed of wood, strengthened by layers of flax, mixed with tar, the rim is bound with iron, it is ornamented with a large copan, or boss, and has but one handle.'

fortunes shrank and now the island of Inchbuie, just downstream from the Falls of Dochart, is the only remaining clan land. A few years ago, the Chief conveyed the island and its ancient burial ground to a trust to ensure its ownership by the clan in perpetuity and its continued use as a final resting place for chiefs and their families.

FERGUSON   337

There were many branches of the Ferguson family established in Scotland – in Perthshire, Aberdeenshire, Fife, Dumfries, Argyll and Ayrshire. Despite the number and geographical spread there appear to have

been only two tartans – the straightforward clan tartan shown here and the Ferguson of Balquhidder sett. The Fergusons of Perthshire were recognized as the principal Highland branch of the clan and the chiefship belonged to 'MacFhearghuis' of Dunfallandy near Pitlochry. The present-day chief is Sir Charles Fergusson of Kilkerran, Ayrshire.

FERGUSON THE ASTRONOMER   1551

A plaid in Kingussie Museum said to have been made at Banff for Ferguson the Astronomer. He was a remarkable character who was born in 1710 in Banffshire and became a self-taught mechanician, astronomer and one of the first writers on elementary science. According to the *Dictionary of National Biography*, 'He brought the complex theories of advanced science to the layman in his ingenious writing and impassioned lectures, and in his quest to make the world of science accessible to the general public, he invented amazing machines and didactic mechanisms with which to visually demonstrate the basic principles of scientific study.'

When or by whom the tartan was designed is not known.

GRAHAM OF MENTEITH   698

Not far south of Balquhidder is the Lake of Menteith. The use of the word 'Lake' is unusual in the land of 'Lochs'; it's believed to be a corruption of 'laich' which in Lowland Scots simply means 'low place'.

The tartan is similar to the Montrose and first appeared in Wilsons' 1819 Pattern Book as Cobourg. There's also a Menteith district tartan which was reportedly rescued from oblivion in 1941. It's the same as the Graham of Menteith except that the azure overchecks have been replaced by white, in all probability a misreading of a faded piece of this Graham sett.

BUCHANAN   151

The Buchanans are from Stirlingshire and north of Loch Lomond and the Buchanan Highlander is probably the most popular of Ronald McIan's 1845 Victorian illustrations in *The Clans of the Scottish Highlands*. In executing it, however, McIan bequeathed a bit of a tangle to the tartan world. Without apportioning blame to McIan or his researcher, author James Logan, the figure isn't

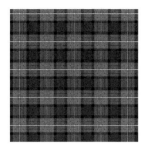

Ferguson   337

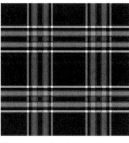

Ferguson the Astronomer 1551

Graham of Menteith   698

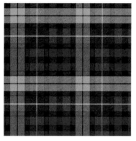

Buchanan   151

MacFarlane   947

A Buchanan in the dress of around 1730, from William Stewart's 1928 book Clanland

wearing the Buchanan tartan as recorded by Logan – presumably from a woven sample from Wilsons of Bannockburn. That sample would have been symmetrical but McIan – for whatever reason – painted it as asymmetrical.

In a very short space of time the wrong sett was established and in their 1850 book *The Authenticated Tartans of the Clans and Families of Scotland* William and Andrew Smith of Mauchline wrote: 'The pattern here given seems to be universally considered the genuine Buchanan Tartan and we know that it is worn by Archibald Buchanan Esq., of Catrinebank, Ayrshire, whose father's name is identified with one of the first cotton manufactories established in Scotland with Arkwright's improvements.' Even today, the bulk of woven Buchanan repeats that error although some weavers also offer the correct version (pictured here above) and name it Old Buchanan.

MACFARLANE   947

On the other side of Loch Lomond from the Buchanans were the Colquhouns and the MacFarlanes, the latter's destiny being to join the ranks of the broken (dispossessed) clans. According to their clan website www.macfarlane.org, despite being a small clan

> the MacFarlanes were a very turbulent lot. Their rallying cry, 'Loch Sloy', signalled many a night raid to 'collect' cattle from their richer neighbors to the south and east. Their march-piobaireachd [marching tune] *'Thogail nam Bo theid sinn'* (To Lift the Cows We Shall Go) gives ample notice of intent. They were so competent that the full moon was known as 'MacFarlane's Lantern'.

In 1594 an Act denounced them as being in the habit of committing theft, robbery, and oppression and in July 1624 many of the clan were tried and convicted of theft and robbery. Some of them were punished, some pardoned, while others were removed to the highlands of Aberdeenshire, and to Strathaven in Banffshire, where they assumed the names of Stewart, M'Caudy, Greisock, M'James, and M'Innes.

Their tartan came from Wilsons of Bannockburn and probably dates to about 1800. The clan also has a dress, hunting and a black and white tartan.

Tartan Myths

There is an old saying that a lie has travelled halfway round the world before truth has got its trousers (or kilt) on! Nowhere is that more evident than in the world of tartan and Highland dress. As the octogenarian tartan guru Jamie Scarlett commented recently, 'Germs of truth frequently multiply into an epidemic of myths.'

MYTH
Originally the kind of tartan that you wore indicated your rank or position. If it was just one colour you were a servant; two a farmer; three an officer, four a priest, five a chieftain, six a poet and seven a chief.

REALITY
This myth appears to have originated in Ireland from the time of the Druids where it's claimed that the colours of one's robes were of social significance. Be that as it may, the idea seems to have been transferred to tartan, carved in granite and exported as reality. It's an attractive theory but totally unsupported by the facts. The only possible connection between one's station in life and the colours in one's tartan could have been the use of an imported – and thus expensive – dye such as cochineal.

MYTH
A keen eye could link a colour with a particular island – like a wine-taster can identify the years and the vineyard.

REALITY
Gross exaggeration! The dyeing processes were crude and mostly used natural materials whose consistency couldn't be guaranteed. Closely replicating a colour in each dye batch was therefore difficult. However, some weavers such as Wilsons of Bannockburn did develop a particular range of colours, which *could* be standardized.

MYTH
In Scotland during the prohibition of tartan (1746–82) Highlanders would often go to church on a Sunday with a tiny scrap of tartan secreted next to their heart. At a particular juncture in the service, they would place a hand on the tartan and join in a silent prayer that the Lord would restore their ancient tartans, or words to that effect.

REALITY
This is an interesting myth that seems to have been invented to sanctify the peculiarly American custom of Kirkin' the Tartan, an annual church service where many clan societies and other such bodies take their tartan banners to church to have them blessed.

MYTH
The penalty for wearing tartan during the prohibition was death.

REALITY
Not so! For a first offence it was six months in prison or, if you were fit, join the army. For a second it was transportation for seven years. Whilst those were the available punishments to hand out, very few ever were since the law was widely ignored.

MYTH

You can't wear a tartan unless you have the same name as the tartan.

REALITY

This is a very old-fashioned idea that has fortunately fallen into disuse. Highland dress is not a uniform restricted in its use. You can wear almost any tartan that you like but most people will want to wear one with which they feel they have some genetic link. If you can't find a tartan for your own name, then look back at the surnames on both the male and female sides of your family and you may find one that has a clan – and therefore a tartan – link.

MYTH

If you're a Scot you have your own tartan.

REALITY

Many enquirers seem openly aggrieved when told that there's no tartan for their surname. Tartan was a Highland phenomenon and in 1906 there were only 140 clan tartans featured in a popular tartan book. Despite there now being over 1,500 there are still very many thousands of surnames which don't have their own tartan.

MYTH

A true Scotsman doesn't wear anything under his kilt.

REALITY

Nonsense! Most kilt wearers will, in the interests of hygiene and decency, don their conventional underwear . . . but you can never be sure!

MYTH

You must wear white hose with Highland dress for evening functions.

REALITY

No. You should wear hose that tones in with your kilt. The only people who conventionally (and inexplicably) wear white hose are pipe bands.

MYTH

If you're wearing a kilt then you must have the proper clothing to go with it.

REALITY

No . . . you should look upon a kilt as a substitute for trousers or shorts and if it's for casual use, you can wear whatever else you fancy. If, however, you're using it at a formal affair then there are certain standards to which you should adhere to avoid embarrassing your host, yourself or other guests.

A glamorous bevy of models at the Los Angeles Tartan Show, none the worse for wearing it in an unorthodox fashion!

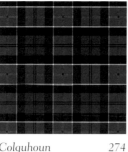

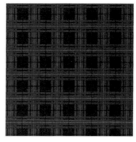

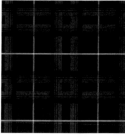

| Colquhoun | 274 | MacAulay of Ardincaple 1164 | Macnaughton | 1066 | Stuart of Bute | 1485 |

COLQUHOUN   274

Frequently the Colquhouns seemed to suffer greatly from the attentions of their northern neighbours the MacGregors. After the Battle of Glenfruin in 1603 in which the Colquhouns were defeated, the MacGregors rubbed salt in the wounds by plundering and destroying the whole Colquhoun estate. They drove off 600 cattle, 800 sheep and goats, and 280 horses and burned every house and barnyard. Retaliation was swift and effective: some

A McIan depiction of a sprightly Colquhoun

sixty Colquhoun widows in deep mourning, carrying their husbands' bloody shirts on poles, appeared before James VI at Stirling. It has been suggested that just like modern footballers taking a dive, this parade was not all it seemed, that not all the women were widows and not all the blood on the shirts had been shed at Glenfruin! However, it worked and the King was sufficiently moved to grant letters of fire and sword against the MacGregors which resulted in the near-extinction of the clan.

A Wilsons' sample of the Colquhoun tartan appeared in the Cockburn Collection of 1810 and another was certified by the Chief with his seal and signature and deposited around 1816 in the archives of the Highland Society of London.

MacAULAY OF ARDINCAPLE   1164

The Colquhouns shared their western boundary with the MacAulays, and the old adage of being judged by the company you keep certainly applied to the MacAulays in earlier times. They claimed kinship with the MacGregors, which wasn't a very safe policy and resulted in their featuring in the Roll of Broken Clans in 1594. They did manage to hang on to the lands of Ardencaple until the 12th Chief sold them to the Duke of Argyll in 1787. Those lands included what is now the town of Helensburgh and the Trident submarine base at Faslane.

Territorial suffixes on tartan names usually indicate a different branch of the family but now and again they represent two totally unconnected clans who just happen to have the same name. That's the case with the MacAulays. The mainland MacAulays of Ardincaple are from Dumbarton and stem from a 13th-century progenitor called Aulay, whereas the MacAulays of Lewis in the Outer Hebrides stem from Aula or Olave the Black, King of Man (the Isle of Man) in the 13th century. In 1992 some MacAulays of Lewis decided it was time they had their own tartan, which is dealt with in the Islands section (see page 87).

There seems to have been a bit of a mix-up in the 1800s with this mainland MacAulay tartan. The original 1831 thread count from James Logan (as used by the artist McIan) somehow became that for the Cummings 200 miles north and was then shortened to become the MacAulay of today which has a striking similarity to the tartan of their adopted kin, the MacGregors.

MACNAUGHTON   1066

Adjoining what used to be MacNab territory to the west were the holdings of the Macnaughtons. For centuries they were extremely influential and powerful but – as with so many clans – the vicissitudes of fate, clan and royal politics had by 1747 rendered them a broken clan with no chief

and the majority of their landholdings lost into the maw of their powerful neighbours, the Campbells.

A touching example of Highland honour involved a Macnaughton during the '45. Ordered to deliver a fine charger to Prince Charles Edward as he entered England, he was subsequently captured and tried at Carlisle. He was offered a pardon and his life if he divulged the giver of the horse but he asked with indignation if they supposed that he could be such a villain. The offer was repeated to him on the scaffold but he died, 'firm to his notion of fidelity'.

The Macnaughton tartan was another one documented by James Logan in *The Scottish Gael* and collected between 1826 and 1831.

STUART OF BUTE   1485

Bute is an island 15 miles long by 5 wide and its port of Rothesay has been a favourite tourist destination since Victorian times. One of the many smaller clans on the periphery of Campbell country, the

Rothesay, the pretty main port on the island of Bute

Campbell

Very many clans had cause to rue the day they upset the mighty Campbells – without doubt the most powerful of Highland clans. The name is said to come from a facial deformity – *Cam* 'wry' and *beul* 'mouth' – and first appeared in 1216 in the Stirling area. The Duke of Argyll is Scotland's most senior peer and his full title gives a flavour of the long lineage and enormous influence and power wielded by the major clan chiefs of old:

THE most high, potent and noble prince his Grace Torquhil Ian Campbell, Duke of Argyll, Marquess of Kintyre and Lorne, Earl of Argyll, Campbell and Cowal, Viscount Lochawe and Glenyla, Lord Campbell, Lorne, Kintyre, Inveraray, Mull, Morven and Tyrie in the peerage of Scotland, Baron Sundbridge of Coombank and Baron Hamilton of Hameldon in the peerage of Great Britain, Duke of Argyll in the peerage of the United Kingdom, Baronet of Nova Scotia, Hereditary Master of the Royal Household in Scotland, Hereditary Keeper of the Great Seal of Scotland, Hereditary Keeper of the royal castles of Dunoon, Carrick, Dunstaffnage and Tarbet, Admiral of the Western coasts and isles, and Chief of the Honourable Clan Campbell, MacCailein Mor.

But fortunately he only has *one* clan tartan, although as a major clan there are many branches including Campbell of Breadalbane, of Cawdor,

Above: Kilchurn Castle on Loch Awe, the family seat of the Campbells until the 18th century

of Glenlyon, Loch Awe, Lochlane and Loudoun that have their own setts. The family seat is Inveraray Castle, 64 miles north of Glasgow.

CAMPBELL 1

Which came first, the chicken or the egg . . . or the Black Watch or Campbell tartan? Genteel debate has puzzled over this for very many a year. Is the tartan worn by the Duke of Argyll the Black Watch in lighter shades, or is the Black Watch the Campbell tartan in darker shades? This was really a Victorian debate and in the early 1800s there was no difference between the two. The Cockburn Collection of 1810 contains five samples of the same pattern, named Sutherland, Campbell, Argyll, Munro and Grant of Grant!

The tartan appointed for the Highland Companies in 1725 and later for the Black Watch in 1739 may in fact have been worn by the Campbells at an earlier date and there's a strong possibility that many others wore the same sett or something similar before the idea of distinctive clan tartans took hold.

CAMPBELL OF BREADALBANE 1046

Breadalbane is all that area stretching from Glenorchy in the west to Aberfeldy in the east, and the first Earl of Breadalbane was John Campbell of Glenorchy (1636–1717). A more able and cunning member of the nobility during that tumultuous period would be difficult to identify. Nicknamed Slippery John, he was indirectly associated with the 1692 Massacre of Glencoe, Scotland's most notorious atrocity, which saw 38 MacDonald men murdered by soldiers commanded by Captain Robert Campbell, with the full approval of King William III.

Breadalbane acquired massive landholdings and titles and lived to the ripe old age of 81. He expanded the family seat of Kilchurn Castle in Loch Awe but in 1740 the family moved east to Taymouth Castle in Kenmore to spend time developing their Perthshire estates. In 1760 Kilchurn was abandoned altogether after lightning damage.

The Breadalbane tartan was first marketed as No. 64 in 1819 by its creators, Wilsons of Bannockburn. It then had a name change to Breadalbane and then to Breadalbane Campbell and finally to Campbell of Breadalbane. This kind of progression was common in the early days of tartan.

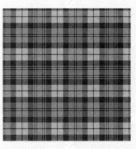

Campbell 1

Campbell of Breadalbane 1046

Left: Campbell of Breadalbane by McIan

Left: The infamous Massacre of Glencoe, as depicted by Victorian artist James Hamilton

Lamont 216

MacLachlan 732

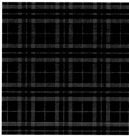

MacTavish 3598

Stuarts of Bute are said to be descended from the natural son of King Robert II and this is one of the tartans prepared for *Vestiarium Scoticum* but excluded from the published version. The popular commercial rendition of this tartan uses maroon in place of red and is called Hunting, but where that change came from is not known and apparently it didn't have the approval of the Marquis of Bute of the time. Today's Chief is the 7th Marquis of Bute, the ex-Formula 1 racing driver Johnny Dumfries.

The 'Stuart' rather than 'Stewart' spelling arose because there was no letter 'w' in the French language and Mary Queen of Scots thus became Mary *Stuart* on her marriage in 1558 to the Dauphin of France, later King Francis II.

Gordon Highlander kiltmakers working outside their Aberdeen barracks in 1904

LAMONT 216

Providing a bit of a buffer between the Stuarts and the Campbells on the mainland were the Lamonts. Their tartan – which is very close to the Campbells' – was verified with the clan seal and deposited in the Highland Society of London Collection on 9 January 1817. In that sample, the white line is silk – a not uncommon enhancement in those days which added a 'sparkle'. This and the Forbes tartan (see page 52) are so similar that each has at times been called – and worn as – the other!

The dispersal of Scots around the world and the changing circumstances of the clans is typified by the current Chief of Clan Lamont who is a parish priest in a Sydney suburb – Father Peter Noel Lamont of that Ilk is the 29th Chief and his branch of the family emigrated to Australia in 1855.

MACLACHLAN 732

Another very attractive colour variation of Black Watch, this rendering from Thomas Smibert's 1850 book *The Clans of the Highlands of Scotland* is the one woven today. Also in 1850, the Smiths wrote of it: 'There are several Fancy MacLachland Tartans in the market, but we have no hesitation in giving this as the genuine Tartan. A lady of very high rank obtained the cloth for us from a member of the family – besides which, it has been confirmed by all the authorities we have consulted.'

The MacLachlans originate from Cowal in Argyleshire and the present Chief, Euan MacLachlan of MacLachlan, lives in Castle Lachlan on the shores of Loch Fyne. As in so many clans, changing fortunes over the years forced many young men to emigrate, and the clan has an illustrious heritage of high achievers in all walks of public and commercial life in many far-flung parts of the world.

MACTAVISH 3598

The MacTavishes were a minor sept of the Campbells and their territory was a stretch of land running along the Sound of Jura, west of Lochgilphead. This is the MacTavish tartan as it appeared in W. & A.K. Johnston's 1906 publication *Tartans of the Clans and Septs of Scotland*, and in October 2003 Lord Lyon was requested by Dugald MacTavish of Dunardry, 26th Chief of Clan MacTavish, to record this as the official MacTavish tartan and not the sett previously

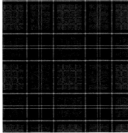

MacMillan   2025   Hunting MacMillan   668

accepted. The change was minor – a thin blue line changed to black. The clan underwent an unsettled period during the recent combative reign of the late 26th Chief, a resident of Florida, who wrestled with officialdom, competing websites and the responsibilities of chiefship. He has been succeeded by his son Steven Edward Dugald MacTavish, who lives with his family in Ontario, Canada.

MacMillan   2025

There's lots of room for debate in academic circles about the Ancient MacMillan and its near-twin the Buchanan. However, received wisdom in the clan maintains that the Buchanans, who at one stage were related to the MacMillans, added the white stripe to the MacMillan and called it their own. Both the Buchanan and MacMillan – as they're represented today – were included in the 1880 *Clans Originaux*.

When MacMillan landholdings of the past are mapped, they're dotted in over 20 locations in Scotland, stretching from Glenurquhart in the north to Galloway in the south and across to the Outer Hebrides, but the main territory was in Knapdale opposite the Isle of Jura; although the chief's seat is now the Finlaystone Country Estate in Renfrewshire on the south side of the Clyde Estuary.

Hunting MacMillan   668

This was designed in 1890 by Baillie Donald (or Cameron) Macmillan, who owned a Highland outfitter's shop in Partick, Glasgow. Addressing the first meeting of the Society – formed in 1892 – the Society Chief said:

> "There is only one thing we have to find fault with in connection with our clan, and that is its

an, pinxit   *I. Dickinson, Lith.*

tartan. Very few people have ever seen it, and those that have do not admire its discordant combination of yellow and red checks and stripes. I am glad that a member of our clan has remedied this defect and patented a hunting form of our tartan which is as harmonious as it is elegant and appropriate. And I trust that it will become so popular that in a few years it will have acquired the charm of antiquity, like the smell of the peat smoke which guarantees the genuineness of the Harris Tweed, and so take its place as a true tartan."

A MacMillan warrior in a 'small kilt' fighting Cromwellian forces, in a historically inaccurate depiction by McIan – in reality the full plaid would have been worn at this time.

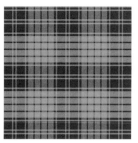
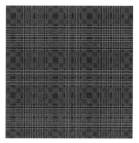
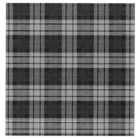

| MacMillan Dress | 1723 | MacAlister | 1465 | MacCallum | 767 | MacDougall | 1519 |

MacMillan Dress 1723

This is the tartan that the Scottish novelist and nationalist Sir Compton MacKenzie (1883–1972) referred to as 'a marmalade stain'! Its earliest documented showing seems to be in the 1880 *Clans Originaux* but if the claim on the clan website that it was 'reputed to have been worn by Robert the Bruce and passed to members of Clan MacMillan' turns out to be true, then the timing is over 500 years adrift. The jury's still out on that claim however.

But there's no argument with the clan comment that 'Being only red and yellow, it can be rather garish for ordinary day use and is uncommon.'

MacAlister 1465

This complex MacAlister tartan was said to have been certified by the Chief in 1845 but definitely was included in the Smiths' book of 1850. MacAlisters are descendants of Donald of Islay, Lord of the Isles, and 18th-century accounts of Flora MacDonald suggest that MacAlisters wore the MacDonald tartan at that time.

MacCallum 767

The MacCallums were a small clan and their territory appears to have been that stretch of coast from Craignish Point up to Loch Melfort. It's believed that around the 1830s the MacCallum family lost trace of the old tartan for 50 or 60 years and had another one woven that was based on the recollections of the older members of the clan. As so often happens, memories are not to be relied upon and when the original tartan eventually surfaced it proved to be substantially different from the remembered one.

MacDougall 1519

The MacDougalls were recorded in the Oban area as far back as 1164 and, just north of Oban, the clan seat was the now ruined Dunolly Castle, dating back to the 15th century when John Stewart of Lorn returned the estates to the clan, which had lost them when fighting against Robert the Bruce.

Early tartan researchers were presented with a bewildering array of options for the MacDougall tartan. The complexity of the design was such that misinterpretations of thread counts and colours were common and five different versions were recorded, including one from the *Vestiarium Scoticum* in which the illustration didn't match the written description! Even some modern weavers and clan branches are unsure but the version shown here seems to win by a short head – even though it wasn't one of the original five *or* either of the two signed and sealed samples in the Highland Society of London collection!

A Raphael Tuck postcard of the MacDougalls' family seat, the ruined Dunolly Castle

Dress Tartans

Inevitably, weavers wanted to proliferate tartans and reasons for wearing them, and the 'dress tartan' was a perfect opportunity. But the real basis for white-grounded men's evening dress tartans appears to have been the ancient women's dress, the arisaid.

I N broad terms, this was the feminine equivalent of the belted plaid and can be fashioned out of a piece of material the size of a blanket. In fact, it seems probable that the first arisaid *was* a blanket – plaide (pronounced pladjer) in Gaelic – caught up and draped rather hurriedly at some time of need. Some support is given to the supposition by the tradition that tartans worn by the women were light-coloured and decorated with an open pattern of red, green and/or black lines, characteristics shared with blankets to this day.

The Sobieski brothers introduced the white ground for men with their 'Roialle' (Royal) tartans, Stewarte and Duke of Rothesaye, and it needed only a tiny verbal amputation to transform 'women's dress tartans' to 'dress tartans', and the great Victorian need for ostentation was more than adequately fed.

Of recent years it has become common for arisaid setts, based upon clan tartans, to be designed for the use of clanswomen and there is now also a vast range of 'dressy' tartans of no great merit or significance, originally designed for competition dancers hoping to catch a judge's eye.

Jamie Scarlett

The Christina Young arisaid, of which this modern version in the Tartans Museum in Franklin, North Carolina is a copy. The original blanket – one of the oldest and most completely preserved specimens of homespun handlooming – was spun, dyed and woven in 1726 by Christina, who embroidered her initials and the date into the edge. With its preponderance of white it is the forerunner of today's many dress tartans.

Stewart

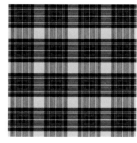

Royal Stewart 1370	Dress Stewart 1790

Of all the tartans in existence, there is the greatest profusion of those for the Stewarts. The reason for this is that they're not just one clan, but many branches evolving from the descendants of the various High Stewards of Scotland.

The International Tartan Index maintained by the Scottish Tartans Authority includes over a hundred different versions of Stewart tartans. Many of them are for family branches – Stewart of Appin, of Argyll, of Ardshiel, of Atholl, Bute, Fingask, Galloway, Rothesay, Urrard. Others are regarded as universal tartans that can be worn by anyone and many others are fashion variants produced by weavers on both sides of the Atlantic.

Not all Stewarts had royal connections, of course, and a Gaelic proverb refers to 'Stewarts, the race of Kings and Tinkers'. Stewart was also a common name amongst tinkers – Scotland's travelling people, not Gypsies but the descendants of the traditional tinsmiths who were metal workers and armourers who travelled between the warring clans repairing weapons and making fine silver jewellery.

ROYAL STEWART   1370
Probably the most popular tartan in the world is the Royal Stewart. Little is known of its origins beyond the fact that it's a development of the early pattern commonly called Prince Charles Edward, which is indeed a great shame, for it is the archetypal Scottish tartan, with colours and proportions that seem to be universally pleasing. It's known that it was *not* an invention of the Sobieski Stuarts but *could* have been an inspired output of Wilsons of Bannockburn at the turn of the 18th century.

Theoretically this is the personal tartan of the ruling monarch of the day but the genie has been out of the bottle now for over 200 years and there's no chance of enticing it back!

DRESS STEWART   1790
Hand in hand with the ubiquitous Royal Stewart goes the Dress Stewart, which spans the fashion spectrum from rough lumberjack shirts to silk evening gowns. The pattern is simply produced by changing the wide red band of the Royal Stewart to white; something like it first appeared in the *Vestiarium* of 1842 followed by Grant's *Tartans of the Clans of Scotland* in 1850. Queen Victoria apparently liked it and a slight variation was produced and called Victoria.

OLD STEWART   160
In his publication of 1893, D.W. Stewart said: 'The use of this design as Stewart tartan for a period extending back to 1745 at least, is vouched by the records of manufacturers and collectors alike.' He then went on to relate that he had been shown – by Mrs Stuart of Dalness – a remarkable example of the old belted plaid, 'of a design differing from the above in certain particulars but having the same dominant features. It is reported to be two centuries old, and to represent the original sett of the tartan.' If that was accurate, it would place the forerunner of this tartan at around the 1690s. This version is from D.W. Stewart's son, D.C. Stewart, who carried on his father's work with his 1950 publication *The Setts of the Scottish Tartans*.

An interesting observation is that the highly thought of William and Alexander Keith Johnston who wrote the 1906 *Tartans of the Clans and Septs of Scotland* – a standard reference work for historians – were not above lifting complete sections

A Stewart weeps as Bonnie Prince Charlie's ship vanishes over the horizon.

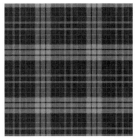

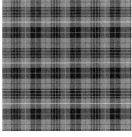

Old Stewart   160   *Stewart Hunting*   6327

of other researchers' work and presenting them verbatim as their own. When talking of this Old Stewart tartan they say: 'This tartan has been known for more than a hundred years as the "Stewart" tartan, and is supposed to have been worn in former times by such families as the Stewarts of Grandtully, etc.' The words were not theirs but those of James Grant in *The Tartans of the Clans of Scotland* published by the Johnstons 20 years earlier! In the interest of historical accuracy one would have expected them to, at least, adjust the time frame accordingly, but not so!

STEWART HUNTING   6327

The pattern books of the Bannockburn weavers William Wilson provide the first record of this sett in 1819 where they described it as a 'cheek' pattern, i.e. an asymmetric or non-reversing one.

The Johnston brothers in 1906 said: 'Although we have failed to trace the history of this tartan, or fix the date of its introduction, as it has long been a favourite with the people of Scotland, we thought it right to preserve in this work a record of one of the most beautiful tartans associated with the Royal Stewarts.' James Grant would certainly have agreed with them because again, the words were his, written 20 years before. D.C. Stewart in 1950 commented that the Hunting Stewart was much worn in Grant's time 'as now' by those having no claim to any other recognized tartan.

Hunting Tartans

IT is rarely possible to set a date on the introduction of new tartan legends and they often appear spontaneously as a result of some unguarded and, at the time, irrelevant remark. There was certainly no need for 'hunting' tartans until the early synthetic dyes came along to make colours that would frighten any animal within eyeshot. George Buchanan is the culprit this time, though possibly by proxy, for his story, published in 1581, was in Latin.

An iconic image from the Scottish Highlands

> They delight in variegated garments, especially stripes, and their favourite colours are purple and blue. Their ancestors wore plaids of many colours, and numbers still retain this custom, but the majority now in their dress prefer a dark brown, imitating nearly the leaves of the heather, that when lying upon the heath in the day, they may not be discovered by the appearance of their clothes; in these wrapped rather than covered, they brave the severest storms in the open air, and sometimes lay themselves down to sleep even in the midst of snow.

Translators dealing with tartan matters are inclined to add their own ideas, even when translating from English to English, and it is difficult to agree with much of this attribution to Buchanan. Certainly, as we have seen, eighteenth- and early-nineteenth-century tartans were superb camouflage and brown rarely figured in the colour schemes, except from fading or where a dye-lot went wrong, in which case there was no hesitation in making a pattern to use it. Nevertheless, Buchanan's remarks produced hunting tartans, usually by changing a red ground to brown, blue or green; in parallel with this, it became the custom, if a clan had claim to a dark tartan as well as a bright one, to refer to the dark sett as 'Hunting' and the bright one as 'Dress'.

Jamie Scarlett

0   10   20   30   40   50 kilometres

0   10   20   30 miles

Dunblane
Dollar
Tillicoultry
Stirling

BRUCE

Falkirk

Firth of Forth

DALZEIL

Edinburgh   **SETON**

NAPIER

Firth of Clyde

Kilbarchan   **ERSKINE**   Glasgow
Paisley

Largs
BOYD   Motherwell

MONTGOMERY   East Kilbride

CUNNINGHAM   **HAMILTON**   **LOCKHART**

Kilmarnock

Arran

Ayr

Ailsa Craig

THE LOWLANDS

This is very much an arbitrary division that encompasses the northern fringe of the Borders and the Lowlands proper – that central belt that links the Atlantic with the North Sea, bordered in the west by Glasgow and in the east by Edinburgh. It has always been the predominant wealth-creating heart of Scotland, a population magnet and the crucible for ambitious entrepreneurs.

Whilst clans and tartans were an integral part of Highland life, they certainly didn't feature in Lowland culture until the Sassenachs[1] were bitten by the tartan bug after George IV's Edinburgh visit in 1822. It's not surprising therefore that there are relatively few early clan and family tartans in the Lowlands but a wealth of district and corporate ones, many of which provide fascinating glimpses into the past and emphasize tartan's ability to act as an historical time capsule.

1 *Everyone south of the Highland line in those days was a Sassenach,*
which is the anglicization of the Gaelic 'sasunnach' meaning Saxon. Nowadays its use ranges
from the good-humoured to the pejorative and is always aimed at someone from England.

Goat Fell, the 2,867ft mountain that towers over the Isle of Arran

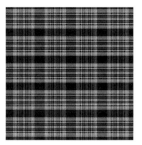

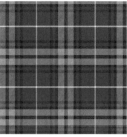

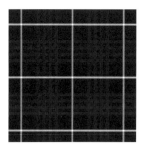

The 7th Cavalry 644	*Dollar* 2668	*Dollar Academy* 290

THE 7TH CAVALRY 644

In 1949 the *People's Journal*, a publication from the D.C. Thomson stable, interviewed one of the directors of Patons – the famous weavers at Tillicoultry established in 1815. The article spoke of an entry in the firm's 19th-century records that showed a scrap of largely blue and red tartan with the thread count falling in sevens, entitled 'The 7th Cavalry Tartan'.

No British military formation ever had such a title and it was assumed that this was for the famous American 7th Cavalry, part of which was annihilated at Custer's Last Stand. It was well known that Custer had a liking for military bands: indeed in 1867 one of his first official acts with the 7th was to organize a regimental band, and it is possible that they wrote to Patons to commission a tartan since the regiment contained many Americans of Scottish descent.

It is a poignant thought that tartan woven in Tillicoultry may well have been witness to that scorching Montana Sunday in June 1876 in the valley of the Little Bighorn when Lt Col. George Armstrong Custer and 262 soldiers and attached personnel of the 7th Cavalry met defeat and death by an overwhelming force of over 1,500 Lakota Sioux, Cheyenne and Arapaho warriors.

DOLLAR 2668
DOLLAR ACADEMY 290

Along the glen, three miles east of Tillicoultry, is the town of Dollar and it was here in the 18th century that John McNabb was born. A life at sea brought him a captaincy and great success as a London merchant but he never forgot his humble beginnings at the foot of the Ochils. On his death in 1802 he left the interest on his fortune – some £60,000 a year – to provide 'a charity or school for the poor of the parish of Dollar wheir I was born'. His wishes were enacted and being educated at Dollar Academy has been a

Below right: Dollar Academy

Below: Tillicoultry, where the famous weavers Patons were based – and perhaps designed a tartan that saw action at Little Bighorn

Mary Queen of Scots

As lads, John McNabb, John Husband and indeed many thousands of pupils would know about Castle Gloom (from the Gaelic *glom* meaning chasm) lying above the town of Dollar at the head of Dollar Glen and protected by the deep ravines of the Burn of Care and the Burn of Sorrow. Both John Knox (1513–72) and Mary Queen of Scots (1542–87) stayed here at one time and Knox would no doubt have breathed hellfire on something so frivolous as the tartan on the alleged Mary Queen of Scots chair.

THIS tartan started life in 1870 when Frederick Parker and Sons was founded in the East End of London. Frederick built up a collection of very fine chairs as examples for his craftsmen to adapt or copy.

Around 1920 Tom Parker (*c*.1886–1965) acquired one particularly fine old chair and, on taking the seat covering off to renovate it, discovered what appeared to be a very old tartan. He is said to have remarked at the time something like: 'Wouldn't it be exciting if this proved to be a chair that belonged to Mary Queen of Scots?'

Some thirty years later, a portion of the tartan was cut off and sent up to Scotland but identification eluded the experts. They did however take the thread count which has ended up in that most modern of recording mediums the computer database, where a much-respected museum curator's comments were noted: 'This sett is taken from a piece of very old hard-spun tartan which was used to cover the seat of a 16th-century chair known as Mary, Queen of Scots chair, said to have come from Holyrood House. Now in the possession of Messrs Parker Knoll of Bucks.' An excellent case of how easy it is for

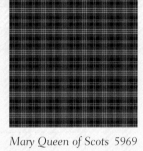

Mary Queen of Scots 5969

whimsical speculation to become incontrovertible fact.

As is discussed elsewhere in the book, tartans certainly did exist at the time of Mary but were possibly just no more than textile designs and of no deeper significance than that of polka dots or pinstripes in the modern world. What tartans *were* in circulation were probably just part of everyday working dress produced by one of the district's weavers. If chiefs were travelling to any corridors of power outside the isolated Highlands, that working dress would doubtless be quickly discarded in favour of the court clothes of the day.

In 1997 on a change of company ownership, Parker Knoll disposed of its valuable chair collection at Sotheby's: family and friends clubbed together and managed to buy about half of them and those 170 chairs became the Frederick Parker Chair Collection, now on permanent display at Furniture Works in Whitechapel, London. Sadly the 'Mary chair' was not amongst them and its present whereabouts are unknown.

Mary Queen of Scots, in a miniature painted by a follower of Francois Clouet; unfortunately the tartan named after her bears no relation to her whatsoever

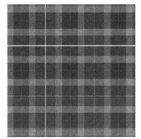

The Boys' Brigade   1466

Stirling   1536

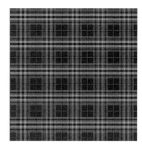
Dunblane   1022

THE BOYS' BRIGADE   1466

Readers of a certain age may remember with nostalgia the pillbox hats worn at a jaunty angle by lads of the Boys' Brigade. The movement was founded in 1883 by William Alexander Smith. He was born in 1854 in Pennyland House in Thurso in the far north of Scotland, and as a young man taught at Sunday School (Sabbath School) in Glasgow. He found it difficult to keep the older boys' teenage exuberance in check at times and came up with the idea of introducing them to the military discipline that he himself experienced and dispensed as a lieutenant in the Volunteers.

Thus was born the Boys' Brigade with a programme including games as well as discipline, gymnastics, sport and hymns. The movement caught the general imagination and the Brigade went from strength to strength and spread to America, Canada and even Nigeria. Over 120 years later and it's still going strong!

This tartan came from the archives of the old weaving company Patons of Tillicoultry – east of Stirling at the foot of the Ochil Hills – and was tantalisingly named 'B.B. Special Tartan'. In Scotland the traditional meaning of BB was of course 'Boys' Brigade' and in recent times the tartan has been brought back to life for the Brigade by one of Scotland's major weavers.

mark of great pride for many generations of pupils.

In the early 1930s, McNabb's coffin was discovered in a crypt below a disused meeting house at Mile End in London. Former pupils cremated the remains, and the ashes of Capt. John McNabb are said to rest in a niche above Dollar Academy's entrance doors, while some of the lead from the coffin was made into commemorative paperweights.

In that same decade it was another former pupil, John Husband, who designed the first Dollar Academy tartan. He was a fruit trader in London before emigrating to New Zealand. Almost seventy years later in 1999 a new version of the tartan was commissioned and the design, from The Strathmore Woollen Company in Forfar, became part of the school uniform for all the girls.

STIRLING   1536

North of Glasgow and Edinburgh lies the ancient town of Stirling, whose tartan started life in the 1840s as the property of the Stirling & Bannockburn Caledonian Society who used it to clothe their officers and the boys being educated by them. In more recent times it has happily been recognised as the district tartan for the town.

DUNBLANE   1022

The surname Dunblane owes its origin to the delightful little cathedral town just north of Stirling – in 1296 there was a Laurence of Dunblane who was a Burgess of Stirling. In Hornby Castle, Yorkshire, there is a portrait of Perigrene, 2nd Viscount Dunblane who died in 1729, and in it he wears this tartan. It was revived in 1822, doubtless on the occasion of George IV's visit to Edinburgh, and has now come to be regarded as a district tartan for the town.

Stirling, pictured in an engraving from the beginning of the 18th century

The Scouts

Many people were put off the idea of joining the Boys' Brigade by its focus on drill and religion and some of the BB officers felt that teaching 'scouting' techniques such as observation, tracking and initiative would widen the BB's appeal. General Robert Baden-Powell had recently returned to England as a national hero after defending the town of Mafeking for seven months from the besieging Boer troops and he was invited to start up a 'scouting' programme.

THE Boys' Brigade display at the Royal Albert Hall in 1903 was of special significance because it was there that Baden-Powell's friendship with BB founder William Smith blossomed. B-P, as he was known, saw the huge potential of teaching the art of scouting to youngsters and initiated the founding of the Scout movement and its subsequent spread around the globe. To onlookers, the Scout movement became a competitor to the Boys' Brigade but it's not known if the two friends regarded them as such.

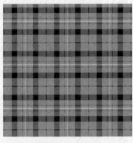

Scottish Scouts   1463

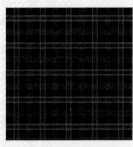

Cub Scouts of America 4119

limited its popularity. In 1989 a weaver changed the light grey to white and it was soon being sold commercially as 'Dress Grey Watch'. As always, the industry showed its great adaptability!

The current Scottish Scouts tartan was designed by an A.G. or J. Porteus of Alva around 1957 and based on the MacLaren tartan in honour of a benefactor. The wider red overcheck represents the Rover Scouts, the finer red lines the Scouts and Senior Scouts and the yellow represents the Wolf Cubs.

Bearing in mind the Patons of Tillicoultry connection with the Boys' Brigade and the fact that Alva is adjacent to Tillicoultry, it's logical to assume that Porteus may well have worked for that company.

Kilted scouts, depicted in an issue of stamps from the Summer Isles off the West Coast of Scotland

SCOTTISH SCOUTS   1463

The first Scout tartan was designed in the early 1920s by the Chief Commissioner of the Scout Association of Scotland, Lord Glentanar, who was George Coats of Paisley thread-making fame. Based on the Black Watch and rendered in three shades of grey, Lord Glentanar intended it for use by Scouts having no tartan of their own or for Scout troops requiring a uniform tartan. Perhaps it was its plainness or similarity to some of the Victorian mourning tartans that

CUB SCOUTS OF AMERICA   4119

In 1918 a Mr W.F. de Bois Maclaren, District Commissioner for Rosneath in Dumbartonshire, dined with Baden-Powell in London and they discussed the need for a permanent camping ground for London Scouts. Maclaren generously said: 'You find what you want and I'll buy it,' which is how Gilwell Park – then a run-down 108-acre estate on the edge of Epping Forest – became the training ground for generations of Scouts from around the world.

This tartan is a very specific one only used on neckerchiefs by the American-based Webelos Cub Scouts (**We'll Be Lo**yal **S**couts) and symbolizes the Scouting tradition inherited from Britain.

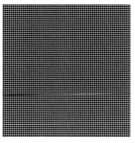

| *Falkirk* | 1253 | *Falkirk District* | 2347 |

Roman occupation of the area around AD 250. Made from Celtic tweed, it used undyed natural and brown yarns woven in a herringbone pattern and was found stuffed into the neck of a pot filled with over 2,000 silver coins. Herringbone weaving on a frame loom is quite technically advanced and therefore a decorated multicoloured cloth would have been far from commonplace. Although often referred to as a tartan, it is in fact a simple two-colour check which is the forerunner of tartan.

FALKIRK 1253

South-east of Stirling on the route to Edinburgh lies the industrial town of Falkirk – site of the 1298 Battle of Falkirk that saw William Wallace and the Scots army routed by Edward I, 'the Hammer of the Scots'. It was also the place where the original 'Falkirk' tartan or check was found that is now in the National Museum of Scotland. One of the earliest examples of Scottish cloth in existence, this is a direct link to the

FALKIRK DISTRICT 2347

This Falkirk district tartan was the winner in a 1989 design competition to 'create a new image for an area that [was] rising from the ashes of its former industrial glory'. The colours are explained as follows: brown represents the dominant colour of the original cloth; blue the River Forth and the canals. Red is the colour of the blast furnace flames from the Falkirk foundries, yellow signifies prosperity and black

Connecting the Union Canal with the Forth & Clyde Canal, the futuristic Falkirk Wheel is the world's only rotating boat lift and is now a major tourist attraction.

represents the road network of the region, all of which passes through the Falkirk area.

BRUCE OF KINNAIRD   1483

The sett of the Bruce of Kinnaird tartan – authorized as the tartan for ordinary wear by Lord Bruce of Kinnaird around 1953 – is taken from a coat claimed to be from the mid-18th century and it combines elements of Wilsons' Old Bruce and the Prince Charles Edward Stuart tartan.

One of the most celebrated Scots of that era was James Bruce of Kinnaird, who was born in 1730 at Kinnaird House, some 3 miles from Falkirk. In adulthood he became a larger-than-life character whose explorations in Africa enthralled not only his own generation but, long after his death, the Victorians too, who regarded him as the prototype gentleman explorer.

Amongst his many achievements, he discovered the source of the Blue Nile. He was nicknamed 'The Abyssinian' and was well remembered in the neighbourhood at 6ft 4in in height, corpulent and beturbanned, travelling around his estate grounds with a long staff. On his overseas travels he habitually took a huge telescope that needed six men to carry. His explanation being: 'exclusive of its utility, it inspired the nations through which he passed with great awe, as they thought he had some immediate

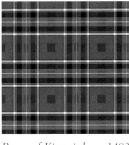
Bruce of Kinnaird   1483

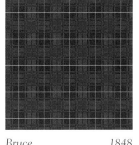
Bruce   1848

Bruce County   1778

connexion with Heaven; and they paid more attention to it than they did to himself'.

BRUCE   1848

It may be that the Sobieski brothers did *not* invent the Bruce tartan that appeared in their *Vestiarium Scoticum*, but based it on a pre-existing one for the clan. In 1967 Lord Bruce, Earl of Elgin, believed that he had independent evidence dating back to 1571 – a weaver's chart with thread count. Regrettably it was subsequently lost, and with it an opportunity to extend the tartan's timeline back into the sixteenth century. Interestingly, the Sobieski Stuarts' version of the Bruce managed to supplant two pre-existing Bruce tartans produced by Wilsons in the early nineteenth century.

The original *Vestiarium Scoticum* Bruce had black guards on the white and yellow but for this personal variation Lord Bruce dropped them.

BRUCE COUNTY   1778

Bruce County in Ontario, two and a half hours northwest of Toronto, is bordered by Lake Huron, Georgian Bay and the Niagara Escarpment. There are over 530 miles of coastline to explore and a broad range of place names which indicate the geographic diversity of its founders – Paisley, Southampton, Tiverton, Tobermory, Chepstow, Dunkeld, Kincardine and Cargill.

In 1963 it was decided to adopt a tartan for the county and permission was sought from the Chief of Clan Bruce to use a colour variation of the Bruce sett. With some input from the Lord Lyon the present tartan was arrived at in 1965. As can be seen, the sett is the same as the Bruce but with blue guards on the white overcheck.

James Bruce of Kinnaird, gentleman-explorer

Tartans in Education

Educational establishments around the world have not been slow to realize the benefits of having a school or university tartan and almost 100 have subscribed to the idea – from America, Canada, South Africa, Japan, Germany, Spain, England and of course Scotland itself. In many schools, parents and the authorities have great problems in persuading youngsters to wear a school uniform because 'it isn't cool' but somehow or other, tartan is *always* 'cool' – especially if the pupils themselves have had a hand in choosing or designing the tartan in question. One of the most touching examples of a new tartan bringing a whole school together as a 'clan' is that of the All As One.

ALL AS ONE   6617

St Stephen's Primary School in Sighthill, Glasgow is a low, single-storey building dropped in the midst of an overshadowing and depressing 1950s tower block complex. The diverse school community is made up of some 35 nationalities, most of whom are the youngsters of refugees housed in the surrounding flats. Many cultures are represented, and for their tartan the children used the most common colours found in the 35 national flags. The symbolism of weaving those together in harmony was not lost on the children, their parents or the Scottish media and represented the coming together of diverse cultures, religions and ethnic heritage to form a new 'clan' in its new country. Would that adults could so easily promote international harmony by designing a new tartan together!

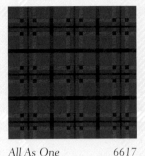

All As One   6617

Hutchesons' Grammar School   6518

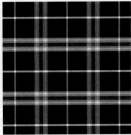

Avalon   6361

Calgary University   4004

Toyokawa Check   6467

Hutcheson's Grammar School in 1841

HUTCHESONS' GRAMMAR SCHOOL   6518

In 1641 two Glasgow merchants, George and Thomas Hutcheson, set aside money for the establishment of a school for orphans and, in the words of the school historian, 'lit an educational torch which has been burning brightly ever since'.

In 1643 their first Hutchesonian or Hutchie, as pupils are affectionately called, was orphan Archibald Edmiston, and over the next three and a half centuries the school expanded until it was one of Britain's leading independent schools with an enviable reputation and a host of loyal alumni.

After a lifetime in the weaving industry, Colin Hutcheson, a governor of the Scottish Tartans Authority and possibly a descendant of the founders, modified his own Hutcheson tartan to incorporate the school colours, thereby creating a much welcomed new symbol for this ancient and venerated Glasgow institution.

AVALON   6361

Avalon School is in Rockville, Maryland, USA, an independent boys' school founded in 2002. There they have adapted the 'clan' concept in a very interesting way and have a total of *five* tartans. One is the 'master' tartan shown here that signifies the school's corporate identity, while the others are variations on that design to provide a distinctively different tartan for each 'house'. The designer was staff member James Bostick and the tartans are woven in Vancouver by Fraser & Kirkbright.

CALGARY UNIVERSITY   4004

University of Calgary education and fine arts graduate James Odell is a member of the university's Pipe Band and Highland Dance Club and designed this official tartan incorporating the university colours of red, black and gold.

TOYOKAWA CHECK   6467

The Japanese have been great fans of tartan in modern times and quite a few corporate bodies have had their own designed. This one is for the pupils of Toyokawa Kindergarten and Elementary schools in Aichi, Japan, 150 miles south-west of Tokyo.

STRATHCLYDE UNIVERSITY   2419

The ancient name of Strathclyde is preserved in many walks of life, one of them being in Strathclyde University whose history stretches back to 1796. Almost exactly 200 years later the 'Uni' acquired its own tartan designed by weaver Kenny Dalgliesh of Selkirk. It was based on the Anderson tartan in honour of Professor John Anderson (1726–96), founder of Anderson's Institution, the antecedent of the University. The tartan incorporates red and green from the City of Glasgow's tartan and the red, blue and gold from the University's crest.

Strathclyde University
2419

Glasgow   515

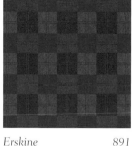

Erskine   891

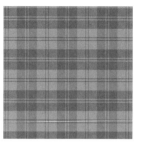

Erskine Hunting   755

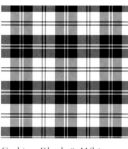

Erskine Black & White
1246

Alloa Tower is the largest surviving keep in Scotland and dates from the 14th century. Home to successive generations of the Earls of Mar – the Erskine family – it retains many of its medieval features such as its dungeon, first-floor well and magnificent oak roof timbers. It's now managed by the National Trust for Scotland.

GLASGOW   515

This City of Glasgow tartan started life as a Wilsons of Bannockburn fancy pattern and is now regarded as the district tartan for the city. Wilsons were producing it around 1800 but subsequently ceased to weave it when the clan tartan fad took off, and it lay dormant for many years. It was revived in the 1960s when the thread count was taken from a manuscript account book in the National Museum of Antiquities of Scotland in Edinburgh.

ERSKINE   891

Although branches of the Erskine clan established themselves in other areas of Scotland, their roots were in Renfrewshire – the town of Erskine is on the south bank of the River Clyde west of Glasgow. Like so many of the Scottish nobility, their fortune and position waxed and waned – indeed, one of their number in the 18th century was known as 'Bobbing John', so frequently did he switch his allegiance. Erskines were prominent in the Scots Guards in France and fought against the English under the leadership of Joan of Arc.

The first published version of the tartan appeared in 1842 in the *Vestiarium Scoticum* and the suspicion is that the Sobieski brothers produced this at the end of a long day, for they just took one of their earlier creations – the Cunningham – changed the background to green and took away the white line . . . and there was the Erskine!

ERSKINE HUNTING   755

The progenitor of the Royal Scots Fusiliers was raised in 1678 when a commission was issued to Charles Erskine, fifth Earl of Mar, as colonel of a new foot regiment which soon became popularly known as the 'Earl of Mar's Greybreeks' ('breeks' being trousers). Some sources say that in 1948 approval was given to the wearing of Hunting Erskine, said to be the family tartan of the Earls of Mar. However, the following year the *People's Journal* of 5 March reported: 'The firm of J and P Paton have just designed a new tartan for the Royal Scots Fusiliers. It is based on the Erskine and may be known as the Hunting Erskine.'

The regiment was presented with the Freedom of the Royal Burgh of Ayr in June 1945, and had the right to march through the town with drums beating, bayonets fixed and Colours flying. Having

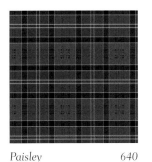

Paisley   640

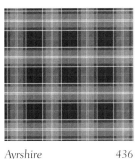

Ayrshire   436

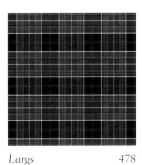

Largs   478

Arran   381

amalgamated to become the Royal Highland Fusiliers or RHF, the regiment was further amalgamated in April 2006 to become the 2nd Battalion, The Royal Regiment of Scotland.

ERSKINE BLACK & WHITE   1246

No one seems too sure of the origins of this version of Erskine but it could have been one of the very many dance tartans designed by Hugh MacPherson of Edinburgh. Regardless of its start in life, it's now widely accepted as a genuine Erskine tartan.

PAISLEY   640

The Paisley tartan was designed in 1952 by Allan C. Drennan, who worked for cotton thread manufacturers Anchor Mills in Paisley. Allan designed it as a district tartan for the town and obviously had a sample woven, for he entered it in the Kelso Highland Show where it won first prize. Although it started out as a district tartan, it was soon in demand by people *called* Paisley and one weaver also produced it for all the Drennans!

The records of Wilsons of Bannockburn are liberally sprinkled with similar examples of this flexible attitude towards the naming and apportioning of tartans. In a hundred years the Paisley tartan will doubtless be looked upon as a venerable historic tartan. Just as in Wilsons' day, time lends respectability.

AYRSHIRE   436

Designed in 1985 by tartan scholar and researcher Dr Phil Smith of the US at the suggestion of the Cunninghams and Boyds who didn't want their family tartans being inadvertently used as district tartans. Phil therefore dedicated this to 'Ayrshire folk who have no family tartan'. Although initially

categorized as 'fashion' in the absence of any documented 'official' acceptance, it has been reclassified as 'district' due to common usage.

LARGS   478

When Phil Smith designed the Ayrshire tartan he put in the yellow line to represent the sun and nowhere is it enjoyed by more visitors than at Largs – a favourite seaside holiday spot on the Firth of Clyde within easy reach of the great Glasgow conurbation. A Knickerbocker Glory at Nardinis and a short boat trip to Millport on nearby Great Cumbrae Island made for an exciting day out for all. Even better would have been a trip on the *Waverley* – the last sea-going paddle steamer in the world.

The Largs tartan was designed in 1981 by Sidney Samuels of whom, regrettably, nothing is recorded other than his name.

ARRAN   381

Anyone clanking and swishing their way down the Clyde Estuary from Largs in the *Waverley* paddle steamer would soon see Goat Fell appearing off the starboard bow – the 2,867ft mountain that towers over the Isle of Arran. The name Arran means 'peaked island' in Gaelic and that language was spoken there well into the twentieth century.

At the foot of Goat Fell nestles the red sandstone Brodick Castle, the ancient seat of the Dukes of Hamilton and a fortress in Viking times. Together with the gardens and country park it's now owned by the National Trust for Scotland.

Some uncertainties surround the Arran tartan but it's thought that it was copied from or based on a nineteenth-century shawl and not designed – as is sometimes claimed – in modern times. The design features are reminiscent of some Outer Hebrides

Law Enforcement

At first glance, law enforcement agencies and tartans don't seem to have a great affinity but the link is quite logical when one learns of the number of pipe bands in police forces around the world. The great majority of them will wear a long-established tartan but a growing number seek the individuality that their own tartan bestows. Inevitably, what starts out as a pipe band tartan gradually comes to be regarded as a corporate tartan for the whole force. Here are just a tiny number of those in existence.

SILLITOE   6430

This is the name given to the chequered band worn round the hats of many of the world's police officers. Strictly speaking it isn't a tartan but a simple check pattern and Glasgow Chief Constable Sir Percy Sillitoe didn't actually design it – it had existed for centuries as a heraldic symbol in many Scottish coats of arms. Highland soldiers are said to have woven white ribbons into their black hat bands, thus creating the familiar chequered effect.

Sir Percy – answering criticism that it was difficult for the public to differentiate between the police and bus conductors and other uniformed officials – introduced the three-line chequered bands in 1932. The experiment was a success and the idea spread across the world with the ultimate accolade being its adoption by the European Union as the universal symbol of the police. Sir Percy had established Britain's first forensic science laboratory in 1929 and as Chief Constable of Glasgow developed a reputation as an effective gangbuster. He went on to head MI5 and had to deal with the problems of Soviet spies, Philby, Burgess, Maclean and Blunt.

The 'Sillitoe tartan', brought into use by Sir Percy Sillitoe, Chief Constable of Glasgow in the 1930s

ROYAL CANADIAN MOUNTED POLICE

2447

When Hugh Macdonald and Helen Shaw met in Glasgow in 1811, they could never have foreseen the momentous events of which their son John Alexander would be the architect. In 1820 Hugh's business failed and the five-year-old John sailed with his parents to a new life in Ontario, Canada. As an adult John embarked on a legal career but it was his move into politics at the age of twenty-nine which was the springboard for Sir John Alexander Macdonald to become Canada's first Prime Minister. One of his early tasks was to establish law and order in the rapidly expanding Canadian Northwest and thus was born the North West Mounted Police, the forerunners of the Royal Canadian Mounted Police.

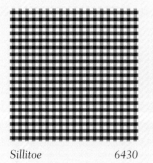

Sillitoe   6430

Royal Canadian Mounted
Police   2447

Federal Bureau of
Investigation (FBI)   83

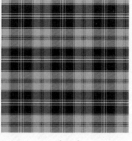

International Police
Association   3991

In 1997 the Mounties decided to mark the 125th anniversary by having their own tartan designed, and Violet Holmes of British Columbia won the national competition and produced the design that was presented to the force by Her Royal Highness Princess Anne in June 1988. The official description explains: 'The tartan colours are as rich and varied as the heritage they represent. They are true to the RCMP tradition as they are derived from the colours of the Force's uniform and badge. The colours weave into a perfectly balanced tartan design. The overall effect is pleasingly subtle, reflecting a harmonious interplay of colour that provides an excellent complement to the Force's world-renowned Red Serge tunic.'

FEDERAL BUREAU OF INVESTIGATION (FBI)   83

America's most famous law enforcement agency is of course the FBI and this tartan was commissioned from Thomas Gordon & Sons of Glasgow, initially for the use of the Bureau's pipe band but now regarded as being a general tartan for the FBI. Other noted 'crime-busting' units to acquire their own tartan included, amongst others, the LAPD (Los Angeles Police Department), the California Highway Patrol, New York State Police, and the forces of Connecticut, Charleston, Detroit, Orlando, Palm Beach and Atlanta.

INTERNATIONAL POLICE ASSOCIATION   3991

Behind this simple tartan lies an inspiring story of how, through dogged determination in the face of official apathy – he was regarded as an eccentric – a Lincolnshire police sergeant called Arthur Troop

The Mounties, or Royal Canadian Mounted Police, one of the world's most famous police forces

was responsible in 1950 for founding the largest police organization in the world with a membership of over 300,000 and branches in 60 countries. He had always had great faith in the positive power of friendship, reflected in the IPA's Esperanto motto of *Servo per Amikeco* (Service through Friendship). Arthur has inspired two generations of law enforcement officers and it was the Lothian and Borders committee of the IPA which instigated this tartan which can be worn by members around the world.

Boyd 1820

tartans and that fact, and the very large sett of 14 inches, suggest that the shawl origins are probably accurate.

BOYD 1820

Designed in 1956 by James Scarlett for Lord Kilmarnock and noted by Lord Lyon in March of that year. The Lords Kilmarnock are descended from both the Hays (the Earls of Errol) and the Stewarts, and the design incorporates elements from the Hay-Leith tartan (the red section) and the Hunting Stewart (the green section) with minor alterations to each. The Boyd family is closely associated with the town of Kilmarnock, which is said to owe its transformation from market town to major industrial hub to one man, William Boyd, Lord Kilmarnock, who made the mistake of backing the Jacobites in the 1745 uprising and, as a result, was beheaded in London. As was the norm in those days, his estates were forfeited and there was no longer any real control over development in Kilmarnock, so entrepreneurs reportedly flocked there to establish businesses.

MONTGOMERY 1082

This was originally Wilsons' No. 7 or 'Eglinton' referring to the fact that Hugh, the 3rd Lord Montgomery, was created the Earl of Eglinton in 1507. D.W. Stewart's research suggested that this tartan was adopted by the Montgomerys of Ayrshire around the time of the Union between Scotland and England (1707). James Scarlett comments that if that was correct, it must be one of the earliest genuine Lowland tartans recorded. Although often rendered in purple today, the Wilsons' specimen uses their standard blue.

D.W. Stewart also had a very interesting comment to make in his book's introduction:

In connection with the plantation of Ulster by Scots colonists towards the end of the sixteenth century, there is evidence that tartan was manufactured in Ireland at that period. Concerning Lady Montgomery, wife of Sir Hugh Montgomery of the Eglinton family, who was a daughter of the Laird of Greenock, we read: 'She set up and encouraged linen and

One of the beautiful beaches of Arran, with Goat Fell rearing up in the distance

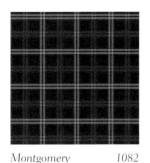
Montgomery   1082

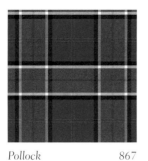
Pollock   867

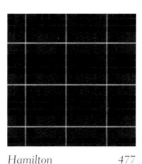
Hamilton   477

Cunningham   4644

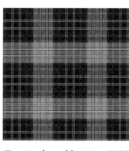
Cunningham Hunting   1972

woollen manufactory which soon brought down the prices of the breakens (i.e. tartans) and narrow cloths of both sorts.'

The Montgomerys and the Cunninghams had one of the longest-running feuds in Scotland; it started in 1448 and lasted for 213 years! Apparently it arose when Sir Alexander Montgomery was appointed Baillie of Cunninghame – a title which belonged to his brother-in-law Sir Robert Cunningham. The families only buried the hatchet when William Cunningham, Lord High Chancellor of Scotland, married Margaret Montgomery, daughter of Alexander, 6th Earl of Eglinton.

POLLOCK   867
Sandwiched between Montgomery lands south-west of Glasgow were the Maxwells, whose main seat was in the Borders. One of their feudal dependents was the Pollock family and in 1979 some Pollocks in the United States formed a clan society and adopted this tartan. For historical continuity it was based on the Maxwell sett.

HAMILTON   477
This was first recorded in the *Vestiarium Scoticum* and there was no evidence of a Hamilton tartan prior to the publication in 1842 of that spectacular work. As has been said elsewhere, the authors, the Sobieski Stuart brothers, enjoyed a popular following amongst the Scottish gentry of the period, and it is probable that the design can be attributed to Charles Edward Stuart (alias Allan Hay). In his book *The Tartans of the Scottish Clans* Jamie Scarlett expresses disappointment that the Sobieskis didn't 'offer something a trifle more inspiring than one of their almost off-the-peg fittings'.

Douglas Douglas-Hamilton, 14th Duke of Hamilton and 11th Duke of Brandon (1903–73), took a great interest in flying from an early age and in 1932 was the first man to fly over Mount Everest. During the Second World War he was responsible for air defence in Scotland. In May 1941 Rudolf Hess parachuted into Scotland, ostensibly to meet with the Duke and plot a secret peace treaty that would lead to the overthrow of Winston Churchill and his government. In reality it was a trap to which the Duke was party, and Hess was captured.

CUNNINGHAM   4644
Being a Lowland family the Cunninghams of old would not have had a tartan but the Sobieskis didn't let that prevent them inventing one for them in *Vestiarium Scoticum*. The name is a territorial one and the District of Cunninghame today forms part of North Ayrshire. Cunningham was also one of the names adopted by the MacGregors when the clan was broken and scattered, and this pattern certainly seems to have been based on the old black and red MacGregor sett.

CUNNINGHAM HUNTING   1972
A labelled sample of this tartan was found at the Kilbarchan Weaver's Cottage in North Ayrshire (5 miles south of Glasgow Airport) and the thread count is taken from that. The problem with dating the Kilbarchan samples is that the handloom weaving of tartans didn't cease there until the early 1950s. This tartan also appears in the collection of James MacKinlay of Aberdeen who collected samples of tartan between 1930 and 1950. Unfortunately, like many early researchers, he didn't provide details of the origins of the specimens.

Burns   1539   Burns Check   1736

The statue of Robert Burns in Kilmarnock

This is also claimed as the MacNicol/Nicolson Hunting or Green tartan although no plausible connection with this clan has yet been uncovered.

BURNS   1539

West of Lee Castle lies Robert Burns's country and whilst the poet had a close relationship with *one* of Scotland's other iconic products ('Freedom and Whisky gang thegither'), the same couldn't be said of tartan. Burns (1759–96) was born into a farming family in Alloway in Ayrshire and was indisputably a Lowlander: in his time, tartan was still viewed as a quaint habit of those rather dangerous Highlanders. Indeed its production and wearing in the Highlands was officially banned (1746–82) during the bulk of his lifetime, though he did touch on it in briefly in his 'Battle of Sherramuir': 'To hear the thuds, and see the cluds/ O' clans frae woods in tartan duds [clothes]'.

It's thought therefore that this very attractive Burns tartan was not specifically designed with the poet in mind but was more likely to have been a family tartan for all Burnses. It was discovered by the Aberdeen researcher James MacKinlay between 1930 and 1950 in the well-known Highlandware shop of R.W. Forsyths in Edinburgh. The first half of the 20th century saw many such lesser clan, sept and family tartans designed.

BURNS CHECK   1736

One design that was produced with Robert Burns in mind was this Burns Check. Almost fifty years ago Baron Marchand of Messrs George Harrison & Co. of Edinburgh explained to E.S. Harrison of Johnstons of Elgin how it came about. He related that he had been approached by a friend from the *Scotsman* newspaper with the suggestion that he create a Robert Burns tartan. The first idea had been to base it on the Campbell – a clan with which the Burns family was connected – but after much discussion it was decided more appropriate to model it on the Shepherd's Check. The overcheck introduced 'the hodden grey and a' that' and a little flavour of green fields was added. There was thought of calling it the 'Ayr tartan' but that was discarded in favour of the present name which celebrated the bicentenary of the poet's birth. In June 1959 the Burns Federation accepted the design with the condition that all goods should be made in Scotland.

Lockhart

A modern tartan that cloaks a fascinating history is the Lockhart –

designed in 1996 by the Chief, Angus Lockhart of the Lee.

THE Locards arrived in Lanarkshire and Ayrshire in the wake of the 1066 Norman invasion of England and their passage through history is marked in many ways. In the thirteenth century, Stephen Locard founded the village of Stevenson in Ayrshire and his son Symon, after acquiring lands in Lanarkshire, called a village which he founded Symons Town – today called Symington.

The Lockhart clan crest bears the motto *Corda Serrata Pando* – 'I open locked hearts', which offers a clue to the modern-day spelling of the surname. Symon fought alongside Robert the Bruce and for his service and loyalty was knighted. As related elsewhere, Symon Locard carried the key and Sir James Douglas the casket in their quest to carry Bruce's heart into battle 'against the infedils'. To honour the family and commemorate Symon's part in that campaign, the family name was changed to Lockheart in the fifteenth century, later spelled Lockhart.

The fascinating intertwining of so many players on the Scottish historical stage is further evidenced by the marriage of a distant relative John Gibson Lockhart – a young genius who went up to Oxford University at the age of thirteen – to Sir Walter Scott's daughter Sophia. Her father in his famous novel *The Talisman* drew on Sir Symon's Crusade experience of capturing a Moorish amir in Spain. As part of the ransom, the Moor's mother included an amulet with healing powers, and that precious talisman is still in the Lockhart family today.

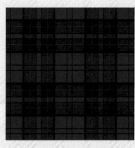
Lockhart 2258

Peter of Lee 1055

Peter of Lee Chief 5507

PETER OF LEE 1055

Although the present Chief, Angus Lockhart, runs the family estate, the original family seat Lee Castle – and the barony that went with it – was sold in 1950. In the late 1980s it was acquired by a larger-than-life American phenomenon, Edward Leslie Peter. A multi-millionaire business tycoon and international socializer, he numbered among his friends and acquaintances three US Presidents and even the King of Thailand.

The 34th Baron of Lee enthusiastically – and sumptuously – set about restoring the one-time Lockhart stronghold and entered into a love affair with Scotland's history, its ancient customs and its pomp and ceremony. He was a great music lover who founded and funded the Pipes and Drums of the Baron of Lee, and was known for his approachability, his pearls of wisdom, enormous generosity and his tremendous capacity for laughter.

The symbolism of Bruce's heart carried to the Crusades was not lost on Leslie Peter, Baron of Lee. His heart too was carried in a casket – from Tampa, Florida where he died in 2001 to the grounds of Castle Lee so that it might for ever rest in Scotland.

In keeping with his total absorption in Scottish culture, Leslie Peter had this tartan designed in 1988 by Harry Lindley of Kinloch Anderson and stocked the castle with kilts so that his visiting American friends could wear 'his' tartan. It's based on the Johnston, a prominent Border family, and created by replacing the yellow line of the Johnston with the red shown here.

PETER OF LEE CHIEF 5507

In 1996 he had this slightly different version produced for his own personal use – a 'Chief's tartan' as it were.

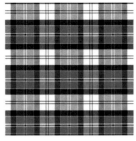

Ailsa Craig   1673

Ailsa Craig

AILSA CRAIG   1673

One sight with which Burns would have been very familiar – he mentioned it in one of his songs – was the rocky hump of Ailsa Craig, a craggy island ten miles out in the Firth of Clyde. Said to derive from the Gaelic for 'Fairy Rock', Ailsa Craig is today uninhabited and an important bird sanctuary.

Famous in curling circles since the early 1800s as the source of the best curling stones in the world, this 1,114ft-high tower of granite was known locally as Paddy's Milestone because of its position halfway between Belfast and Glasgow.

In 1972, inspired by this *weel kent* sight, a Miss Ailean Robertson of Ayr decided that it merited its own tartan. The grey-blue is based on the famous

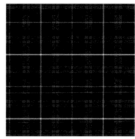

East Kilbride   2147

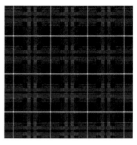

Edinburgh   1163

Ailsa Craig microgranite used for the curling stone and the original material was produced by Thomas Gordon of Glasgow. Fortunately for posterity, the thread count of this tartan was taken from Miss Robertson's 'kilt' by Tony Murray of Stirling.

East Kilbride 2147

Some 12 miles south of Glasgow lies East Kilbride, once a rural Lanarkshire village but destined for growth when it was designated a New Town in 1947. Now Scotland's sixth-largest town, it enjoys the dubious sobriquet of 'Polomint City', signifying that it has the most roundabouts of any Scottish town.

This tartan was commissioned in 1990 by East Kilbride Development Corporation for use by its many friends and visitors and by the people of the town. Designed by Gordon Teal of the old Tartans Society, the design echoes the symbolism of the ensigns armorial granted by the Lord Lyon King of Arms. The first material was woven into rugs presented to Her Majesty the Queen, who visited East Kilbride in July 1990 with the Duke of Edinburgh.

Edinburgh 1163

Just as with Glasgow, there's a proliferation of tartans prefixed with the city name but only one that has become popular and is now regarded as the city's own.

Girvan Harbour, the starting place for trips to Ailsa Craig

Whisky Tartans

Distilleries are most frequently associated with picturesque Highland glens and mist-shrouded moors and mountains. Whilst this is true of very many of them, the corporate powerhouses and modern marketing infrastructures are often located in the country's commercial heartland of the Lowlands – far away from the bubbling springs and tumbling burns! Here are just a few of them.

BELL
4155

The city of Perth has great cause to be thankful to the whisky dynasty of the Bell family. In 1825 T.R. Sandeman opened a small whisky shop near the Kirk of St John in the city centre where he was joined by Arthur Bell, who by 1865 controlled the business. He was succeeded on his death by his son Arthur Kinmont Bell – A.K. Bell – an outstanding philanthropist whose legacy to the city and its people is still very much part of modern life. True to the spirit of 'A.K.', when the firm wanted a new tartan it stayed within the city and this was designed in 2000 by Claire Donaldson of the House of Edgar for the launch of new packaging for the company.

The design appears to be based on the Perth tartan, a pattern with strong Jacobite associations in the area.

BLACK & WHITE
2042

Black & White whisky celebrated its centenary in 1984, which is when this tartan was designed – presumably to celebrate that event. The original bottle was black with a white label and when customers persistently asked for 'that black and white whisky', its astute founder John Buchanan changed its name. It was supplied to the House of Commons in the nineteenth century and the label included a quotation from the respected medical journal *The Lancet*: 'Our Analysis shows this to be a Remarkably Pure Spirit, and therefore well adapted for Medicinally dietetic purposes.' One can easily imagine the 'Hear, hear!'s and murmurs of approval from the green benches in the House of Commons!

DRAMBUIE
2474

It must be natural to raise a quizzical eyebrow at a claim that the recipe for your hugely successful product was given to a forebear by Bonnie Prince Charlie, but in this case it is well-documented, a gift from the Prince to his trusted lieutenant Captain John MacKinnon. The writer Vivian Devlin relates how the ancient recipe was preserved by the MacKinnon family, who concocted variations of it – which became known locally on Skye as *dram buidhe*, the yellow drink, or *Dram Buidheach*, meaning the drink that satisfies. This is the origin of the Drambuie Liqueur we know across the world today.

The trio of tartans for this truly historic liqueur were designed in 1998 by Kinloch Anderson of Edinburgh and are said to be based on the MacKinnon Hunting tartan – the MacKinnon family is still the proud owner of Drambuie and the secret recipe is only handed down the matriarchal line. Following the death of managing director Norman MacKinnon in 1989, his widow Mary became chairman and took charge of the secret family recipe. That has now been passed on to Pamela, wife of Norman and Mary's eldest son Calum.

HAIG & HAIG
1609

Probably the most famous product from the Haig stable is Haig's Dimple, said to be the fourth-largest blended de luxe whisky in the world. In the USA it's known as 'Pinch' and its distinctive triangular and dimpled bottle still has the hand-applied wire mesh which was originally designed to prevent the cork coming out during export

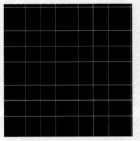

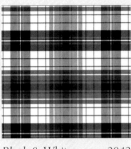

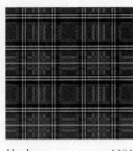

| Bell's | 4155 | Black & White | 2042 | Drambuie | 2474 | Haig & Haig | 1609 | Hepburn | 1381 |

shipments through rough seas. So prized was the design that in 1958 it was the first bottle to be patented in the USA. The Haig & Haig tartan first appeared around 1979 and was from the Johnstons textile mill in Elgin.

HEPBURN 1381

A confusing plethora of notes surround this Royal Stewart-based tartan, with four claimants to its design. Tartan doyen D.C. Stewart wrote in 1970 that he had designed it for a Captain Chas. Hepburn 'only a few years ago'. Another source states that it was designed for Charles Hepburn in 1968 by Andersons of Edinburgh. Further notes say it was researched and produced by a totally different Edinburgh retailer.

The most appealing claim however – and the one that justifies its inclusion in this section – is that it was designed by Captain Charles Hepburn of Red Hackle whisky for the film star Audrey Hepburn . . . fanciful but very romantic! It's thought that the D.C. Stewart claim is the most likely and perhaps Capt. Hepburn did send some to Audrey (its weaving organized by Andersons of Edinburgh), and in later years it may have been ordered through the other Edinburgh retailer. It's recorded that Charles Hepburn had a Rolls-Royce converted into a delivery van with black and red coachwork strips – perhaps the inspiration for his tartan.

Those unfamiliar with the term 'Red Hackle' will be interested to learn that it was the famous cap badge of the Black Watch, first officially issued to the Regiment at a parade in 1795. In 1821 the Regiment was confirmed as having the sole right to wear the Red Hackle amongst all the regiments in the British Army. In April 2006 the

To friends everywhere we send Greetings and all Best Wishes for
A MERRY CHRISTMAS AND A GOOD NEW YEAR
"BLACK & WHITE"
SCOTCH WHISKY
JAMES BUCHANAN & CO. LTD., SCOTCH WHISKY DISTILLERS, GLASGOW & LONDON

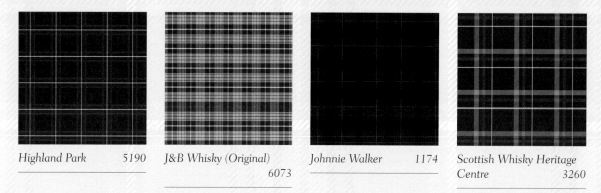

Highland Park   5190   *J&B Whisky (Original)*   *Johnnie Walker*   1174   *Scottish Whisky Heritage*

                                       6073   *Centre*   3260

Black Watch became the 3rd Battalion, The Royal Regiment of Scotland. The 3rd, together with one company of the 7th Battalion, continue to wear the Red Hackle to denote their antecedent regiment.

HIGHLAND PARK   5190

Another great single malt whisky from a distillery that stands on a hill above Orkney's capital Kirkwall, overlooking the vast natural harbour of Scapa Flow. Read what its makers say of it: 'Born in the unforgiving Orkney Islands off the North coast of Scotland, every day is a challenge. With gale force winds, crashing waves and rain every other day, we have had to try harder than most distilleries to create our whisky over the last 200 years. With the long list of accolades and awards against each of our single malt expressions – the struggle is well worth it.'

Their tartan was designed by Lochcarron in May 1996 and used the colours from the company logo.

J&B WHISKY (ORIGINAL)   6073

Three years after the Battle of Culloden (1746), Giacomo Justerini – a distiller and wine merchant from Bologna – fell in love with an opera singer and followed her to London. So began a distilling dynasty that produces one of the most popular brands of blended whisky, which contains 42 individual malt and grain whiskies that together are 'Reminiscent of honey, herbs, hay and delicate aromas revealing a subtle, rather gentle style. Smooth entry with a soft, rounded palate showing faint sweet impressions.' Now you know!

Little is known of the tartan except that it appears to take its vibrant colours from the J&B bottle label.

JOHNNIE WALKER   1174

In 1820, John Walker bought a grocery, wine and spirit business in Kilmarnock and this famous brand – now said to be the largest-selling standard blend worldwide – was originally known as Walker's Kilmarnock Whisky. Despite being relatively modern there are no details of this company tartan except that it dates to 1985.

SCOTTISH WHISKY HERITAGE CENTRE   3260

To round off the representative entries for *uisge beatha* (Gaelic for 'water of life', the origin of the word 'whisky') comes this asymmetric (non-repeating) tartan from the Scottish Whisky Heritage Centre on Edinburgh's Royal Mile.

Its choice was almost by accident: the Centre Director had an appointment with the much mentioned Harry Lindley of Kinloch Anderson, the purpose of which was to discuss the design of a tartan for the centre. On entering the Kinloch establishment, the director spotted one of that season's tartans and apparently said quite firmly, 'That one will do nicely.' Harry is said to have protested that it was just a transient fashion check and besides that, it was asymmetrical and quite unsuited for the purpose. The director insisted and so survived this unique tartan.

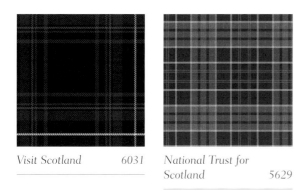

Visit Scotland   6031   National Trust for
                                 Scotland   5629

The Edinburgh tartan was designed and registered in 1970 by Councillor Hugh Macpherson of Edinburgh to mark the Commonwealth Games being held there that year. Several attempts had been made over the years to develop a special tartan for the residents of Edinburgh but none was successful until Hugh produced this one for another purpose altogether!

VISIT SCOTLAND   6031

In 1981 the Scottish Tourist Board, as it was then called, commissioned its first tartan. In 1990, emulating some of the football teams, it dropped that in favour of a fresh design and then in 2003 – to celebrate its new title – it commissioned the current version from Lochcarron's Galashiels mill. Its greens, blues and purples have become very popular in the last decade, reflecting Scotland's rural hues with the white on blue representing the Scottish flag – the St Andrew's Cross. Fortunately, the traditional clans don't change their tartans to stay in line with fashion!

NATIONAL TRUST FOR SCOTLAND   5629

This greatest of Scotland's institutions has over 270,000 members and depends entirely for its support on donations, legacies, grants and membership subscriptions. Established in 1931 as a charity, its remarkable achievements in renovating,

The Edinburgh Military Tattoo, one of the capital's greatest spectacles, featuring military bands from across Scotland and beyond

Historic Scotland   2547   *Scotsman*   2645

protecting and promoting Scotland's natural and cultural heritage have resulted in it acquiring a diverse range of properties – historic houses, castles, gardens, battlefields, whole islands, coastlines and even mountains! In its own words it is 'the guardian of the nation's magnificent heritage of architectural, scenic and historic treasures'. Its aims have appealed to Scots around the globe and in 2000 the National Trust for Scotland Foundation USA (NTSF) was established by a group of US citizen volunteers with a passion for Scotland and the Trust's work.

This tartan was designed in 1999 by Edinburgh resident and Trust member Colin Hutcheson, working with northern weavers Johnstons of Elgin. It's based on the Old Stewart tartan which was a favourite of the Trust's then Patron, the Queen Mother.

HISTORIC SCOTLAND   2547

Historic Scotland is a government agency that conserves over 300 of Scotland's monuments and buildings of special architectural or historic interest. Visitors to some of its major properties such as Stirling Castle and Edinburgh Castle will see staff dressed in this very appropriately coloured tartan designed in 1998 by Betty Davis of Scottish Fashion International in Edinburgh.

SCOTSMAN   2645

The *Scotsman*'s own history web page explains that the much respected newspaper was (on Robert Burns's birthday on 25 January 1817) 'Born in indignation, felt by Fife-born solicitor William Ritchie and customs official Charles Maclaren, at the "unblushing subserviency" of local newspapers to the establishment . . . The idea for an eight-page, quarto Saturday journal with a break-even weekly

Kilbarchan Weaver's Cottage

With its original working looms and spinning wheels, this traditional 1723 weaver's cottage comes vividly to life. Given to the National Trust in 1954 by the family of a Miss Christie – the last weaver in the cottage – it houses the last of 800 handlooms once working in the village of Kilbarchan. Weavers today use the 200-year-old loom, specialising in the making of tartan. They regularly spin and dye their own wool using natural dyes, many of which are obtained from plants and herbs in the pretty cottage garden. Visitors can try their hand at spinning, pirn-winding and weaving – costumed guides are always on hand to help. There is also a DVD presentation on the village's involvement in the making of Paisley shawls.

The 200-year-old loom at Kilbarchan Weaver's Cottage, still in use today

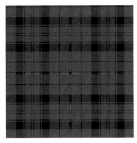

| Leith | 2333 |

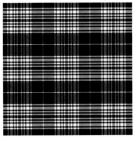

| Napier | 1242 |

embarkation and entry point for a historical tide of humans, imports and exports. On a light-hearted note, it also gave the world one of the English language's shortest and most famous tongue-twisters, said to have been used by the local constabulary as a test for drunkenness, 'The Leith police dismisseth us.'

In 1995 the town hosted the year's hugely successful Cutty Sark Tall Ships Race and this tartan was designed by Kinloch Anderson to mark the event. Based on the Robertson in honour of Henry Robb, Leith Shipbuilders, the red marks Leith's strong links with the claret trade. The tartan proved very popular and was later adopted as the Leith district tartan.

circulation of 300 copies, came to the two men when city newspapers refused to print, even as an advertisement, a story written by Ritchie on the mismanagement of the Royal (then New) Infirmary.'

Designed in 1999 by that other Edinburgh institution Kinloch Anderson, the colours of this tartan are from the *Scotsman*'s corporate colours and the setts are based on the MacIntosh (Ritchie's tartan) and the MacLaren.

LEITH   2333
Only ten minutes from the centre of Edinburgh, the old town of Leith (first documented in AD 1128) played a central role in Scotland's history for almost 900 years as its principal port. It was a major centre for shipbuilding, milling, rope and sail making, fishing, whaling and over the centuries was the

NAPIER   1242
The Napiers are said to descend from the Lennox family and it's claimed that the name originated with a comment from King Alexander III (1241–86) after a battle in which the great bravery of a young Lennox turned defeat into victory: 'You have all done valiantly, but there is one amongst you who has nae peer.' And he commanded young Donald Lennox to change his name forthwith.

Probably the most famous Napier was John, the eighth Laird of Merchiston in Edinburgh, who was born in 1550 when his father was only 17. He matriculated at St Andrews University at the age of

*The waterside at Leith,
Edinburgh's attractive port*

Dalziel

One of Scotland's old family names that always causes pronunciation problems for visitors is Dalziel with its many spelling variations. Regardless of how it's spelt, it's always pronounced Dee-ell.

Dalziel   969

THE House of Binns at Linlithgow is owned by the National Trust for Scotland and is a living monument to the Dalyells, who have lived there since 1612. It was here in 1681 that General Tam Dalyell formed the legendary regiment of Royal Scots Greys.

Bluidy Tam, as he was known, first attracted notoriety for his merciless suppression of the Covenanters at the Battle of Rullion Green in 1666. Little more than a thousand Protestant 'rebels' had marched from Dumfries towards Edinburgh, armed only with scythes, pitchforks and staves, wanting to air their grievances about the religious persecution inspired by Charles II. Their march was blocked however and they were turned back into the arms of General Tam – a royalist supporter since his youth. He and his well-armed government troops killed about 50 Covenanters before darkness stopped the slaughter. Of the 80 prisoners captured, 21 were later hanged and others were transported to America as slaves.

Tam Dalyell had led an adventurous early life and even managed to escape from the Tower of London, where he had been imprisoned by Oliver Cromwell, fleeing to Russia where he joined the army of Tsar Alexei Mikhailovich and achieved high rank. When Charles II summoned him back to Scotland to be commander-in-chief of his forces, Tam brought back with him a rather fiendish Russian invention – the thumb-screw – and earned himself the additional sobriquet of 'the Muscovite De'il'.

This tartan, with slight amendments, has had a variety of names over the years. Originally produced by the Bannockburn weavers Wm Wilson & Sons as 'Locheil', they had reworked it by 1824 when it was sold as 'King George IV'. Attribution of the name 'Dalyell' appeared first in the publication *The Scottish Gael* in which James Logan documented samples collected between 1826 and 1831.

Another variation appeared about 1850 as 'Munro' and continues to be used by that clan today as their 'true clan tartan'. Slight differences exist between all four and it is a good example of just how confusing the tartan scene can become.

Above: *The House of the Binns, ancient home of the Dalziel family*

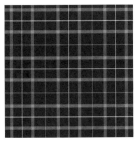

Scottish Canals 3916

Scottish Airports 2510

Seton 932

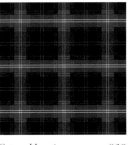

Seton Hunting 938

13 and later invented logarithms and the decimal point.

The origins of the Napier tartan are unclear but its structure suggests that it's a fancy pattern from the late nineteenth or early twentieth century.

SCOTTISH CANALS 3916

The thought of canals in Scotland sometimes bemuses visitors but there are four – the Caledonian, the Crinan, the Forth & Clyde and the Union. These were all built between 1768 and 1822, the year that King George IV made his famous visit to Edinburgh and sparked off the world's great love affair with tartan.

The most spectacular waterway has to be the 60-mile-long Caledonian Canal, 38 miles of which traverse the lengths of Loch Lochy, Loch Oich and Loch Ness. The Forth & Clyde and the Union canals run for 69 miles and join the two great cities of Glasgow and Edinburgh and two oceans, the Atlantic and the North Sea. The Crinan Canal is only 9 miles long but links Loch Fyne to the Sound of Jura and cuts out the long and treacherous sea voyage around the Mull of Kintyre.

The Scottish Canals tartan was designed in 2001 by Claire Donaldson of the House of Edgar for the British Waterways Board and after a couple of false starts with names – Highland Canals and then Caledonian Canal – it settled down with its present title in 2003.

SCOTTISH AIRPORTS 2510

Four years before the Wright brothers conquered the skies of North Carolina, a British inventor almost beat them to it, but fate stepped in and Percy Pilcher's life ended 'as the result of a rapid and unforeseen reduction in the distance between his homemade wooden glider, the Hawk, and the well-kept lawns of Stanford Hall in Leicestershire'. His Scottish connections are not too well known except that his mother was a Robinson and when he was a naval cadet he was disciplined for 'not wearing drawers when the order was given'.

When Kinloch Anderson of Edinburgh designed the Scottish Airports tartan in 1998 they commemorated Pilcher's early work by basing the design on the Gunn (the tartan for Robinson) and using the colours of the British Airports Authority with a purple line added for the Scottish thistle.

SETON 932

One yardstick for measuring the importance of a nineteenth-century family is whether it attracted the design talents of the Sobieski brothers in their *Vestiarium Scoticum*. In that case, the Setons were certainly important! Great supporters of Mary Queen of Scots – they were instrumental in her escape from Loch Leven – and of the Jacobite cause, they built the Palace of Seton east of Edinburgh, which in 1791 was replaced by Seton Castle, designed by Robert Adam. They were very much involved in the early economic development of the local area and were instrumental in establishing the port of Seton on the Firth of Forth, today known as Cockenzie & Port Seton.

SETON HUNTING 938

The hunting version of Seton is the *Vestiarium* sett with colour changes and is thought to date to the 1920s. The romantic explanation of the surname was that they came from the village of Sai near Exmes in Normandy. A more prosaic suggestion was that it came from their place of abode – the 'sea town' of Tranent near Edinburgh.

The famous Napier of logarithm fame, celebrated on this 1927 cigarette card

Sports Tartans

Spectator sports attract legions of followers and it didn't take long for tartan to commend itself as a unique club identifier and a great rallying symbol for the 'fan clan'. Such tartans cover football, rugby, ice hockey, squash, curling and of course Scotland's 'gift to the world' – golf. With over 60 such sports tartans now and the number growing each year, only a small selection can be covered here.

Most of the football clubs are based in the Lowland belt with the occasional foray outwith Scotland's borders. Supreme amongst the football giants of course are Rangers and Celtic and such is their huge fan base that it has attracted the illegal copying skills of some Far Eastern entrepreneurs. Both clubs have brand managers keeping an eye on such infringements and seizure raids on market traders by the local authorities are not unknown. Football teams quite often change the design and colours of their strip and this is – confusingly – often extended by the major clubs to their tartans and they end up with a portfolio of discarded designs.

Scottish football clubs with their own tartans include Aberdeen, Celtic, Dundee, Dundee United, Dunfermline Athletic, Falkirk, Hearts, Hibernian, Kilmarnock, Livingston, Montrose, Motherwell, Partick Thistle, Queen of the South, Raith Rovers, Rangers, Stenhousemuir, St Johnstone and St Mirren.

RANGERS F.C. 2171
The original tartan for Rangers Football Club was designed in 1989 and based on the Government or Black Watch tartan. Designer Chris Aitken increased the size of the sett and changed the shade of blue to suit the Rangers team colours.

CELTIC F.C. 6496
Designed by Claire Donaldson of the House of Edgar for Celtic Football Club, updating the club's tartan for 2005.

SHENZHEN 6250
A striking 2004 design by Peter Gerlam of Lochcarron of Scotland together with Rangers Football Club for a Chinese team with which Rangers have a twin club agreement – a three-year deal to help coach their players while also developing merchandise and sponsorship links. A new joint strip in bright orange with both club badges was produced and immediately sold 3,000, and the tartan is also used for Shenzhen ties.

Old rivals Glasgow-based Rangers and Celtic battle it out on the pitch

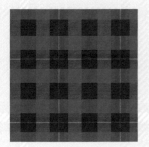

Rangers F.C.   2171

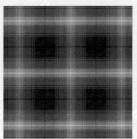

Celtic F.C.   6496

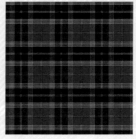

Shenzhen   6250

Hammarby F.C.   2661

Toronto Blue Jays   5103

HAMMARBY F.C.   2661

From the days of Scandinavian invaders, there has always been a very close bond between Scotland and the Norse countries, and in previous centuries a steady stream of Scots mercenaries and entrepreneurs crossed the North Sea in search of excitement and fortune. Whether or not this Swedish club has any roots in the 'old country', it obviously decided that the international appeal of tartan justified commissioning this design by the Strathmore Woollen Company of Forfar in 2000.

TORONTO BLUE JAYS   5103

Toronto's famous baseball team, the Blue Jays, do their spring training down south in Florida and a local doctor and long-time fan, Pat Snair, decided to present them with their own tartan in 1996. Designed and woven by Lochcarron of Scotland the tartan is, of course, predominantly blue and the Jays were the first major-league baseball team to have their own tartan.

ROYAL & ANCIENT   2193

The use of eye-shattering tartan by many competition golfers has a long pedigree but good taste has won the day and many golf clubs around the world are commissioning their own subdued designs. The home of golf – St Andrews – understandably has a handful of such tartans, with that of the Royal & Ancient occupying the place of honour. Based on the Earl of St Andrews tartan, this was designed by Kinloch Anderson of Edinburgh in 1993 to help with fund-raising for the restoration of the Club's historic buildings.

RYDER CUP 2006   6836

In 1926 the St Albans seed merchant Samuel Ryder – a keen golfer – set up a competition between American and British players. His golfing mentor was Abe Mitchell and Sam Ryder insisted that the gold figure atop the Ryder trophy should be modelled on Abe.

The Scottish Tartans Authority – commissioned by the Professional Golfers Association at Wentworth – followed Sam Ryder's lead and based this subdued design on the Mitchell tartan, introducing dark green for the fairways and a lighter shade for the greens. Specifically for the 2006 competition, over a mile of this tartan was woven for officials' clothing and accessories.

Royal & Ancient   2193

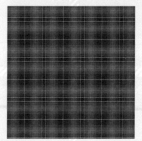

Ryder Cup 2006   6836

The Royal and Ancient in St Andrews, one of the world's oldest and most illustrious golf courses

LAUDER
Ayton
Berwick-on-Tweed
Tweedmouth
MAITLAND
HOME
Coldstream
Peebles
Galashiels
Kelso
Melrose
Selkirk
Roxburgh
DOUGLAS
KERR
Ayr
BUCCLEUCH
Jedburgh
SCOTT
Denholm
Hawick
Moffat
JOHNSTON
ELLIOT
KENNEDY
MCKERRELL
ARMSTRONG
JARDINE
Dumfries
MAXWELL
AGNEW
MURRAY
Solway Firth

Tweed
Teviot

0   10   20   30   40   50 kilometres

0   10   20   30 miles

THE BORDER LANDS

South of Scotland's densely populated central belt lie the Southern
Uplands, which embrace the Scottish Borders and Dumfries and Galloway.
Although this gently rolling buffer zone between Scotland and England
is far removed from the Highlands, it has seen more than its fair share of
violence through the centuries.

At the time of the Roman invasion Scotland and England did not
exist as separate regions and it was probably Emperor Hadrian who,
with his 70-mile wall from the Solway to the Tyne, was the architect
of the division between England and that part of the country that the
Romans often called Britannia Barbarica.

The River Tweed at Coldstream, the border between Scotland and England

After the Roman invasion came the Norse incursions, then the Saxons and the Normans and then the warring factions of great Border families. Overlaid on those were the continual battles between the Kings of Scotland and England that invariably laid waste to villages, towns, castles and churches.

Despite their specialization in textiles in later centuries, tartan was not part of the inhabitants' heritage and indeed the great families there went out of their way to stress that they were just that – families and *not* clans. It's not known who was the first to buckle, whether under the sales pitch of weavers Wilsons of Bannockburn or the social pressure of George IV's 1822 visit to Edinburgh. The initial trickle of converts became a flood when the Sobieski Stuart brothers produced their *Vestiarium Scoticum* in which almost half the featured tartans purported to be those of Lowland and Border

families. As the authors of the 1980 publication *Scotland's Forged Tartans* commented: 'they provided a welcome source for many who had never before thought to lay claim to any tartan at all'.

COLDSTREAM 2650

An appropriate place to start this Border tartan tour is undoubtedly Coldstream with its bridge straddling the Scottish/English border. The town was once a serious rival to Gretna Green for runaway lovers wanting to dash over the border and get married without prior public notice – a privilege which was abolished in 1856.

The town is also the birthplace of the famous Coldstream Guards – the oldest regular regiment in continuous service in the British Army. The story of how it acquired its name is a long and complicated one; suffice to say that it was in 1670 that it was

The Coldstream Guards – the oldest continuously serving regular regiment of the British Army, being directly descended from General Monck's Regiment of Foot, founded in 1650 during the Civil War, and renamed the Coldstream Regiment of Foot in 1670

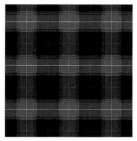

Coldstream   2650

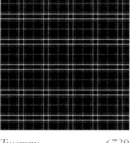

Twempy   6739

Northumberland   6765

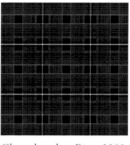

Chattahoochee River 2203

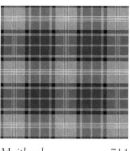

Maitland   714

officially given the name by which it had been unofficially known for many years – 'His Majesty's Coldstream Regiment of Foot Guards'.

In 1787 Robert Burns stepped over the centre line of the Coldstream bridge and set foot for the first time on 'foreign soil'. He also wrote 'The Cotter's Saturday Night' in the town – a fact celebrated by a commemorative plaque on the bridge.

There are a good few other Coldstreams dotted around the world – British Columbia, Kentucky, California, Australia – but it's not known if those are named after cold streams in the vicinity or after this ancient Scottish border town. The Scottish Coldstream is certainly the only one that appears to have a tartan, chosen in 1999 by the townspeople from a shortlist of four from local tartan designer Ronnie Hek.

TWEMPY   6739
Also right on the border – this time just over on the English side – is Tweedmouth which lies immediately opposite Berwick-upon-Tweed. Ronnie Hek designed this tartan for the inhabitants of Tweedmouth, Twempy being a good-natured nickname for the residents there.

NORTHUMBERLAND   6765
Traditionally Border shepherds wore a simple black and white checked plaid or shawl – useful for keeping not only themselves warmed but also their orphaned lambs. Whether it's called the Shepherd's Check or Shepherd's Plaid, the Northumberland tartan, the Border Check or the Border Riever, this design is the 'mother of all tartans'. Early weavers with artistic aspirations would have used the simplest of materials to hand to fashion this ubiquitous check – the black and white wool plucked from primitive sheep breeds.

The fleeting permanence of fabrics in a northern climate results in the earliest example of this pattern dating back only to Roman times – an earthenware jar of coins with a chequered cloth stopper was discovered at Falkirk and dated to AD 260.

During the infamous 18th- and 19th-century Highland Clearances, when crofters were often ousted to make way for sheep, experienced shepherds from the Borders were encouraged to move north and they took with them their traditional checks, which formed the basis of very many estate tweeds.

In 1760 the Duke of Northumberland designated this tartan for his personal pipers and it was later adopted as the plaid for the pipers of the Northumberland Fusiliers, the official tartan of Northumberland County and that of the Shepherd family. It was also very popular in London in the 19th century, thanks, it is said, to Sir Walter Scott's liking for wearing trews in the 'Border Drabs', as the family of checks were known.

CHATTAHOOCHEE RIVER   2203
In 1993, Scottish Border Enterprise suggested celebrating the twinning of the River Tweed and the Chattahoochee River in Georgia (USA), and this tartan was designed and woven by Lochcarron of Galashiels.

MAITLAND   714
The visit of George IV to Edinburgh in 1822 saw many clan chiefs hurriedly trying to identify and acquire their clan tartans. Fascinatingly, history repeated itself 131 years later in the preparations for Queen Elizabeth II's Progress through Edinburgh after her 1953 Coronation. The honour and duty of acting as Hereditary Bearer for the Sovereign of the National Flag of Scotland fell to the then Master of

District Tartans

There can be little doubt that it was the events following the '45 (see page 9) that set tartan on the road to its spectacular success. There had been Scottish settlements in the New World for many years and these had imported tartan for their own use and doubtless for trade with the native American Indians. In the West Indies, tartan was popular for clothing slaves, being cheap, cheerful and durable, but the story that its bright colours aided the recapture of escapees will not hold water; the soft colours and diffuse patterns of the tartans of the day disappear into the landscape at a very short distance and, in most cases, would have helped rather than hindered an absconder.

After the '45, increased emigration and Highland regiments engaging in Continental and American wars stepped up demand and the large weaving settlements that grew up on the Highland fringes waxed fat for many years. By the time the wars had ceased and the colonies had become independent and self-sufficient, Sir Walter Scott and his friends had set off the Romantic Revival of the Highlands and another wave of prosperity ensued.

It's ironic that the Lowlanders happily joined this movement, despite their having, not so long before, despised and feared the Highlanders. Queen Victoria went for tartan in a big way, the myth makers kept up their work and tartan has never seriously looked back.

All this was very good for trade but it had to be matched by a corresponding plenitude of tartans and excuses for wearing them, and this was where the myth makers came into their own. Meticulous combing of old reports and taking them both in and out of context provided the tartan trade and the general public with just what was needed. The clan tartans had been expanded to cover as much ground as possible, but to those who could not squeeze under that umbrella, Martin Martin's 1703 book *A Description of the Western Islands of Scotland* gave them the following:

> Every Isle differs from each other in their fancy of making *Plaids*, as to the Stripes in Breadth and Colours. This Humour is as different thro' the main Land of the *Highlands* in so far that they who have seen those Places is able, at the first view of a Man's *Plaid*, to guess the place of his Residence.

Thus was born the concept of district tartans, not as an established 'official' system, but as a natural evolution of the local weaver's output. Many of those happenstance district tartans became so closely associated with the extended family that wore them that what started out as a district sett became a clan sett.

A ROYAL REEL;
OR, THE QUEEN IN THE HIGHLANDS.

Tune—"Tullochgorum."

ALBERT.—Dat is goot, mein tear, you vare goot at a reel—how you like me midout mein Breeches?
VIC.—Oh! always much better than with them.

An 1842 cartoon in the Penny Satirist, mocking Queen Victoria and Prince Albert's love for the Highlands

Jamie Scarlett

Lauderdale, deputizing for his brother the 16th Earl.

The authorities argued that the Bearer should appear in appropriate clan tartan but it was not at all clear what that should be. Lord Lyon King of Arms, presiding over the Scottish College of Heralds, pronounced that although the Maitlands were by origin Lowlanders, it was quite proper for them to wear tartan and he suggested a modification of the known and accepted Lauder tartan – the Maitland Chief being Earl of Lauderdale.

In consultation with Harry Lindley of Kinloch Anderson, Lyon suggested that the thin red line in the Lauder should be bordered or guarded by two yellow lines on either side to reproduce the gold from the family's coat of arms. Thus was born the Maitland tartan!

LAUDER 709

Sir Dick Lauder was a particular friend and benefactor of the Sobieski brothers and it's thought that they made a slight modification to the proportions of the Gunn tartan and recycled it in their *Vestiarium Scoticum* as Lauder. It was this tartan that Lyon further modified in 1953 to produce the Maitland.

HOME 127

Although spelt 'Home' the name is pronounced 'Hume'. Like so many Border families the fortunes of the Homes waxed and waned with Scotland's ever-present political upheavals. The 5th Lord Home supported the Reformation, then supported Mary's marriage to Bothwell only to later contribute to her imprisonment in Lochleven. He was then imprisoned by James VI for treason but his son supported the King and was rewarded with the title of Earl of Home. The 7th Earl supported the Jacobites, the 8th didn't and rose to the rank of Lieutenant General and Governor of Gibraltar.

The Home tartan, although differing in colour, has the same sett as the Grey Douglas which also began life in the *Vestiarium Scoticum*.

AYTON 328

Readers will have realized that many tartans have sprung into life through the strangest of circumstances, and the Ayton tartan is another fine

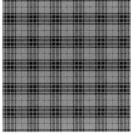
Lauder 709

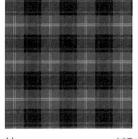
Home 127

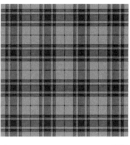
Ayton 328

example. Ayton Castle is just a few miles north of Berwick-upon-Tweed and close to the site of the 12th-century Ayton family stronghold which the English demolished in 1497.

The first official Gathering and the founding of the Ayton Family Society took place 498 years later at the relatively modern castle built in 1851 – a magnificent sandstone example of classic Scottish architecture. Its imposing silhouette will be familiar to many Edinburgh-bound train passengers speeding north from Berwick.

The Ayton tartan is said to have been designed and woven in 1979 in the occupational therapy department of the Bellsdyke psychiatric hospital near Falkirk and then consigned to be an orphan in the Scottish Tartans Society until it was adopted by the new family society.

Queen Elizabeth II's Progress through Edinburgh following her 1953 Coronation

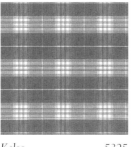

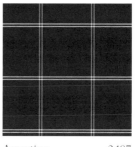

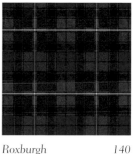

Kelso 5325	*Sprouston* 6231	*Argentina* 2487	*Roxburgh* 140

KELSO 5325

The next settlement upstream from Coldstream on the River Tweed is Kelso and the graceful five-arched bridge over the river there was the model for London's Waterloo Bridge. Kelso has never had a district tartan of its own; Scottish designers Laird Portch did design a Kelso tartan in the early 1980s but that was almost certainly a sett designed for the fashion market only.

SPROUSTON 6231

Sprouston is a small town near Kelso and this is a Hek design for its local primary school. The name is thought to come from the Old English *tun*, 'farmstead', owned by someone called 'Sprow'.

Kelso Bridge, the model for London's Waterloo Bridge

ARGENTINA 2487

One overseas tartan that has a very definite link with Kelso is the Argentine tartan. It was designed by a Scottish-Argentine, Eduardo Macrae Moir, to honour two Kelso men – John and William Robertson, who started the first settlement of Scottish immigrants in Argentina. Two hundred and twenty emigrants left the port of Leith on board the *Symmetry* and arrived in Buenos Aires on 8 August 1825, settling in a ranch 20 miles south-west of the city, bought by the Robertson brothers in the area of Monte Grande and called 'Santa Catalina'. The tartan combines the colours of the Argentine and Scottish flags, showing the amalgamation of the two cultures. Blue, navy blue and white are used in sports and national symbols representing Argentina.

ROXBURGH 140

Just a couple of miles south-west of Kelso lies the old village of Roxburgh on the banks of the Teviot. The town grew up around the castle – a favourite residence of the Kings of Scotland in the Middle Ages – and with the castle's demise, the population drifted to nearby Kelso leaving behind a sparsely populated village. Probably the best-known 'resident' was Andrew Gemmels, a blue-coat gaberlunzie (a licensed tramp) who died aged 106 and who inspired Sir Walter Scott's Edie Ochiltree in *The Antiquary*.

Andrew died in 1793 and missed the unveiling of the red Roxburgh tartan that first appeared about forty years later, probably the work of the famous weaving firm Wilsons of Bannockburn. It gradually fell into disuse and only reappeared around 1988 when it was resurrected by a Selkirk weaver. It soon ousted the Roxburgh Green tartan, a Johnny-come-lately that first appeared in a gents' tie between the two World Wars.

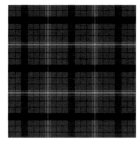

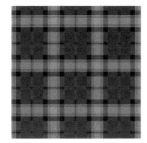

| Jedburgh | 2314 | Kerr | 791 |

JEDBURGH 2314

Further south lies Jedburgh, or Jethart to give it its local name. Historically it lay too close to the English border for comfort and was forever being invaded. Its bloodthirsty background has given rise to the Jethart Axe, the Jethart Staff (a lethal spear!) and worst of all the infamous Jethart Justice: 'When in the morn men hang and draw . . . And sit in judgement after.'

The February event of Jedburgh or Candlemas Hand Ba' is reputed to date from 1548 when the local residents recaptured Ferniehurst Castle from the English. Two teams – the 'uppies' and the 'downies' (born above or below the Mercat Cross) – fight over leather balls which are 'thrown, run away with, smuggled from hand to hand, but never kicked' through the streets of Jedburgh. In 1548 the balls were of course English heads!

In 1947 the two-week-long Jedburgh Callants Festival was inaugurated, which includes ceremonial rides to places of historic interest including Ferniehurst Castle and Redeswire – site of another battle victory over the English. Polly Wittering from the weavers Macnaughtons designed the Jethart tartan to celebrate the 50th anniversary of the Festival.

KERR 791

The Kerrs are believed to be of Viking descent, arriving in the Borders of Scotland by way of Normandy in France. Two main branches traditionally descended from the two brothers who settled near Jedburgh about 1330. Ralph was said to be progenitor of the Kerrs of Ferniehurst whose traditional home is Ferniehurst Castle, which has a fascinating claim to fame connected with the left-handedness of the Kerr family.

Most castle staircases spiral clockwise but Ferniehurst has anticlockwise ones, which allow left-handed defending swordsmen the freedom to move over the open railing. The trait probably goes back to Andrew Kerr, founder of the family's Ferniehurst dynasty in 1457, who was certainly left-handed and found the characteristic a powerful asset in battle. It's said that he specifically taught his sons and armed menservants (who, by custom, took the family name) to wield their weapons with the left hand and they, in turn, taught their own sons the same skills. The association between the Kerr name and left-handedness was so well known through Scotland that the expression Kerr-handed, or kerry- or corry-fisted, is said to have been commonly used to mean left-handed.

With its close proximity to the English border, Jedburgh was no stranger to the frequent passage of English armies marching north and Scots armies marching south. This is the ancient town's Mercat Cross, 'Mercat' being the Scots for 'market'.

The Kerr tartan was first depicted in the much referenced *Vestiarium Scoticum* where the Sobieskis appear to have used the same sett for quite a few tartans including the Lindsay, Stewart of Atholl and Armstrong.

KERR SHEPHERD'S PLAID 3936

A very welcome return to an old tradition is the Kerr Shepherd's Plaid, designed in 2002 for the Chief of Clan Kerr, the Marquis of Lothian, KCVO, of Ferniehurst Castle.

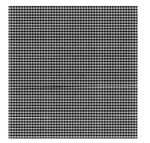

Kerr Shepherd's Plaid 3936   *Melrose* 3926

MELROSE 3926

Upstream a few more miles is Melrose, another Border town with its annual festival – instituted in 1938 – which celebrates with ride-outs to local historic sites, the final event taking place at Melrose Abbey where over 800 years of history are celebrated and the granting of the Foundation Charter by King David I is re-enacted.

In 2002 Melrose was the final venue for a visit by Her Majesty the Queen during the Queen's Jubilee

Celebrations in Scotland. To mark the occasion the town had a new tartan designed specifically for a gift to her and for future use as the Melrose district tartan. It was designed and woven by Lochcarron in nearby Galashiels.

Above: Another town that suffered from invading English armies was Melrose; its high street is much more peaceful nowadays!

Below: Melrose Abbey, founded in about 660; the current, very beautiful, ruins date from the 15th century

Galashiels

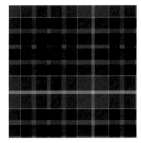

Gallowater, New 1571

Galashiels – or Gala as it's known – was granted its Royal Charter in 1599, an event celebrated annually with the Braw Lads Gathering during which all the burgh boundaries are inspected by a group on horseback – The Braw Lads. The Gala Water itself runs through the town, hence its name Gala Shiels – the shiels or dwellings on the Gala.

The bustling town has been at the heart of the textile industry from 1585 and specialized in tweeds and woollen hosiery. Hand in hand with those went the dyeing of yarns. and the motto of the Galashiels Manufacturers Corporation was 'We dye to live and live to die.'

The Gala Water was the early driving force for many of the mills and a working water turbine could be seen until very recently at the world's largest tartan weavers, Lochcarron of Scotland. A move from Galashiels to Selkirk to make way for a shopping mall has greatly increased the firm's capacity and the turbine may well remain to become a feature of the new mall. With Gala's importance in the textile industry it is hardly surprising that the river had its own tartan designed by Wilsons of Bannockburn in 1793. Perhaps they were spurred on by the publishing in 1783 of 'Braw, Braw Lads' with words by Robert Burns. Sung every year at the Braw Lads Gathering, its earliest verses are thought to be:

> Braw, braw lads of Gala Water,
> O! braw lads of Gala Water,
> I'll kilt my coats aboon my knee,
> And follow my love through the water.
> Sae fair her hair sae brent her brow,
> Sae bonnie blue her een, and cheerie,
> Sae white her teeth, sae sweet her mou',
> I aften kiss her till I'm weary.

Above: The Borough Chambers in Galashiels

Left: Music for Robert Burns' famous song, 'Braw, Braw Lads', still sung annually at the Braw Lads Gathering in Galashields

GALLOWATER, NEW   1571

The names 'Gala Water' and 'Gallowater' seem to be interchangeable and which is used seems to depend on the source. The Old Gallowater tartan first appeared in the records of Wilsons of Bannockburn

Scott

Just on the southern outskirts of Galashiels lies Abbotsford – the home of Sir Walter Scott (1771–1832). The worlds of literature, history and tartan owe a great debt to Scott. With his romantic historical novels he was instrumental in popularizing the Highlands and their disappearing clan culture. He was also the gifted organizer of the spectacular levee to celebrate George IV's visit to Edinburgh in 1822. This heralded an upsurge in popularity of Highland dress as clan chiefs scrambled to find their traditional tartans or new ones that they could claim as their own. By around 1840 Scott was so popular that Wilsons got in on the act and produced a variant of their Pattern No. 150 as Sir Walter Scott.

Sir Walter Scott, who made the Highlands – and tartan – fashionable, in a portrait by Sir Edwin Landseer

THIS was the era of the Sobieski Stuarts and their skilled but spurious *Vestiarium Scoticum* – supposedly detailing over seventy historical clan tartans. Scott's friend – and assistant at the 1822 royal visit – Sir Thomas Dick Lauder was the gullible patron of the Hay brothers (the real name of the Sobieskis) and wrote excitedly to Sir Walter in 1829 telling him that he had seen the 'Scott Tartan' in a manuscript prepared for the brothers. Scott, with great prescience, rejected the idea very firmly. Forged or not, however, that tartan went on to establish itself in modern times as the most popular Scott tartan.

RED SCOTT   1005
This is the Scott tartan, about which Sir Thomas Lauder got excited.

SCOTT BLACK & WHITE   1826
Thomas Smibert published this design in 1850, saying that it 'was produced for his own use by Sir Walter Scott in 1822, and he wore this in private in the form of a Lowland shepherd's plaid'.

GREEN SCOTT   825
This is sometimes called the Green Hunting Scott and is generally available today. The Chief of the Scotts is His Grace the 9th Duke of Buccleuch and 10th of Queensberry who lives in Selkirk in the Borders region of Scotland.

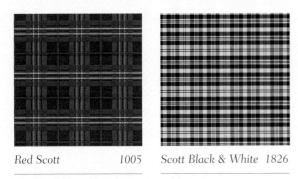

Red Scott 1005	Scott Black & White 1826

Green Scott 825	Meg Merrilees 1602

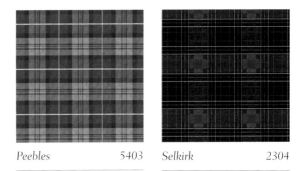

Peebles 5403	Selkirk 2304

MEG MERRILEES   1602

In 1815 Sir Walter Scott wrote *Guy Mannering*; one of the novel's characters was a gypsy named Meg Merrilees. Only fourteen years later William Wilson of Bannockburn produced the Meg Merrilees tartan and it was soon being sold in Inverness by a draper named MacDougal of 27 High Street as 'Meg Merrilees tartan plaids for ladies'.

By the turn of that century the name was shortened to Merrilees and the tartan was being bought as a clan/family tartan by those of the name. A hundred years later another Scottish weaver reversed two of the colours and produced the Merrilees Dress tartan.

This admirably demonstrates the fascinating journey of Meg from world of fiction to a weaver's drawing board, to clattering looms 170 years apart and to Merrilees societies and individuals around the globe.

in the late 18th century. However, they were not above recycling patterns that had outlived their original usefulness and to celebrate the Battle of Waterloo (1815), they changed the size and proportions of the pattern and named it 'Wellington' in honour of the victorious Duke.

Perhaps by public demand, or commercial acumen, by 1793 they had embellished the Old Gallowater by introducing a red stripe. Within about twenty years they had further 'improved' the design adding a thin white stripe, and named it the New Gallowater.

PEEBLES   5403

Continuing westwards towards the source of the River Tweed, the wool town and Royal Burgh of Peebles is thought to have received its Royal Charter from King Alexander III in 1367.

Five hundred and thirty years later saw Queen Victoria's Diamond Jubilee in 1897 and to mark the occasion the burgh revived the old ceremony of 'riding the marches' and linked it to the Beltane Fair – an ancient pagan festival to celebrate the coming of the summer sun when people would light fires and burn their winter bedding and floor coverings, ready to be replaced afresh.

Another century later, the Peebles Callants Club gifted a new tartan to the town to celebrate that centenary and it is much in evidence at the modern Beltane Festival, a hugely successful annual event with its own Cornet and Beltane Queen.

SELKIRK   2304

High above the Ettrick and Yarrow Valleys between Galashiels and Hawick lies the Ancient and Royal Burgh of Selkirk. Sir Walter Scott was its Sheriff for 33 years, and it was here in the 13th century that

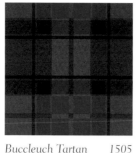

Buccleuch Tartan   1505

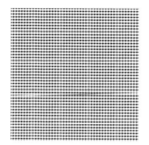

Buccleuch Check   647

Selkirk High School   6846

Hawick   2220

William Wallace was declared Overlord of Scotland. Remnants of the industrial background of Selkirk are seen not only in the architectural heritage of many of its old mills, now serving new purposes, but also in those that are still alive with the deafening clatter of looms ancient and modern inching out tartans and tweeds to be shipped to all corners of the world.

Selkirk's main link with a turbulent past is the Common Riding in June, when up to 500 riders saddle their horses at daybreak to ride the Marches. The Casting of the Colours remembers the story of Flodden when Selkirk sent 80 men with the Scottish King and only one returned, bearing a bloodstained English flag.

Selkirk has become the nucleus of the Scottish tartan weaving industry and Andrew Elliot's small mill, pictured here, is one of a handful of long-established traditional weavers in the area.

Despite its weaving background, the town had to wait until 1996 to get its own tartan – designed by Andrew Elliot of Forest Mill on the banks of the Ettrick in Selkirk. It's not so surprising when one remembers that tartan was essentially a Highland art form that was alien to Border folk. The tartans that *did* appear in the early days were for the powerful Border families, some of whom may have had roots in the Highlands or whose need had been sparked by the tartan mania of the early 19th century.

BUCCLEUCH TARTAN   1505

The Buccleuch family seat is Bowhill, three miles outside Selkirk, and this family tartan is from Wilsons of Bannockburn and dates to the period 1800–40. The current Duke of Buccleuch is the largest private landowner in the United Kingdom.

BUCCLEUCH CHECK   647

This popular check started life as a military sett, designed in 1908 by Sir Richard Waldie Griffiths, Colonel of the 4th Battalion King's Own Scottish Borderers, who used it for the pipers' plaids. It was also called Haig – Earl Haig's family adopted it because he also had been a colonel of the battalion. A third name by which it was known was Gladstone – the reason for that has yet to be discovered.

According to research conducted in the 1960s by James Cant of Dundee, the correct version of this has nine black squares between the blue overstripe, but leading estate tweed expert and author Edward Harrison (1878–1977), Chairman and Managing Director of Johnstons of Elgin for 46 years, claimed there was no fixed number. Probably both of them were correct: in the days when the Buccleuch was woven specifically for the KOSB by Ballantynes of Walkerburn, there were doubtless very strict controls over the design, but when the check became more of an estate tweed, the early criteria would have been relaxed.

SELKIRK HIGH SCHOOL   6846

Designed by Lochcarron in 2005 in conjunction with pupils from Selkirk High School and using colours from the school tie.

HAWICK   2220

Due south of Selkirk, Hawick lies on the River Teviot and is the largest of the Border towns, internationally famous for its fine-quality woollens and tweeds. Many generations of families have gone into the mills since water power replaced the hand knitters of the 17th century – by 1800 up to 3,000 people were employed in the industry.

Over fifty textile mills clustered around a network of fast-running lades produced hosiery, carpets, linen, tartan and knitwear, whilst related support industries sprang up to provide dyeing, textile finishing and light engineering. By 1870 over 450 tons of wool were being converted into a range of goods that were exported around the world.

Like Selkirk, its tartan was designed and woven in 1996, by Andrew Elliot from Forest Mill.

The imposing Town Hall in Hawick – the largest town in the Scottish Borders

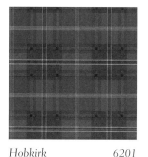

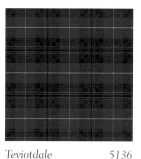

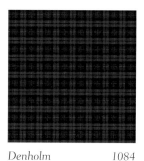

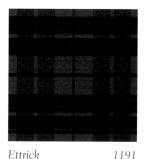

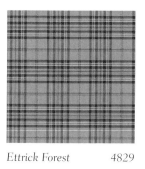

| Hobkirk | 6201 | Teviotdale | 5136 | Denholm | 1084 | Ettrick | 1191 | Ettrick Forest | 4829 |

There has been a church at remote Ettrick for at least 800 years.

HOBKIRK 6201

Another Hek creation, this time for Hobkirk School in Bonchester Bridge, south-east of Hawick.

TEVIOTDALE 5136

The River Teviot, flowing through Hawick, joins the Tweed at Kelso and the 23-mile-long valley is called Teviotdale which has its own district tartan designed and woven in 1996 by Lochcarron in their historic Galashiels mill. The colours of blue, green, brown, gold and black are the major colours found in the valley.

DENHOLM 1084

Five miles north-east of Hawick on the Jedburgh road lies the quiet village of Denholm, which Wilsons of Bannockburn chose for another of their ubiquitous tartans that changed name depending upon where it was: if it was sold in the Scottish Borders it was Denholm but in north-east England they sold it as Durham, once again demonstrating their commercial acumen!

ETTRICK 1191

The Borders village of Ettrick, south-west of Selkirk, is just a scattering of houses in a magnificent and extremely remote spot in what in bygone centuries was the heavily wooded wilderness country known as Ettrick Forest. There is a school, community hall and an ancient church – last rebuilt in 1824. Probably the most famous inhabitant of the graveyard there is James Hogg (1770–1835), the famous Ettrick Shepherd, poet, novelist and balladeer.

The tartan first came to notice in a 1900 pattern book and may have deliberately been modelled on the Wallace clan tartan since both William Wallace and Robert the Bruce based themselves in the forest for their guerrilla campaigns against the English. The Wallace has a yellow line on black in place of the Ettrick's red on black.

Moffat District 1139

Moffat Clan 1129

ETTRICK FOREST 4829

An altogether more modern tartan is the Ettrick Forest from the Lochcarron mill in Galashiels. Its colours depict those found in and around the Ettrick Valley and River Ettrick.

MOFFAT DISTRICT 1139

Just east of the A74(M) motorway lies the town of Moffat – well known to generations of north–south travellers until it was eventually bypassed by the motorway. The town was of sufficient strategic importance even in the 16th century to be included in one of his maps by the noted Flemish cartographer Gerardus Mercator.

MOFFAT CLAN 1129

This design came about after a new clan chief – the first for 420 years – was recognized by Lord Lyon in 1983. A family tartan was introduced and to commemorate early family connections it was based on the Grey Douglas.

The Border Families

THE range of tartans for the great Border 'families' – they never regarded themselves as clans – illustrates how the tartan cult spread south of the Highlands. The historian Thomas Smibert wrote in his 1850 publication *The Clans of the Highlands of Scotland*:

> The Scotts . . . Kers, Elliotts, Armstrongs, Homes, Pringles, Johnstones, Maxwells, Jardines, Kennedies, and the like, were no trifling septs in their day and generation. But neither by them, nor by such great inland houses as the Hamiltons and Hays, were tartan ever worn, assuredly. As little were they ever worn, in all likelihood, by those southern houses, such as the Maclellans, Macullochs, Macdoualls . . . neither they or any of the people south of the Forth and Clyde can be shown to have ever habitually adopted the Highland dress, either in respect of form or materials.
>
> The fighting dress of the Borderer, unlike that of his Highland counterpart, was light armour or other dress as worn by the soldiers of his time, and he had no need of tartan.

Scottish 'reivers' setting out to raid cattle across the border with England – a common pastime in the 16th century

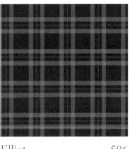

Elliot 596

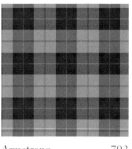

Armstrong 793

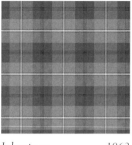

Johnstone 1063

West Point Military Academy 1130

ELLIOT 596

First recorded in the 1880 *Clans Originaux* and then by the Johnstons in their 1906 book *The Tartans of the Clans and Septs of Scotland*, along with many others in use at the time. The colouring is unique among traditional tartans, being described as maroon and blue. The Elliots are a Border clan, founders of the Minto family. The chiefship once belonged to the Elliots of Redheugh but passed to the Elliots of Stobs near Hawick in Roxburghshire. In 1993 Andrew Elliot of Elliot Fine Fabrics in Selkirk produced – for the Chief – an evening version with a smaller sett and the blue changed to midnight blue.

ARMSTRONG 793

The Armstrong name has an almost mythical origin that has the family's progenitor Fairbairn saving the King of Scotland. It's said that after the King's horse had been killed under him in battle, Fairbairn, although dressed in full armour, swung the king up onto his own horse with one arm. The reward was a land grant and the bestowal of the famous Armstrong name.

Among the great Border families, the Armstrongs are said to have been the most feared and at one time could put 3,000 riders into the saddle and wreak havoc on both sides of the Scottish border. Reiving – cattle stealing – was their stock in trade and one of the most notorious and ruthless was Johnnie Armstrong of Gilnockie – 16th-century Gilnockie Tower is a couple of miles north of Canonbie in Dumfries and Galloway and now houses a Clan Armstrong Centre and Museum.

King James V of Scotland, worried by Johnnie's excesses – he ran a protection racket right across the borderland – called him to a meeting near Hawick

in 1530 and summarily hanged him along with forty of his followers. King James VI finished the job in 1611 when he hanged the remaining Armstrong leaders in the marketplace in Newcastle. Amongst them was the last Chief, whose son fled with no trace, so the clan has been 'heidless' ever since.

This Armstrong tartan shows the pragmatic approach the Sobieskis took to tartan design – it's not known which they designed first but the similarity between the structure, if not the colours, of the Armstrong and Kerr tartans can be clearly seen.

JOHNSTONE 1063

The progenitor of the Border Johnstons seems to have been one John who named his Annandale estate John's Toun and whose son called himself Gilbert de Jonistoun, probably signalling his Norman lineage. These were different Johnstons from the Aberdeenshire branch whose origins lay in Perth. which was originally called St John's Town – a fact commemorated by the city's St Johnston football team.

The Border Johnstons grew to be extremely powerful, and their ascendancy threatened the Maxwells and precipitated what has been described as the greatest of all Border feuds, which lasted until the 1620s.

Like so many of the Border tartans, this one was first published in the *Vestiarium Scoticum* in 1842.

WEST POINT MILITARY ACADEMY 1130

In 1983, America's famed West Point Military Academy wished to commemorate General Douglas MacArthur, and Harry Lindlay of Edinburgh was commissioned to design an appropriate tartan. In a simple move he took the

Agnew   182

Maxwell   1500

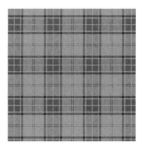

Maxwell Hunting   865

Because the Highlands, the traditional home of tartan, lay some 100 miles to the north, the family ironically referred to the new creation as the MacAgnew tartan.

MAXWELL   1500

The wealthy Maxwells became so powerful in the Borders that the Scottish Crown looked to them to uphold the law in the area and act as a bulwark against English incursions. Their long-running feud with the Johnstons took its toll however and in 1613 Lord Maxwell was beheaded for his murder of the Laird of Johnston five years previously; in 1715 his brother Robert joined the Jacobites and lost his title of Earl of Nithsdale.

Once again *Vestiarium Scoticum* is to be thanked for producing yet another Border tartan. Time bestows much-needed historical credibility on all these 'new boys' of 1842 and now the Maxwell and all its stablemates are venerated tartans.

MAXWELL HUNTING   865

An even newer Maxwell is the hunting version developed by the first President and Chieftain of the US Clan Maxwell Society, Scotty Maxwell. It is the same pattern as the red sett but with the red and green colours switched.

Grey Douglas and in place of the twin black lines on grey, he used gold to represent the uniform braids. The new tartan was used for the first time in the academic year of 1985/86.

AGNEW   182

Another connection with the Douglases is the Agnew tartan. The Lochnaw family of this name were originally appointed hereditary sheriffs of Galloway by King David in 1363 but it wasn't until over 600 years later in 1978 that they acquired a tartan.

Sir Crispin Agnew of Lochnaw Bt. became interested in 1966 in the idea of a tartan for the family but his father – head of the family at the time – was not interested and asked Sir Crispin not to pursue the matter until after his father's death.

When I succeeded in 1975 I was in Northern Ireland with my Regiment, the Royal Highland Fusiliers after which I went to climb Mt. Everest. On my return in June 1976 I approached Kinloch Anderson for advice on tartan design and had a useful discussion with Mr Harry Lindley. My initial thoughts were, that as a lowland family, we should have a design that was more of a tweed, rather than a fussy Highland tartan. At this meeting I settled on the idea of a tartan based on the Douglas with a red stripe from the Agnew livery colours.

I adopted this idea, because I liked the Douglas colours and because the Agnews were granted Lochnaw by William Douglas of Leswalt in 1426 and I thought it a good reason for showing a tartan 'allegiance' to the old Lords of Galloway.

Built in the 14th century by the Maxwell family, Caerlaverock Castle, just seven miles south of Dumfries, now shows the ravages of time and warfare.

Douglas

Probably the most charismatic and romantic figure of the powerful Douglas family from the Borders was Sir James Douglas, regarded by many as the 'greatest Captain' to serve under King Robert the Bruce in the War of Independence and held to be 'the third of Scotland's finest patriots only after Bruce and William Wallace'.

THE following stirring extracts come from a work by James Taylor, MA, DD, FSA published in 1887. Bruce's deathbed statement is given in such remarkable detail that it would be charitable and heartwarming to assume that its contents were *not* Victorian invention but the result of 550 years of Scotland's great tradition of oral history.

In the year 1329, when King Robert was on his deathbed . . . he called to him the brave and gentle knight Sir James Douglas, and said: 'Sir James, my dear friend, none knows better than you how great labour and suffering I have undergone in my day for the maintenance of the rights of this kingdom, and when I was hardest beset I made a vow . . . that if I should live to see the end of my wars, and be enabled to govern this realm in peace and security, I would then set out in person and carry on war against the enemies of my Lord and Saviour to the best of my power.

'Since my body cannot go thither and accomplish that which my heart hath so much

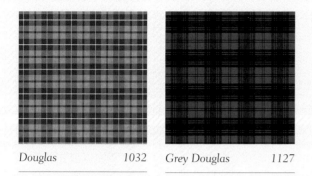

| Douglas | 1032 | Grey Douglas | 1127 |

| Nithsdale | 533 | Murray of Elibank | 340 |

desired, I have resolved to send my heart there in place of my body to fulfil my vow; and I know not any knight more hardy than yourself, or more thoroughly furnished with all knightly qualities for the accomplishment of the vow in place of myself, therefore I entreat thee, my dear and tried friend, that for the love you have to me you will undertake this voyage and acquit my soul of its debt to my Saviour . . . I will, then, that as soon as I am dead you take the heart out of my body and cause it to be embalmed, and carry it along with you and deposit it in the Holy Sepulchre of our Lord, since this poor body cannot go thither.'

The 'Good Sir James' carried the casket and Sir Symon Locard held the key. Unfortunately Sir James was to die in the most heroic of circumstances before completing that journey and Melrose Abbey was destined to become the home for Bruce's heart rather than the Holy Land.

DOUGLAS 1032
This is the accepted Douglas family tartan which first appeared in Wilsons' 1819 list as No. 148 where they used a dark purple in place of today's blue. It's possible that the Douglas label was given to it in the 1820s after the great increase in demand for named tartans following George IV's 1822 visit to Edinburgh.

GREY DOUGLAS 1127
The Grey Douglas came along later, in 1842, when the Sobieskis included it in their *Vestiarium Scoticum*.

A one time Douglas stronghold, Threave Castle probably got its name from the Old Welsh word 'Tref' meaning 'homestead'. This suggests settlement at least as far back as the 500s, before the Old Welsh-speaking residents of Galloway were displaced by Gaels.

NITHSDALE 533
John Hannay had a hand in the design of the Nithsdale tartan, together with Arthur Galt of Hugh Galt & Sons. Dumfries lies in Nithsdale on the River Nith, which stretches over 50 miles from north to south and flows through great swathes of Johnston and Maxwell country.

MURRAY OF ELIBANK 340
Elibank Castle is a few miles from Walkerburn in the Borders and was the home of Sir Gideon Murray, a King's Privy Councillor between 1610 and 1620. Agnes Murray was the last of his unmarried daughters and was said to have been unbelievably ugly and nicknamed 'Muckle Moo'ed [big-mouthed] Meg'. Providence appeared to smile on 'Meg' however in the form of William (Watt) Scott of Harden who was wont to indulge in the Border pursuit of 'reiving' – cattle stealing.

Sir Gideon was forewarned of a raid on his lands and Watt was captured and destined to be hanged the next morning. But Lady Murray intervened and suggested – because he came from a good family – that he be given the choice of being hanged or marrying their daughter 'Meg'. It's said that having seen the hopeful bride, the young William stated that he would rather hang. When the rope was placed around his neck, however, he was persuaded to view her in a more attractive light. He and Meg entered into a very happy marriage which was most fortuitous for the world of tartan and literature, too, because one of their descendants was none other than Sir Walter Scott.

The tartan was first recorded at some time between 1930 and 1950 and its origin is unknown.

Kennedy   5334

Kennedy Dress   1263

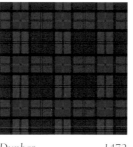

Dunbar   1472

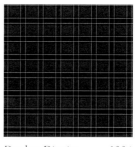

Dunbar District   1236

Jardine of Castlemilk   1432

KENNEDY   5334

Just across the water from Ailsa Craig lies Culzean (pronounced *Cullane*) Castle, the family seat of the Kennedys. About the time that the Kennedy tartan was designed, in the 1830s to '40s, Archibald Kennedy the 12th Earl of Cassilis was created 1st Marquis of Ailsa by his good friend King William IV.

In the eighteenth century, on behalf of the 10th Earl, the famous Scottish architect Robert Adam had extensively repaired and renovated the rambling

Culzean Castle, the family seat of the Kennedys

fortified tower house. In 1945 the 5th Marquis of Ailsa gifted this cliff-top Italianate castle to the National Trust on condition that a top-floor apartment was kept for the use of General Dwight D. Eisenhower in gratitude for his wartime role. That apartment is now run as a small country-house hotel.

The Kennedy tartan first appeared in McIan's 1847 *The Clans of the Scottish Highlands*. Later authors claimed the origins of the Kennedy tartan lay with the Kennedy families that settled in Lochaber who first wore the design. Careful reading of McIan reveals an example of the sloppy research that has so often bedevilled tartan studies and which is then taken as historical fact. McIan states that the design was 'taken from a plaid in possession of Dr. Kennedy, Fort William'. Thus, we can see that a Kennedy in Lochaber had a plaid in this rough design about 1840–5. There is nothing to suggest that this plaid was necessarily old, or that it had always been in the possession of the good doctor, let alone was used more widely by the Kennedys. That said, its use as a clan tartan is as old as many others commonly seen today.

KENNEDY DRESS   1263

Hugh MacPherson, a kilt maker in Edinburgh, designed very many tartans for the world of Highland dancing including this one shown here. His method was to take the conventional clan tartan and substitute white for one of the ground colours. This was confusing enough but he also just added the suffix of 'Dress' to the original tartan name. This gave the impression that the new tartan was approved and many clan and family societies inadvertently adopted the adulterated version as a genuine clan tartan.

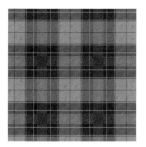

Jardine Dress   2084

Galloway Green   1467

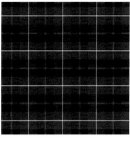

Galloway Red   843

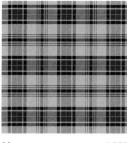

Hanna   1255

DUNBAR 1472

The passage of centuries has seen many Scottish clans and families spread to the four winds and the Dunbars are an excellent example. The present Chief is Sir James Michael Dunbar, 14th Baronet of Mochrum (a parish in south-west Scotland), a dental surgeon, and ex-colonel in the United States Air Force. His father was a jockey and naturalised American, Sir Jean Ivor Dunbar. The origin of the name is said to be from the old barony of Dunbar – 30 miles due east of Edinburgh – and the name was first used in the 11th century.

One of many famous Dunbars was Agnes Randolph, known as Black Agnes, who put up a spirited defence of Dunbar Castle against the English in 1338 during the absence of her husband who was fighting away from home. Legend has it that after a fierce cannon bombardment of the castle she appeared on the ramparts with her maids and joined them in calmly dusting the cannon-ball damage with their lace handkerchiefs!

This sett first appeared in 1842 in *Vestiarium Scoticum* and is the favoured sett for the family. A comparison with the Maxwell shows again the Sobieski Stuarts' use of a common theme to produce a number of 'old' tartans.

DUNBAR DISTRICT 1236

Life is never simple with tartans and here we have another Dunbar tartan, this one from Wilsons of Bannockburn, *c.*1840. Scholars have assumed that Wilsons intended this as a district tartan but it may equally have been so named simply to help it sell.

JARDINE OF CASTLEMILK 1432

This was designed in 1978 and approved by Colonel Jardine, clan Chief. The chiefly house is Jardine of Applegirth, a baronetcy created in 1672; the Jardines of Castlemilk in Dumfriesshire settled there in the early fourteenth century. A 1979 letter from the founder of the Scottish Tartans Society, Capt. Stuart Davidson, says: 'As you know Col. Jardine has always firmly rejected the two Jardine tartans as trade inventions but he now appears to have been pressurised by the family to adopt a Jardine tartan.'

JARDINE DRESS 2084

In stark contrast to the clan tartan this dress version, designed by Strathmore Woollens of Forfar in 1991 and approved by the Chief, is unusually bold and bright and makes for a perfect dress tartan.

GALLOWAY GREEN 1467

Councillor John Hannay was a chiropodist in London's Chelsea and a keen collector and designer of tartans. He is said to have designed this 'everyday tartan' in 1950 with four shades of green and a yellow and red stripe. When it came to be woven by Cree Mills of Newton Stewart, however, it only had two greens and the yellow line was replaced with a white.

GALLOWAY RED 843

Whether Hannay's intention was that this should be a dress version of the Galloway is not known, but it has ended up being an alternative district tartan.

HANNA 1255

Despite being Deputy Mayor of Chelsea, John Hannay found time to become Convenor of the newly formed Clan Hanna Society in 1960. In 1950 he had apparently established the clan tartan from an old kilt in his possession that had been worn by

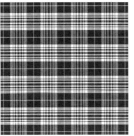

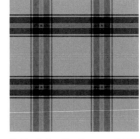

Hanna of Stirlingshire 5150 *Border Bell 370* *Bell of the Borders 1489* *McKerrell of Hillhouse Hunting 1758*

Commander Alex Hannay (1788–1844) and discovered in the proverbial family chest by his descendant Miss Anne Hannay. It's reported that John created the new design based on the old, which had included a red stripe. Why he chose to change the historical sett is not documented.

There are quite a few other Hanna/Hannay tartans but with very few exceptions they're just slight variations on the basic clan tartan.

HANNA OF STIRLINGSHIRE   5150
Very little is known of this tartan except that Lord Lyon's committee looked at it in 1984. It's an excellent illustration of how just a few changes to one tartan can produce what looks like a completely different one.

BORDER BELL   370
This Scottish Bell – as distinct from the next entry, which is the 'American' Bell – was initiated in 1987 by May Roberts (now Madam McKerrell of Hillhouse) and was designed by James Scarlett MBE. It was originally known as 'Bell (Blackethouse)', Blackethouse being the former chiefly home of the Bells, but the Blackethouse reference was removed at the request of the Lord Lyon, who wanted the territorial name reserved for the chief. The tartan was then renamed 'Border Bell'. However, the American-based Clan Bell International Society calls this one 'Bell South'.

BELL OF THE BORDERS   1489
Designed by the American Bob Martin in 1984 for a Col. William Bell of California who, it's believed, was President of Clan Bell International. It suffered a protracted identity crisis: first being called Riverside Bell, then American Bell, then Southern Bell and

finally Bell of the Borders but with a nickname of Dress Bell. William H. Bell penned the following explanation of the colours:

> Black is for the Border and in remembrance of
> our dead,
> Blue is for the sky above and the oceans o'er we
> fled,
> Green is for the Border's hue and the promise
> of nature's plan
> Red is for the blood we've shed, our courage
> and elan
> Yellow is the sunburst,
> Our honor shining bright for all to tell
> That soon, with justice proper
> The reestablishment of Clan Bell!

MCKERRELL OF HILLHOUSE HUNTING   1758
As with many tartans, quite a bit of confusion seems to have been generated about the McKerrell of Hillhouse family tartan because of colour nomenclature, possible misrecording of the thread count by early researchers and then the inability of some computer graphics programs to distinguish between different warps and wefts. The McKerrell of Hillhouse family tartan shown here however is the definitive version recorded in the Lyon Court Books in 1982. Note that the red runs in only one direction and is crossed by a yellow that similarly only runs one way. The earliest illustration of the tartan is in a portrait by de Sange of Robert McKerrell of Hillhouse (1804–75).

McKerrell of Hillhouse
Dress   *6041*

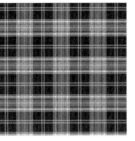

Scottish Borders Tourist
Board   *4040*

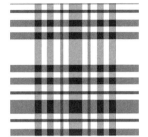

Border Sett   *2458*

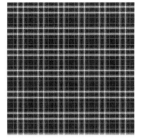

Benson (New England) 6465

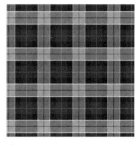

Green Leslie   *1113*

McKerrell of Hillhouse Dress

6041

This was designed by Madam McKerrell of Hillhouse in 1996 and recorded in the Lyon Court Books in 2001.

Scottish Borders Tourist Board

4040

It's difficult to think of a more appropriate corporate identity for a tourist board than its own tartan and in 2000 the Scottish Borders organization went to Lochcarron in Galashiels for this distinctive design.

Border Sett

2458

This offers an amusing example of how a little knowledge can be a dangerous thing. Early researchers quite correctly documented patterns such as this as Border setts and over the ensuing years, many tartan aficionados spoke knowledgeably about the setts or patterns that were special to the Scottish Borders. They eventually found out to their embarrassment that the Border setts had absolutely nothing to do with the Scottish Borders but were the designs used by Wilsons of Bannockburn for the borders or edging on their blankets.

Benson (New England)

6465

This tartan links the Scottish Borders, New England and Alaska and is an excellent example of how many tartanless Scots descendants – long settled in other countries around the globe – choose to have their own tartan designed. Benson was originally a Borders name and some Bensons in Vermont decided upon this design for all of the name wherever they were, and had Molly Manaugh of Alaska weave it for them.

Tartans such as this have a strange status. With no traditional clan or family tartan and an absence of any identifiable clan chief or head of family, the next layer of decision-making would usually be the major clan or family association. If there is none, then it falls to anyone of the name to initiate a tartan but it can't be regarded as an official clan or family tartan, only as a personal tartan which can be worn by all of the name. However, in the world of tartan, age lends respectability and just as with many other historical setts, no doubt this particular one will in a few decades be regarded as the official Benson tartan.

Green Leslie

1113

In 1689 the 25th Regiment of Foot – sometimes known as the Edinburgh Regiment – was raised by David Leslie, 3rd Earl of Leven, and its first action was at the Battle of Killiecrankie on 27 July of that year. This Regiment was to become the famous KOSB, The King's Own Scottish Borderers, and its tartan, the Green Leslie, which first came to notice in the 1850s as the Leslie Hunting, was chosen in memory of David Leslie.

In April 2006 the KOSB amalgamated with The Royal Scots to become a battalion of the newly formed Royal Regiment of Scotland. As a Lowland regiment, the KOSB always wore trews and it will therefore come as a great culture shock that in their new battalion they will, for the first time in their history, wear kilts. Here is just one verse from a poem written during the Korean War by a KOSB soldier, Private Bill Dalziel who went on to win the Military Medal.

Now the Australians they fought like devils
And the Kislies did well I agree
But give me the lads of the tartan trews
The lads of the KOSB!

UNITED STATES, CANADA, AUSTRALIA AND NEW ZEALAND

Regardless of where the Scots emigrated and how well they adapted and coped with the demands of a new life and a new country, they carried with them the spluttering flame of Celtic melancholy – the deep-seated ache for the land that they'd left behind. To quote William Aytoun (1813–65), Professor of Literature at Edinburgh University,

They bore within their breasts the grief that fame can never heal –
the deep, unutterable woe which none save exiles feel.

It's not surprising therefore that, with distance dulling the often tragic reasons for their departure, the early Scots in the New World set about recreating much of what they'd left behind: place names, churches, language, poetry, music, dances, tartans … Such roots don't shrivel with time but grow deeper and stronger and offer increasing stability in a shrinking and insecure world. Today's ever-growing numbers of American, Canadian, Australian and New Zealand tartans are constant and visible reminders of that reassuring legacy.

The Great Smoky Mountains National Park, Tennessee

United States

Alabama   6980

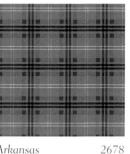

Arizona   5706

Arkansas   2678

The population of the United States is nudging 300 million in 2006 and of those, it's unofficially claimed, between 14 and 20 million are of Scottish extraction. It's hardly surprising therefore that throughout the length and breadth of the US, there are many hundreds of organizations dedicated to celebrating that heritage. One very potent method of doing that is to have a unique State tartan and of the 50 states, 37 have their own – 25 of them official and 12 either unofficial, or in the process of being formally adopted.

ALABAMA   6980

The newest claimant to statehood is the Alabama tartan, designed in 2006 by Joseph Ryan Morrison, member of the planning committee for the first annual Tartan Day celebration in Alabama which will take place in the city of Birmingham in April 2007. The five white stripes represent the region's first flag – the Bonnie Blue Flag which comprised a white, five-pointed star on a blue background; it was later adopted by Texas (the 'Lone Star State') and became an unofficial flag of the Confederate States of America. The bright crimson stripe flanked by the white represents the official state flag, the crimson saltire, and the grey commemorates the state's Confederate heritage.

ARIZONA   5706

Commissioned by a joint committee of the state's Scottish societies in 1995, this was designed by Dr Phil Smith and officially recognized as the Arizona State Tartan by Governor Symington in December of that year. The significance of the colours speaks volumes for the natural resources of this, the 48th state to join the Union in 1912. Green is for the forests that cover half the state; brown is for the desert; azure for copper, white for silver, yellow for gold, red for the Native Americans and the red, white and green stripes from the Mexican flag for the citizens from that neighbouring nation.

ARKANSAS   2678

This official tartan was another one designed by Dr Phil Smith and encompasses the familiar celebration of human and natural resources with the choice of colours: green represents the state's nickname of the 'Natural State', red is for the original settlers, white for the diamonds and black for rich oil reserves. The tartan was approved by Governor Mike Huckabee on 1 September 1998 in the state capital of Little Rock.

Left: The north rim of the Grand Canyon

The Scots in America

It would be difficult to find a more stirring curriculum vitae for the Scot than this extract from George Fraser Black's *Scotland's Mark on America*, published in New York in 1921.

BUT it is perhaps in the intangible things that go to the making of national character that the Scottish contribution to the making of America has been most notable. In 1801, the population of the whole of Scotland was but little over a million and a half, and behind that there were at least eight centuries of national history. Behind that, too, were all the long generations of toil and strife in which the Scottish character was being molded into the forms that Scott and Burns made immortal.

It is a character full of curious contrasts, with its strong predilection for theology and metaphysics on one side, and for poetry and romance on the other. Hard, dry and practical in its attitude to the ordinary affairs of life, it is apt to catch fire from a sudden enthusiasm, as if volatility were its dominant note and instability its only fixed attribute. And so it has come about that side by

side with tomes of Calvinistic divinity, there has been transmitted to Scotsmen an equally characteristic product of the mind of their race – a body of folksong, of ballad poetry, of legend and of story in that quaint and copious Doric speech which makes so direct an appeal to the hearts of men whether they are to the manner born or not. It is surely a paradox that a nation which, in the making, had the hardest kind of work to extract a scanty living from a stubborn soil, and still harder work to defend their independence, their liberties, their faith from foes of their own kindred, should be best known to the world for the romantic ideals they have cherished and the chivalrous follies for which their blood has been shed.

Scots and the American Indians

It may surprise many to learn of the great affinity that existed between some of the early Scots immigrants to North America and the native Americans. Historians cite two major reasons for this: the first is that the social structure of the two cultures was very similar – the Indians had their tribes, the Scots had their clans and both had a chief. Each culture produced fearless and fearsome warriors and the Indians greatly respected the kilted Highlanders that they'd encountered.

The second factor was said to be a fundamental difference between the Scots and English and their treatment of the native population. The English were said to descend upon the Indian territories and demand or take what they wanted. On the other hand, the Scots – perhaps with their inherited egalitarian streak and memories of their own persecution – tended to ask.

The two factors combined to create a remarkable affinity that saw Scots and their descendants become trusted agents, friends, husbands and even – on occasion – tribal chiefs.

The only dedicated tartan museum in the United States is in Franklin, North Carolina

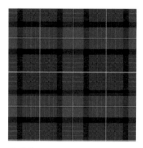

California   2454

CALIFORNIA   2454

This state tartan is based on the Muir and commemorates the famous botanist John Muir (1838–1914) from Dunbar in Scotland. His family emigrated to the United States and there John became a founding father of the world conservation movement, and devoted his life to safeguarding the world's landscapes for future generations. The tartan designers were J. Howard Standing of California and Thomas Ferguson of British Columbia and the Governor was Gray Davis who processed the enabling legislation in July 2003.

It's claimed that the number of Scots descendants in California is the same as the population of the whole of Scotland – 5 million!

CAROLINA   1377

The word Caroline is an adjective traditionally used in connection with Charles I and Charles II and, by extension, any other king called Charles. Part of today's Carolinas had been named Carolina by the Frenchman Ribaut in honour of Charles IX of France, and the English who took possession kept the old name in honour of Charles II.

Below: Enjoying the golden aspen on horseback in Colorado, with Crested Butte in the background

Carolina   1377

Colorado   4554

When it came to a tartan for the Carolinas, Scottish designer, historian and weaver Peter MacDonald suggested that a very slight variation of the Royal Stewart would be appropriate since Charles had belonged to the Stuart/Stewart dynasty. That tartan was officially adopted by North Carolina in 1991 and South Carolina in 2002.

COLORADO   4554

This was designed in 1995 by Rev. John B. Pahls and adopted by the Colorado General Assembly in March 1997. House Joint Resolution 97-1016 described the colour symbolism:

> The crispness of the color blue captures the beauty of the clear Colorado skies and the coolness of forest green renders images of pine and spruce that grace the mountains with dignity . . . The contrasting colors of lavender and white are reflective of the granite mountain peaks and the snow that crowns them in the winter months . . . and are also found in the state flower, the white and lavender columbine. The brilliance of the color gold signifies the vast wealth of mineral resources to which the mining industry was attracted and on which the state's early economy was built; and the color red distinguishes the 'C' on the state flag and signifies the red sandstone soil which gave the area its name Colorado, meaning red in Spanish.

CONNECTICUT   2671

This asymmetric tartan, designed by three professors at Three Rivers Community College in Norwich, Connecticut – Brent A. Maynard (Professor of Nuclear Engineering Technology), Kathleen Swope

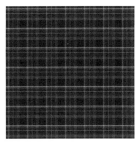

Connecticut   2671

Georgia   794

Hawaii   5163

and Noel Alexis – was adopted and signed into law by Governor John Rowland in May 1995. The blue is for the Long Island sound, green for the forests, red and yellow for the autumn leaves, grey for granite and white for snow – this last colour is clearly offset and symbolizes the irregularity of the Connecticut snowfall.

GEORGIA   794

One of the state's early defenders was the Highland Independent Company of Foot, raised in 1740 and led by a John Mackintosh. Peter MacDonald bore this in mind when designing the Georgia tartan and used the Black Watch – which the Company of Foot were reported as wearing – together with elements of an old Mackintosh tartan. The colours selected were 'blue for beautiful Georgia sky, red for the rich Georgia clay and green for the magnificent forests'. Although designed in 1982 to celebrate the 250th Anniversary of the founding of the state, it wasn't until May 1997 that it was officially adopted.

HAWAII   5163

Hawaii is such a far and exotic location that it's easy to forget that it became the 50th state in 1959. The island group has a surprising number of Scottish societies and there are annual Highland games at famous Waikiki. In 1997 Douglas Herring of the Hawaiian Handweavers Hui designed this tartan, which embodies elements of both Hawaii's heritage and geology: the red and yellow symbolize the monarchy *and* the fire and lava from which the islands arise. Brown is the colour of the lava once it cools and starts to turn into soil, and green represents the plant life that springs from it. Finally, blue is for the sky and the deep surrounding ocean. The tartan hasn't yet been officially accepted by the state Legislature but it's so firmly established now that it can only be a matter of time.

Below: *The Georgia tartan on a handloom*

Left: *Molokini Maui – a partially sunken volcano crater that has formed a volcanic islet just off the coast of Maui in the Hawaiian island group*

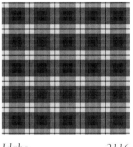

Idaho   2116

Illinois   2051

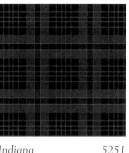

Indiana   5251

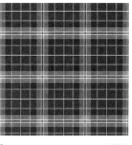

Iowa   6051

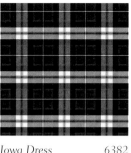

Iowa Dress   6382

IDAHO   2116

It's reported that in the early 1860s when the US Congress was considering organizing a new territory in the Rocky Mountains, an eccentric lobbyist called George Willing invented the name Idaho, claiming that in the Native American Shoshone language it was 'eed-a-hoo' and meant 'gem of the mountains'. Despite his hoax being discovered, the name has stuck.

Jan Crook, a weaver from California, designed the Idaho tartan in 1989 in preparation for the state's centennial in 1990. Based on the Black Watch, the blue represents the lakes, the green is for the pine forests, white the snow-capped mountains, brown the desert areas and the Idaho potato, and red is for the minerals and the Native Americans. Although widely used, this tartan has never been given any official status by the Legislature.

ILLINOIS   2051

Another tartan that is widely regarded as the state tartan but which has never been officially adopted. 1990 was the 150th anniversary of the founding of the charitable organization the Illinois St Andrew Society, and to mark the occasion Francis Gillan designed this tartan, the colours of which reflect the Illinois state flag, the St Andrew's flag of Scotland and the colours of the Chicago sports teams.

INDIANA   5251

This is sometimes called the Indiana Cardinal and is the third tartan in a row with an uncertain future. Designed by Jan Crook again, this time in 1992, it's named after the Indiana state bird and, for many years, was the nearest that the state had to its own tartan. Lately, however, two other contenders have appeared and what the outcome will be is not known.

IOWA   6051

There's no argument about the status of this tartan, designed by Mark Osweiler, for it was approved by the Scottish Heritage Society of Iowa (SHSI) and officially accepted by the Iowa State Legislature in April 2004. The idea originated with the SHSI and a total of 30 designs were submitted to the vote. This sett won the day and a dress tartan was also selected. Blue is for the sky, rivers and lakes; green for the fields, black and brown for the rich soil; white for the snow; red for the barns and the state flower which is the wild rose and yellow for the corn and the Goldfinch – the state bird.

IOWA DRESS   6382

A nail-biting railway bridge in the Des Moines river valley of Iowa

Scottish Societies

As the Romantic Revival of the Highlands got under way, Scottish societies of all kinds rose in its wake: Highland, Caledonian, St Andrew's, Burns. Some of these were of a charitable nature, for the Highlands were still suffering from the after-effects of the '45, the Clearances and periodic famines.

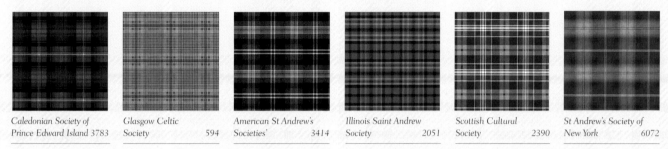

Caledonian Society of Prince Edward Island 3783   Glasgow Celtic Society 594   American St Andrew's Societies' 3414   Illinois Saint Andrew Society 2051   Scottish Cultural Society 2390   St Andrew's Society of New York 6072

SOME set out to preserve their conceptions of the old Highland way of life and naturally, they adopted tartan, some using existing patterns and some devising their own individual setts. In 1835 at the request of a friend in Canada, James Logan designed a tartan for the Caledonian Society of Prince Edward Island (3783); in about 1847 Wilsons of Bannockburn produced a design for the Stirling and Bannockburn Caledonian Society which has since become the Stirling District tartan shown in the Lowlands section; the Glasgow Celtic Society also had its own tartan (594).

The USA was, of course, the favourite destination for Scots emigrants. The 1776–1976 American Bicentennial tartan was cannily recycled to become the American St Andrew's Societies' (3414). Despite being founded by Scots in 1840 for philanthropic purposes, it was not until its 150th anniversary that the Illinois Saint Andrew Society (2051) designed its own tartan – the colours representing the flag of St Andrew, the State of Illinois and various sports teams in the state. Another Illinois charity for members with Scottish interests was the Scottish Cultural Society (2390).

That was followed in 2000 by the St Andrew's Society of Rhode Island (2659) but the nearby St Andrew's Society of New York waited until its 250th anniversary in 2003 before it acquired its own unique tartan (6072).

Dr Herbert and Mrs Ethyl Macneil founded the Council of Scottish Clans & Associations in 2000 and that organization's tartan was appropriately based on the 'red-line Macneil' (3857).

Ten thousand miles to the east lies the Indonesian archipelago and two St Andrew's tartans designed in 2000 for the thriving Java Saint Andrew Society – the Hunting and the Dress (4105 and 5401). Up to the north-east, the Kansai St Andrew's Society of central Japan has two tartans – one for the society (3987) and one for the society Highland games (3988) held annually in Kobe. The Russian capital, almost 5,000 miles to the west, is home to the tartan for the Gaelic Society of Moscow (6494).

In this modern age where national boundaries and characteristics are shrunk by travel, blurred by migration and erased by politics, one's roots assume even more importance, and for Scots and their descendants tartan can supply a unique and comforting umbrella that identifies and unites them in a common purpose.

Council of Scottish Clans & Associations 3857   Java Saint Andrew Society 4105   Java Saint Andrew Society 5401   Kansai St Andrew's Society 3987   Kansai Highland Games 3988   Gaelic Society of Moscow 6494

KENTUCKY 2667

The blue and grey in this official Kentucky state tartan represents the Union and Confederate uniforms and marks the fact that two American presidents were born in the state – Lincoln and Davis, who led opposing sides during the American civil war. The tartan was designed in 2000 by two members of the Scottish Society of Louisville – Rupert Ferguson and Pat Murray-Schweitzer. The blue and green represent the state's bluegrass – a bluish-green grass that is grown for forage. Blue also represents the Ohio and Mississippi rivers and the state's twin lakes, Barkely and Kentucky, which stretch for 184 miles and are the largest man-made lakes in the world. The state bird is the Cardinal, marked by the red, which also symbolizes the blood spilled by Kentuckians who gave their lives defending their nation. Yellow is for the state flower, the Goldenrod, and black represents two major economic resources in the state – oil and coal. Finally, white is for goodness and valour.

LOUISIANA 4126

Named after Louis XIV of France, Louisiana has been governed under ten different flags since 1541 and is a fascinating multi-cultural mix. It's interesting

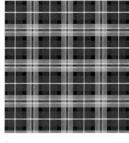

| Kentucky | 2667 | Louisana | 4126 |

to note that when Governor Mike Foster signed the enabling bill for the tartan in 2001, also attending were members of the Caledonian Society of Baton Rouge, St Andrew Society of Baton Rouge, Celtic Society of Louisiana, Caledonian Society of New Orleans, Caldeonian Society of Acadiana, New Orleans Pipes and Drums, Caledonian Society of the Northshore, St Andrew's Society of Louisiana, Members of the Board of the Highland Games of Louisiana, and Baton Rouge Irish Society! The designer was Joe McD. Campbell of the Caledonian Society of Baton Rouge and the passage to legislation was greatly facilitated by Randall Stevenson and Representative Charles MacDonald. Blue is for the sky, lakes, bayous, rivers and waterways, green is for

A carriage in front of the Royal Café, New Orleans

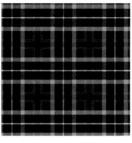

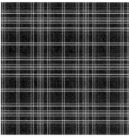

| Maine Dirigo | 3068 | Maryland | 5920 | Massachusetts | 4543 | Michigan Up North | 3473 |

agriculture and forests, white is for rice, sugar cane, cotton and the magnolias and black is for petroleum and natural resources.

MAINE DIRIGO   3068

'Dirigo' means 'I lead' in Latin and is the motto of the state of Maine. The original 'Maine' tartan was the oldest state tartan in America (albeit reportedly unofficial), having been designed in 1964 by Sol Gillis of Yarmouth in the nearby Canadian province of Nova Scotia. It disappeared from sight for many years and was then rediscovered in 1987 and copyrighted by a private company. This appeared to cause problems and the original tartan was modified by the St Andrew's Society of Maine and accepted as the state tartan in 2001. The colours reflect the natural landscapes of the state.

MARYLAND   5920

Founded in 1634, Maryland was named after Queen Henrietta Maria, wife of King Charles I of England and Scotland. The Maryland tartan was designed in 2003 by Cynthia Balfour-Traill of Woodsboro Maryland to commemorate the centenary of the adoption of the Maryland state flag. The design incorporates colours from that flag with the addition of blue for the United States Naval Academy at Annapolis and azure (light blue) for the waters of Chesapeake Bay. At the time of writing the tartan has not yet been officially approved but the legislative wheels are said to be in motion.

MASSACHUSETTS   4543

The first state tartan design was by Nicholas Steward in 1993 but for some reason it never became official. The one that *did*, in 2003, was designed by John R. Austin, a lifetime Massachusetts resident. Its

production is looked after by the St Andrews Society of Massachusetts and the proceeds go towards the Massachusetts Scholarship Fund. The blues in the tartan are for the Atlantic Ocean and all the reservoirs, rivers, and ponds. The green is for the Boston Hills, Worcester Hills and the Berkshire Mountains. The tans are the long beach line, from the North Shore to the South Shore; Cape Cod, the Islands, and Buzzards Bay. Finally the red is for the apple and cranberry harvests.

MICHIGAN UP NORTH   3473

This tartan was designed in 2005 by Kati Meek, a well-known weaver and craft author from Alpena on Lake Huron. There are no formal plans yet for its adoption but as with so many tartans, over a period of 'use and wont' they often gain official acceptance.

The 5-mile long Mackinac Bridge, bridging the Straits of Mackinac, from Mackinaw City, to St Ignace Michigan

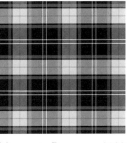

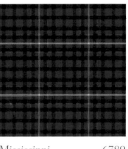

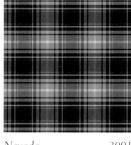

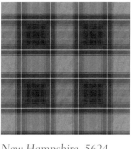

Minnesota 3930	*Minnesota Dress* 3929	*Mississippi* 6789	*Nevada* 3091	*New Hampshire* 5624

MINNESOTA 3930

The state name comes from the Dakota Indian 'Minisota', 'sky-tinted waters', and with 15,291 lakes of over 10 acres, it's not difficult to see where the inspiration for that might have come from!

The decision was made to inaugurate a state tartan, and in 2001 each of the fourteen Scottish organizations forming the Minnesota Tartan Day committee chose a colour. The first choice was blue for the 'sky-tinted waters'. The dark pink and the yellow came from the state flower, the protected Lady's Slipper. Green was for the state tree which is the Norway pine; black represented the Common Loon (the state bird); the white was for milk (the state beverage), rice (the state grain) and snow. In addition to representing the Lady's Slipper, the yellow was for maize, the autumn colours and the 'golden opportunities' of Minnesota.

Armed with those, Minnesotan Mark Osweiler crafted this sett, which was formally adopted by the State Senate in February 2002. Mark also designed a companion dress version.

Paddle steamers – the iconic image of the great Mississippi River

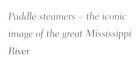

MINNESOTA DRESS 3929

MISSISSIPPI 6789

This state's tartan was designed in 2005 by Karen Green in the aftermath of the horrendous flooding of many parts of the state. Dark green is for the never-ending forests of pine and the evergreen leaves of the state tree, the Magnolia. Light green is for the lustrous leaves of the Great Southern Oaks. Dark blue for the waters of the world-famous Mississippi River and the many lakes within the state. Red is from the state flag and for blood shed in times past. White represents the beautiful sands of the Mississippi Gulf Coast and the 'cotton fields of home' and yellow is for the heart of the Magnolia (the state flower). The official adoption process for the new tartan has been initiated and the 'Magnolia State' should soon have its own tartan to add to the list of state symbols.

NEVADA 3091

Designed by a distant relative of Poland's Lech Walesa, California-born Richard Zygmunt Pawlowski ('Ziggy'), and officially adopted by the state in May 2001. The blue and silver represent Nevada's state colours. Red is for the Virgin Valley black fire opal, the official state precious gemstone, and the red rock formations of southern Nevada. Yellow is for the sagebrush, the state flower; white is for the name of the state – 'Nevada' is a Spanish word meaning 'snowy' or 'snow clad' and is a reference to the US Sierra Nevada mountain range that runs down the eastern border of California, overlooking Nevada.

NEW HAMPSHIRE 5624

In 1623 a Captain John Mason from Portsmouth in Hampshire (England) arrived at the mouth of the

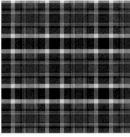

New Mexico   2522   Ohio   651

Piscataqua River to establish a fishing colony, so it takes no great leap to decide where the name New Hampshire came from! With him was a Scot named David Thomson but it took another 370 years before the idea of a New Hampshire tartan appeared. Initially the plan was that it would celebrate the 20th anniversary of the New Hampshire Highland Games but it escalated from there and the tartan was adopted as the official state tartan in May 1995.

Ralf Hartwell, a hand-weaver from Newton, New Hampshire, designed it and the purple represents the state bird and the state flower – the Purple Finch and the Purple Lilac. Green is for the forests, black the granite mountains, white the snow and the red commemorates all the 'state heroes'.

NEW MEXICO   2522

Sometimes the path to acquiring a state tartan is strewn with boulders and that was certainly the case with this sett. Designer Ralf L. Stevenson of Bernalillo County, New Mexico, circumnavigated some and pushed others out of the way to get this tartan onto the statute books in 2003.

The tartan was originally designed back in 1996 when it was known simply as the New Mexico Tartan. With its new official status and name – the State of New Mexico Tartan – it can be freely reproduced after Ralf surrendered the copyright to the public domain. Blue was included for the all-encompassing sky, green for the state's plant life and forests, gold for the minerals and desert and red for the original 'cultural providers'.

OHIO   651

The trustees of the Ohio Scottish Games were far-sighted in 1983 when they had their own tartan designed by one of their trustees, Mary Jayne

McMichael Fishbach. Like quite a few other states, the official state bird is the Cardinal – a North American member of the Finch family – and that gave Mary the red. Blue was for the state's waterways from the Ohio River to Lake Eyrie.

White represented the major cities, azure (light blue) was dedicated to the eight US presidents who came from Ohio. The azure/blue combination represents Ohio as the birthplace of light, flight and the first man on the moon, namely Thomas Edison, The Wright Brothers and Neil Armstrong. Gold is from the State Seal and represents Ohio's leadership in agriculture. No mention was made of the green but it was no doubt connected with the Ohio flora. The tartan was first used on the 1983 Games programme but has never officially become the state tartan.

Las Vegas in Nevada, gambling capital of the world

Oregon 5743

Pennsylvania 3130

Rhode Island 2659

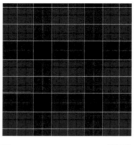

Tennessee 3067

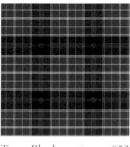

Texas Bluebonnet 852

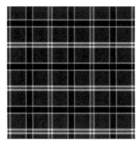

Oklahoma 2429

OKLAHOMA 2429

Ex-US Marine, Treasury Department official and President Emeritus of United Scottish Clans of Oklahoma, the late Jerrel Ray Murray of Oklahoma City designed this tartan with Polly Wittering of the Scottish weavers House of Edgar in 1998. The colours chosen of red, white, black and gold on a field of blue are said to be representative of the people, agricultural and manufactured products and natural resources of Oklahoma. One wonders if the red came from the origin of the name Oklahoma, which was formed from two Choctaw Indian words: 'okla' meaning 'people' and 'humma' meaning red. The tartan was officially adopted by the Oklahoma House of Representatives on 6 April 1999.

OREGON 5743

This tartan was designed in 2002 by Robbie Harding of the Caledonian Society and the High Desert Celtic Society and declared the official tartan of the State of Oregon in April 2003 by Governor Ted Kulongski. The blue represents the state flag, Oregon's rivers and the Pacific Ocean. From the flag also, comes the gold which represents the state's agriculture. White is for the snow-topped mountains, tan is for the deserts and grasslands, azure (light blue) symbolizes the Oregon sky and its streams, creeks, lakes and wetlands. Black is for the obsidian buttes – hills of volcanic glass that are said to have been used for tool making for over 14,000 years.

PENNSYLVANIA 3130

This tartan was designed in 1993 by the late William (Bill) H. Johnston of Skippack PA. Bill based it on the Black Watch tartan to honour that regiment's success at the Battle of Bushy Run in 1763, which ensured that Pennsylvania did not fall under French control. Like the state flag, the background of the tartan is blue, incorporating green, yellow and a touch of red – colours also used in the Great Seal of the Commonwealth of Pennsylvania. A House Bill to designate it as the official state tartan was drawn up in 2001 but after no further action was taken the matter 'died' at the end of the session in 2002.

RHODE ISLAND 2659

The state of Rhode Island is not actually an island and the most credible explanation for the name appears to be that it is derived from Roodt Eylandt, old Dutch for 'red island'. This was apparently the description given to largest island in Narragansett Bay by Dutch explorer Adriaen Block (1567–1627) because of the red clay on the island's shore.

An Act was introduced on 6 April (Tartan Day) in the year 2000: 'The St Andrews Society of RI, Inc. is hereby authorized to create, authenticate and register, at the sole expense of the Society, the official tartan of the state, hereinafter to be called "The State of Rhode Island Tartan."' The designer was Claire Donaldson of the House of Edgar in Perth, Scotland.

TENNESSEE 3067

The Tennessee tartan was adopted by the state of Tennessee on 28 March 1999, having been developed by an organization called the 'Heart of Tennessee Scottish Celebration' in conjunction with all the other Scottish societies in the state. The significance of the colours are: green for agriculture; blue for the famous Smoky Mountains; purple for the state flower which is the Iris; red for the sacrifices of the veterans and pioneers in the state and white to symbolize the Three Grand Divisions of the State of Tennessee – Eastern, Middle and Western.

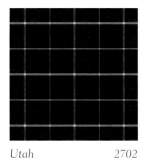

Utah 2702

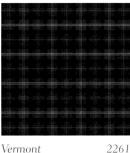

Vermont 2261

TEXAS BLUEBONNET 852

In 1983 June Prescott McRoberts (1922–99) of Saledo in Texas designed this sett as the Sesquicentennial Tartan, basing the colours and proportions on the state flower, the Bluebonnet, a member of the lupin family which changes colour with the passing of time, the brim becoming flecked with wine red. The design proved very popular and was officially adopted as the Texas State Tartan in May 1989.

UTAH 2702

The prevailing opinion on the derivation of 'Utah' seems to favour it being a Native American word meaning 'mountain-top dwellers' or 'those who dwell high up'. The state tartan was commissioned by Gary Bryant in 1995 and designed by Dr Phil Smith, who based it on the Logan tartan – Ephraim Logan being a 'mountain man' and the first American of Scottish descent to leave a permanent mark upon Utah. On visiting Cache Valley in northern Utah in 1824 Logan gave his clan name to the river flowing through it. The tartan was officially adopted by the state in 1996 and Governor Michael Leavitt signed it into law on 28 February.

VERMONT 2261

In 1993 Lilias MacBean Hart of Wilmington, Vermont, teamed up with weaver Andrew Elliot of the Scottish Borders town of Selkirk to design the Vermont tartan. They used the colours from the Vermont landscapes throughout the seasons: the greens of spring and summer, the reds of fall, the white snow of the winter and the dark blue of the moonlit sky. The tartan was officially adopted by the state in 2003 and a dress version was later designed by Andrew Elliot.

Kirkin' the Tartan

WHILE the Kirkin' o' the Tartan service celebrates Scotland and a Scottish heritage, it is truly a Scottish-American custom. If one searches the Web for information, stories abound of the Kirkin's roots being in days of the Act of Proscription, when the wearing of the kilt was banned. According to the legend, Highlanders hid pieces of tartan and brought them to church to be secretly blessed at a particular point in the service.

In his famous collection of Highland folklore, prayers, charms and omens, the *Carmina Gadelica*, Alexander Carmichael does list a prayer for the 'Consecration of the Cloth', but no mention is made of it originating from the days following the '45 or being associated with outlawed tartan. While making for a rather romantic legend, there seems to be no credible source for such a tale. The real history of the Kirkin' service is all-American, with a Scottish twist.

The Rev Peter Marshall, originally from Coatbridge, Scotland, was the pastor of the New York Avenue Presbyterian Church in Washington, DC, and served as Chaplain of the United States Senate before his untimely death in 1949. During the Second World War he held prayer services at New York Avenue to raise funds for British war relief. At one of the services (either in April 1941 or May 1943), he gave a sermon entitled 'the Kirkin' o' the Tartans' – and thus a legend was born.

Kirkin's are held year-round, but St Andrew's Day (30 November) and Tartan Day (6 April) tend to be very popular dates – Kirkin's are also sometimes held at Scottish games and gatherings in an outdoor setting, ironically reminiscent of the secret outdoor services (conventicles) of the Covenanters in Lowland Scotland.

Today, many Scottish, Caledonian and St Andrew's Societies across the United States and Canada hold Kirkin' of the Tartans; while most seem to be in Presbyterian churches, one may also find them in churches of other denominations.

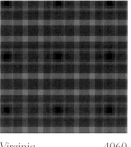

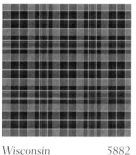

Vermont Dress 4348	*Virginia* 4060	*Washington* 2133	*Wisconsin* 5882

VERMONT DRESS 4348

VIRGINIA 4060

A frequent visitor to the United States, Andrew was also inspired by the colours that he saw when travelling through the Blue Ridge Mountains in Shenandoah, Virginia, and returned home to Scotland to capture them in weave.

WASHINGTON 2133

The state tartan was designed in 1988 by Vancouver, USA country dancers Margaret McLeod van Nus and Frank Cannonita. The occasion was the Washington State Centennial and the colours used were: green for the rich forests (Washington is known as the 'Evergreen State'); blue for the lakes, rivers and Pacific ocean; white for the snow-capped mountains, red for the apple and cherry crops, yellow for the wheat and grain crops and black for the eruption of Mount St Helens. The tartan was formally adopted in 1991 by the State of Washington legislature and thus became the official State Tartan.

WISCONSIN 5882

A great driving force on the Scottish scene in the US, Robert McWilliam of Whitefish Bay, WI, initiated the idea of a state tartan with his friend Dr Phil Smith, who submitted a number of tartan designs based on his discussions with Bob. From that selection the winner was chosen by a committee from the Milwaukee Saint Andrew Society. The significance of the colours is as follows: brown is for the fur trade, grey for the lead mining in the south-west corner of the state. Green is for the lumber industry and Wisconsin's Great Pine Forest; blue is for the two Great Lakes (Michigan and Superior) bordering Wisconsin which generate the state's maritime trade and its fishing and tourism industries. Yellow is for the dairy and brewing sectors and red is for the University of Wisconsin, which plays a vital research and development role in the state.

The Chippewa River & Red Cedar Trail in western Wisconsin

Canada

Alberta   2055

British Columbia   808

Manitoba   144

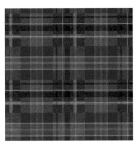

New Brunswick   1880

Canada's ten provinces and three territories combine to make up the world's second largest country in area and were an early and powerful magnet for Scots explorers, adventurers, entrepreneurs and emigrants. Of those thirteen provinces and territories only the relatively new Inuit (First Nation/Eskimo) territory of Nunavut doesn't yet have its own tartan.

ALBERTA   2055
One of Canada's three prairie provinces, Alberta's tartan was designed by Alison Lamb and Ellen Neilsen, two ladies from the Edmonton Rehabilitation Society – a voluntary agency providing work for handicapped students learning to operate handlooms. Adopted by the Provincial Legislature in March 1961, the green represents the forests; the gold is for the wheat and sunshine; the blue is for the lakes and skies; the black for the oil and coal and the pink for Wild Rose – the provincial emblem.

BRITISH COLUMBIA   808
This tartan was designed by Earl K. Ward of Victoria in 1967 as part of the 1966–7 centennial celebrations marking the creation of the province as one colony, and in 1974 it was officially adopted as the provincial tartan. The Pacific Dogwood is the official flower of the province and is represented by white in the tartan. Green is for the BC forests which cover an area twice as big as all of the New England states and New York State. Blue is for the Pacific Ocean, red is for Canada's national emblem of the maple leaf and gold is for the sun and the crown in the provincial flag.

MANITOBA   144
The designer of this tartan was Hugh Kirkwood Rankine, who was born in Winnipeg of Scottish parents. It's said that he became interested in tartan during a leave in Scotland during World War II, and on his return learned how to weave and in time produced this 'history in cloth' which was given Royal Assent in 1962.

The red squares represent the Red River Settlement; the green squares signify the natural resources of the province; the azure blue squares represent Lord Selkirk, the founder of the Red River Settlement, and the dark green lines are for Manitoba's multi-cultural population.

NEW BRUNSWICK   1880
This Atlantic seaboard province acquired its own official tartan in 1959. The design came from the Loomcrofters company in Gagetown – a pretty village on the Saint John River. The colours are forest green for the lumbering; meadow green for

A Canola (rapeseed) field in the prairies of Manitoba

Newfoundland   1543

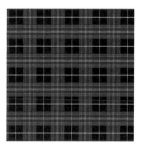

Northwest Territories   662

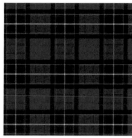

Nova Scotia   1713

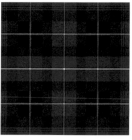

Ontario   6627

Prince Edward Island   918

agriculture; blue for the coastal and inland waters; and an interweaving of gold, symbol of the province's potential wealth. The red blocks signify the loyalty and devotion of the early Loyalist settlers and the New Brunswick Regiment. Another observer adds that the brown band commemorates the 'beaver' from Lord Beaverbrook, the press baron who commissioned the first weaving. Although not born there, he published his first newspaper in the Province at the age of 13 and always regarded it as home.

NEWFOUNDLAND   1543

There are two names connected with the official provincial tartan – Louis Anderson, recorded in old records as the designer, and St Johns clothing-store-owner Sam Wilansky, mostly referred to as the developer. Perhaps both are correct and the designer handed over to the marketing specialist. There seems to be agreement on the year however – 1955 – and on the significance of the colours. Gold represents the sun's rays, green the pine-clad hills, white the snow, brown the minerals in the Province and red to commemorate the Royal Standard of her British origins.

NORTHWEST TERRITORIES   662

Mrs Janet Anderson Thomson first proposed the idea of an NWT tartan after attending an RCMP ball in Yellowknife in 1966 and seeing the official piper dressed rather drably. After having been given the go-ahead Mrs Thomson enlisted the help of Hugh MacPherson of Edinburgh. She chose the colours and Hugh produced three draft designs from which this one was chosen by an official committee. Green represents the forests, white the frozen Arctic Ocean, blue the Northwest Passage,

gold the mineral wealth of the NWT and the red-orange, which she describes as 'autumn colours', represents the barren lands or 'Arctic prairies'. The tartan also contains a thin black line representing the northern treeline. The tartan was officially unveiled at the 48th Session of the Territorial Council in January 1973.

NOVA SCOTIA   1713

The Atlantic province of Nova Scotia – New Scotland – was first mentioned in 1621 on a land

Right: Re-enacting the changing of the guard in Halifax, Nova Scotia

charter. Appropriately, this is the oldest provincial tartan in Canada and was designed in 1953 almost by accident. As President of the Halifax Weavers' Guild, Mrs Bessie Murray designed a trade display on sheep rearing. In it, a shepherd wore a tartan and to avoid showing favouritism she designed a completely new one that proved to be so popular that in 1963 it was adopted as the official provincial tartan. The colours represent the blue of the sea and sky; the dark and light greens of the evergreens and deciduous trees; the white of the rocks and coastline surf; the gold of Nova Scotia's Royal Charter and the red from the lion rampant on the Province's crest.

ONTARIO   6627

Up until 2000 the accepted – but unofficial – tartan for the province appeared to be one called the Ensign of Ontario – a fairly simple sett designed back in

1965. However, championed by Bill Murdoch, member of the Ontario Parliament, a new provincial tartan was designed in 2000 by Jim MacNeil, Chairman of Scottish Studies at Ontario's University at Guelph. A complicated sett, it fell foul of an inaccuracy in the parliamentary private bill which resulted in a six-year delay in getting it officially recognized.

Colours include red and white with three shades of green and two of blue. The greens symbolize the forests and fields of Ontario and the blues depict the huge expanses of water in the province. The First Nations (Canadian Indians) of Ontario are represented by the red, and the sky over the province is depicted by white.

PRINCE EDWARD ISLAND   918

Close to and once part of Nova Scotia, Prince Edward Island lies just north of its old 'parent' in the

Above: Peace and quiet in the solitude of an Ontario lake

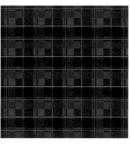

Quebec 1949

Saskatchewan 1817

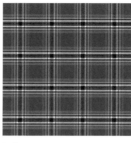

Yukon 2129

huge Gulf of St Lawrence. With its population predominantly of Scottish extraction it's not surprising that an official tartan design competition was held in 1960, which was won by Mrs Jean Reid of Covehead. The colours she chose were described as follows: 'Red for the warmth and glow of the fertile soil, green for the field and tree, yellow and brown for Autumn and white for the surf or a summer snow . . . rust, green, yellow and white.'

QUEBEC 1949

Scottish immigrants first settled in Quebec over 400 years ago and are regarded as one of the founding peoples of the province. Although the Quebec tartan has never been officially adopted, the concept of an annual Tartan Day on 6 April has, so perhaps it's only a matter of time. The designers of the Plaid du Québec circa 1965 are recorded as Rotex Limited, believed to be a clothing manufacturer. The structure and colours of the tartan are based on the three horizontal divisions of the provincial shield.

SASKATCHEWAN 1817

The last of the three prairie provinces, Saskatchewan is half forest and half farmland and has over 100,000 lakes, rivers and marshes. The tartan was designed in 1961 by Mrs F.L. Bastedo, wife of the Lieutenant Governor of Saskatchewan, and has seven colours – the predominant gold representing prairie wheat; brown for the summerfallow (the traditional practice of leaving land fallow over a growing season); green for the forests; red for the provincial flower, the Western Prairie Lily; yellow for the Rapeseed Flower and the Sunflower; white for snow; and black for oil and coal.

YUKON 2129

The Yukon Tartan Act was passed in 1984 and this tartan – designed in 1965 by Janet Couture of Faro – was fully accredited as the official provincial tartan. Faro is a tiny village of 400 situated in the 'overwhelming wilderness of the Campbell Region' in country where 'in winter, ice bridges replace ferries'. The symbolism of the colours has been lyrically described:

The crystalline blue background represents Yukon's sparkling, glacier-fed waters and its clear mountain skies. Magenta reflects the colours of the Yukon's floral emblem, the Firewood of late summer. Green is symbolic of Yukon's great expanses of wilderness forest and purple symbolizes the majestic thrust of mountains into the northern sky. White represents the purity of the winter snow that crowns the peaks and blankets the alpine meadows. The yellow represents the long, soft evenings of the midnight sun and the Yukon's famous deposits of gold.

Such an evocative description makes selling up and emigrating to the Yukon an overwhelmingly attractive prospect!

Australia and New Zealand

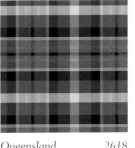

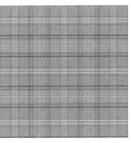

Australia 611	*Queensland* 2618	*New South Wales* 2492

Despite having ample justification to 'splash out' on new tartans over the past 200 years, both Australia and New Zealand have been very restrained, and the number of new sets for both countries totals only about 50. Here is a small selection of the more notable ones.

AUSTRALIA 611

The South Australian Heritage Council mounted a design competition in the early 1980s for a national tartan for Australia and the winning entry was from John Reid, a Melbourne architect. He based his pattern on the MacQuarrie to commemorate Lachlan MacQuarrie, the first Governor of Australia (see also page 82), and he incorporated the colours most used by the native Aborigines – ochre, red/brown, black, white and cobalt blue. The result was a most distinctive and attractive 'un-Scottish' tartan that showed just how flexible the art form can be.

QUEENSLAND 2618

The Queensland state tartan was designed and woven in 1995 by the late Jack Allen of Bundaberg – a coastal city adjacent to the southern tip of the Great Barrier Reef. Royal blue was one of the colours used by Jack to represent the reef and white and light blue signified the sparse cloud in the clear winter skies; yellow was for the sun and sand on the legendary Queensland beaches and green was for the inland tropical forests. Finally, the important sugar cane flower gave the lilac, and the state flower of the Cooktown Orchid provided the crimson.

NEW SOUTH WALES 2492

Designed by Betty and Bradley Johnston of Murrumbateman, it was said to have been originally produced to raise funds for two charities – the Cerebral Palsy Association of Australia and the Motor Neurone Association of Australia. However, it was officially launched as the state tartan on 4 May 2000 at Glen Innes. The red represents the colour of the Waratah, the state flower, and the St George cross on the New South Wales coat of arms. The gold represents the lion and stars on the arms and the colour of the national flower, the Wattle.

No tartan on display in this archetypal Aussie beach scene

Tasmania 2498

Victoria 2509

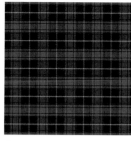

New Zealand 5790

Otago 2317

Dunedin 2114

TASMANIA 2498

Just like its Scottish namesake, the lovely old Tasmanian town of Bothwell lies on its own River Clyde and was the first community to rear a herd of Aberdeen Angus cattle *and* lay the island's first golf course. Appropriately it was also home to Lamont Weaving where Isabella Lamont Shorock designed and wove the Tasmanian state tartan in 1988. The blue-green-grey, the rich red and the yellows are all colours familiar to Tasmanians and found in the deep red soils, Blue Gums and Wattles of the highland and midland landscapes.

VICTORIA 2509

As Australia's leading tartan designer, Betty Johnston turned her attention in 1998 to the state of Victoria, and seven years after she produced this sett, the state government initiated proceedings for its official adoption.

The pink is from the state's floral emblem, the Pink Heath flower, and the blue has its origin in the Eureka Stockade Flag, commemorating a short-lived but important gold miners' revolt in 1854 .

NEW ZEALAND 5790

Helen Clark, the Prime Minister of New Zealand, and the President of the Piping & Dancing Association of NZ, the late Frank MacKinnon, launched the New Zealand Tartan at the country's parliament on 26 February 2003.

OTAGO 2317

The official district tartan for the Otago region on South Island, designed in 1996 by Vilma Ruth Nelson to commemorate the early settlers to Otago — mostly crofters and shepherds from Scotland.

Many other nationalities also came to seek their fortunes in the goldfields of Otago and stayed to form the region's diverse ethnic footprint.

DUNEDIN 2114

The early Scottish settlers are also remembered with this 1988 tartan from Vilma Nelson as they were the first settlers from the Free Church of Scotland who stepped ashore on the 23 March 1848, at Otago Harbour, after a voyage of 116 days. It was at the upper end of this harbour that they established the first settlement which was to become the City of Dunedin, sometimes known as the Edinburgh of the South. The white lines represent the first two ships; the blue strips the sea they crossed; the green for new pastures; the gold for crops grown. The red signifies blood ties left behind and the black, sadness for loved ones missed.

WAIPU 6510

'A proud Scottish history and superb surfing characterise the little town of Waipu' reads one website's introduction to this community on the east coast of Northland – the most northerly of New Zealand's large islands. It was at this spot in the 1850s that seven sailing ships anchored with their immigrant cargoes of Scots settlers after an epic voyage from Nova Scotia. This tartan was designed to celebrate the sesquicentennial of their arrival. There are seven colours in the tartan, one for each ship that anchored out beyond the Waipu sand. Green is for the forest and land that the settlers first saw; red is from the MacFarlane tartan and the yellow and black are in honour of Reverend Norman MacLeod who was the leader of the settlers.

Waipu 6510

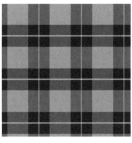

Pride of New Zealand 2632

PRIDE OF NEW ZEALAND   2632

No selection of New Zealand tartans – regardless of how small – would be complete without at least one that paid homage to their famous 'All Blacks' rugby team. This simple classic was designed by Ivan Coward, a bespoke tailor from Dunedin, and John Clark of Alliance Textiles in Timaru. It's for use by all New Zealanders and in addition to the 'beatified' black, is grey for the multi-cultural make-up of the population and white for the snow on New Zealand's many mountains.

It was of course by sailing ship that the original Scottish settlers reached the other side of the world. Now the modern Spirit of New Zealand perpetuates that heritage by offering 'character development' sail training to up to 1200 Kiwi youngsters a year.

Tartan Index

Bibliography and Further Reading

Adam, Frank, *The Clans Septs & Regiments of the Scottish Highlands*, Edinburgh, W & A K Johnston, 1908

Anderson, William, *The Scottish Nation*, Edinburgh & London, Fullarton & Co., 1867

Bain, Robert, *Clans & Tartans of Scotland*, Glasgow & London, Collins, 1938/1961

Barber, E.W., *The Mummies of Ürümchi*, New York, W.W. Norton & Co., 1999

Browne, James, *The History of Scotland. Its Highlands, Regiments and Clans*, Edinburgh, London, Boston, Nicolls & Co., 1909

Cheape Hugh, *Tartan the Highland Habit (3rd edition)*, Edinburgh, National Museums of Scotland, 2006

Clan Map of Scotland, Edinburgh & London, Johnston, W., & A.K., & Bacon, G.W., 1956

Costantino, Maria *The Handbook of Clans & Tartans of Scotland*, Leicester, Silverdale Books, 2002

Harrison, E. P., *Scottish Estate Tweeds*, Elgin, Johnstons of Elgin, 1995

Harrison, E. S., *Our Scottish District Checks*, Edinburgh, NASWM, 1968

Hesketh, Christian, *Tartans*, London, Octopus Books, 1972

Johnston, W.H., & Smith Jr, P.D., *Tartans Abbotsford to Fraser*, Pennsylvania, Schiffer Publishing, 1999

Johnston, W.H., & Smith Jr, P.D., *Tartans Frederickton to MacNeil*, Pennsylvania, Schiffer Publishing, 1999

Johnston, W.H., & Smith Jr, P.D., *Tartans MacNichol to Yukon*, Pennsylvania, Schiffer Publishing, 1999

Johnston, W., & A.K., *The Tartans of the Clans and Septs of Scotland*, Edinburgh & London, W & A K Johnston, 1906

Keltie, John S., *History of the Scottish Highlands*, London & Glasgow, William MacKenzie, 1830

Logan, J., & McIan, R.R., *The Clans of the Scottish Highlands*, London, Ackermann & Co., 1845

MacDonald, Micheil, *The Clans of Scotland*, London, Todd Publishing, 1991

MacDonald, Peter E., *The 1819 Key Pattern Book*, Perth, Jamieson & Munro, 1996

MacKay, J.G., *The Romantic Story of the Highland Garb and the Tartan*, MacKay, Stirling, 1924

MacLeay, R.S.A., Kenneth, *The Highlanders of Scotland Vols I & II*, London & Edinburgh, Mr Mitchell & Blackwood & Sons, 1870

Scarlett, James D., *The Tartan Spotters Guide*, self-published, 1973

Scarlett, James D., *Scotland's Clans & Tartans*, Guildford, Lutterworth Press, 1975

Scarlett, James D., *The Tartans of the Scottish Clans*, Glasgow & London, William Collins, 1975

Scarlett, James D., *The Tartan Weaver's Guide*, London, Shepheard Walwyn, 1985

Scarlett, James D., *Tartan – The Highland Textile*, London, Shepheard Walwyn, 1990

Scarlett, James D., *The Tartans of Clan Chattan*, Tomatin, Clan Chattan Association, 2003

Smibert, T., *The Clans of the Highlands of Scotland*, London, James Hogg, 1850

Smith, W., and Smith, A., *Authenticated Tartans of the Clans and Families of Scotland*, Mauchline, W & A. Smith, 1850

Stewart, D.C., & Thompson, J.C., *Scotland's Forged Tartans*, Edinburgh, Paul Harris Publishing, 1980

Stewart, D.C., *The Setts of the Scottish Tartans*, Edinburgh, Oliver & Boyd, 1950, Revised edition, London, Shepheard Walwyn, 1977

Stewart, D.W., *Old & Rare Scottish Tartans*, Edinburgh, George P. Johnston, 1893

Stewart, William, *Clanland*, Midland & Scottish Railway Company, London, 1926

Stuart, J.S.S., & C.E., *Vestiarium Scoticum*, Edinburgh, William Tait, 1842

Sutton, Ann, & Carr, Richard, *Tartans their Art & History*, New York, Arco Publishing, 1984

Tartan Map of Scotland, Collins, 2003

Taylor, D. D., James, *The Pictorial History of Scotland*, London & New York, J S Virtue, 1859

Teall, D.G., & Smith, P.D., *District Tartans*, Shepheard Walwyn, London, 1992

Picture Credits

p i Lochcarron of Scotland; p ii & iii Glencoe Village and Ballachulish, Michael Macgregor Photography; p iv Lochcarron of Scotland

Introduction
p. viii courtesy of Undiscovered Scotland ; p. ix courtesy of Lochcarron of Scotland; p. 2 courtesy of Lochcarron of Scotland; p. 3 courtesy of Jeffrey MacArthur Fox; p. 4 courtesy of Jeffrey MacArthur Fox; p. 5 courtesy of Rex Features; p. 6 courtesy of the Scottish Tartans Authority; p. 7 courtesy of the Scottish Tartans Authority

North-West
p. 8 courtesy of Undiscovered Scotland; p. 9 R.R. McIan; p. 10 National Gallery of Scotland/Bridgeman Art Library; p. 12 R.R. McIan; p. 14 above from D.W. Stewart, *Old and Rare Scottish Tartans* (1893); p. 14 below courtesy of Lochcarron of Scotland; p. 15 R.R. McIan; p. 16 courtesy of the Royal Society for the Protection of Birds; p. 17 courtesy of Undiscovered Scotland; p. 18 K. MacLeay; p. 19 Raphael Tuck; p. 20 R.R. McIan; p. 21 above courtesy of Harley-Davidson; p. 21 below courtesy of the Summer Isles Stamp Bureau; p. 22 courtesy of the Scottish Tartans Authority; p. 23 above R.R. McIan; p. 23 below courtesy of Undiscovered Scotland; p. 24 courtesy Harrods of Knightsbridge; p. 25 K. MacLeay; p. 26 courtesy of the Scottish Tartans Authority; p. 27 R.R. MacIan; p. 28 courtesy of the Scottish Tartans Authority; p. 29 both R.R. McIan; p. 30 courtesy of Undiscovered Scotland; p. 32 Raphael Tuck; p. 33 courtesy of Undiscovered Scotland; p. 34 William Stewart; p. 35 left courtesy of Undiscovered Scotland; p. 35 right R.R. McIan

North-East
p. 36 courtesy of Undiscovered Scotland; p. 37 R.R. McIan; p. 38 R.R. McIan; p. 39 courtesy of NASA; p. 40 left R.R. McIan; p. 40 right William Stewart; p. 41 R.R. McIan; p. 43 courtesy of Undiscovered Scotland; p. 44 courtesy of the National Trust for Scotland; p. 45 courtesy of Memorial Pegasus of Ranville, France; p. 46 courtesy of Stephen Ervin; p. 47 William Stewart; p. 48 above R.R. McIan; p. 48 below K. MacLeay; p. 49 courtesy of the Canadian Forces Base Pipe Band; p. 50 left K. MacLeay; p. 50 right courtesy of Undiscovered Scotland; p. 51 courtesy of Undiscovered Scotland; p. 52 R.R. McIan; p. 53 courtesy of the National Trust for Scotland; p. 54 courtesy of the Office of the Lord Lyon; p. 56 courtesy of the National Trust for Scotland; p. 57 R.R. McIan; p. 58 R.R. McIan; p. 59 above courtesy of Undiscovered Scotland; p. 59 below courtesy of the National Trust for Scotland

The Islands
p. 60 courtesy of Malcolm MacDonald Photography; p. 61 R.R. McIan; p. 62 courtesy of Michael Macgregor Photography; p. 63 Rachel Tuck; p. 64 courtesy of Undiscovered Scotland; p. 66 R.R. MacIan; p. 67 K. MacLeay; p. 68 courtesy of Scottish National Portrait Gallery/Bridgeman Art Library; p. 70 William Stewart; p. 71 R.R. McIan; p. 72 R.R. McIan; p. 74 Michael Macgregor Photography; p. 75 left R.R. McIan; p. 77 courtesy of the UK Antarctic Heritage Trust; p. 78 courtesy of Vivienne Westwood and Lochcarron Fashion; p. 79 above courtesy of Jimmy Choo and Lochcarron Fashion; p. 79 left courtesy of Howie Nicholsby of Edinburgh's 21st Century Kilts; p. 79 right courtesy of Vivienne Westwood and Lochcarron Fashion; p. 81 courtesy of Michael Macgregor Photography; p. 82 courtesy of Scottish Viewpoint; p. 83 R.R. McIan; p. 84 courtesy of Michel Macgregor Photography; p. 85 courtesy of the Bunnahabhain Distillery; p. 86 courtesy of Scottish Viewpoint; p. 87 Kathie Miller of Southern Oregon Soay Sheep Farms; p. 88 courtesy of Scottish Viewpoint; p. 89 courtesy of Michael Macgregor Photography; p. 91 courtesy of Royal Scottish Country Dance Society

The Central Highlands
p. 92 courtesy of Michael Macgregor Photography; p. 93 R.R. McIan; p. 96 courtesy of RAF Leuchars; p. 97 above courtesy of Peter MacDonald; p. 97 below courtesy of the Scottish Tartans Authority; p. 98 courtesy of the National Trust for Scotland; p. 99 R.R. McIan; p. 100 courtesy of Michael Macgregor Photography; p. 101 courtesy of Michael Macgregor Photography; p. 102 courtesy of Undiscovered Scotland; p. 103 courtesy of Undiscovered Scotland; p. 104 K. MacLeay; p. 105 courtesy of Crieff Hydro Hotel; p. 107 K. MacLeay; p. 108 R.R. McIan; p. 109 William Stewart; p. 111 courtesy of Lochcarron Fashion; p. 112 R.R. McIan; p. 113 courtesy of Undiscovered Scotland; p. 114 courtesy of Michael Macgregor Photography; p. 115 above R.R. McIan; p. 115 below courtesy of Art Gallery and Museum, Glasgow/The Bridgeman Art Library; p. 116 courtesy of J K W Fine Arts, Comrie; p. 117 R.R. McIan; p. 118 Raphael Tuck; p. 119 courtesy of Tartans Museum in Franklin, North Carolina/Matt Newsome; p. 120 William Stewart; p. 121 courtesy of Scottish Natural Heritage/ Laurie Campbell

The Lowlands
p. 122 courtesy of Undiscovered Scotland; p. 124 below and below right courtesy of Undiscovered Scotland; p. 125 courtesy of Victoria & Albert Museum/The Bridgeman Art Library; p. 126 courtesy of the Scottish Tartans Authority; p. 127 courtesy of the Summer Isles Stamp Bureau; p. 128 courtesy of Undiscovered Scotland; p. 129 courtesy of Scottish National Portrait Gallery/The Bridgeman Art Library; p. 130 courtesy of Jamie Simpson; p. 131 courtesy of Hutchesons Grammar School; p. 132 courtesy of the National Trust for Scotland; p. 134 courtesy of the Scottish Tartans Authority; p. 135 courtesy of the Royal Canadian Mounted Police; p. 136 courtesy of Undiscovered Scotland; p. 138 courtesy of Undiscovered Scotland; p. 140 Michael Macgregor Photography; p. 141 courtesy of Undiscovered Scotland; p. 143 courtesy of Mary Evans Picture Library; p. 145 courtesy of Undiscovered Scotland; p. 146 courtesy of the National Trust for Scotland; p. 147 courtesy of Undiscovered Scotland; p. 148 courtesy of the National Trust for Scotland; p. 150 courtesy of Rangers Football Club; p. 151 courtesy of Scottish Viewpoint

The Border Lands
p. 152 courtesy of Undiscovered Scotland; p. 156 courtesy of Mary Evans Picture Library p. 157 courtesy of the Scotsman Publications Ltd; 158 courtesy of Undiscovered Scotland; p. 159 courtesy of Undiscovered Scotland; p. 160 above and below courtesy of Undiscovered Scotland; p. 161 courtesy of Undiscovered Scotland; p. 162 courtesy of Mary Evans Picture Library; p. 164 courtesy of Undiscovered Scotland; p. 165 courtesy of Undiscovered Scotland; p. 166 courtesy of Undiscovered Scotland; p. 167 courtesy of Mary Evans Picture Library; p. 169 courtesy of Undiscovered Scotland; p. 170 courtesy of Undiscovered Scotland; p. 172 courtesy of the National Trust for Scotland

United States, Canada, Australia and New Zealand
p. 176 courtesy Tennessee Dept of Tourist Development; p. 178 courtesy of Arizona Office of Tourism; p. 180 courtesy of Colorado Tourist Office; p. 181 above courtesy of Scottish Tartans Museum, Franklin, North Carolina; p. 181 below courtesy of Hawaii Visitors Convention Bureau/Ron Dahlquist; p. 182 courtesy of Iowa Tourist Office; p. 184 courtesy of New Orleans Convention Bureau; p. 185 courtesy of Great Lakes of North America; p. 186 courtesy of Mississippi Tourist Office; p. 187 courtesy of Nevada Commission on Tourism; p. 189 courtesy of Knox Presbyterian Church /Jean Stafford-Green; p. 190 courtesy of Great Lakes of North America; p. 191 courtesy of Travel Manitoba; p. 192 courtesy of Nova Scotia Tourism, Culture and Heritage; p. 193 courtesy of Image Ontario; p. 195 courtesy of Tourism Queensland; p. 197 courtesy of the Spirit of Adventure Trust

The author and publishers have made every effort to contact the copyright holders for the illustrations used in this book. The publishers should be notified of any omission of credit.